YHWH AND ISRAEL IN THE BOOK OF JUDGES

In the Book of Judges the narrator presents an image of the good parent YHWH whose enduring love and loyalty is offset by his wayward child Israel who defaults on the relationship repeatedly. Biblical scholars have largely concurred, demonstrating the many faults of Israel while siding with YHWH's privileged viewpoint. When object-relations theory (which examines how human beings relate to each other) is applied to Judges, a different story emerges. In its capacity to illuminate why and how relationships can be intense, problematic, rewarding and enduring, object-relations theory reveals how both YHWH and Israel have attachment needs that are played out vividly in the story world. Deryn Guest reveals how its narrator engages in a variety of psychological strategies to mask suppressed rage as he engages in an intriguing but rather dysfunctional masochistic dance with a dominant deity who has reputation needs.

Deryn Guest is Senior Lecturer in Hermeneutics at the University of Birmingham. She is the author of *When Deborah Met Jael, Beyond Feminist Biblical Studies*, the founding co-editor of the best-selling *Queer Bible Commentary*, and co-author of *Transgender, Intersex and Biblical Interpretation*.

SOCIETY FOR OLD TESTAMENT STUDY

MONOGRAPH SERIES

Series Editor: Lena-Sofia Tiemeyer, *University of Aberdeen*

The SOTS monograph series seeks to showcase the best of modern biblical studies. All published books will have the Hebrew Bible/Old Testament as their focal point. There will also be scope for volumes that take an interdisciplinary approach, such as studies which look at the biblical texts from a comparative perspective, in dialogue with ancient Near Eastern studies or modern literary theory. Similarly, volumes which explore the reception history of a particular text or set of texts will be encouraged.

YHWH and Israel in the Book of Judges

An Object-Relations Analysis

DERYN GUEST

University of Birmingham

CAMBRIDGE
UNIVERSITY PRESS

University Printing House, Cambridge CB2 8BS, United Kingdom

One Liberty Plaza, 20th Floor, New York, NY 10006, USA

477 Williamstown Road, Port Melbourne, VIC 3207, Australia

314–321, 3rd Floor, Plot 3, Splendor Forum, Jasola District Centre, New Delhi – 110025, India

79 Anson Road, #06–04/06, Singapore 079906

Cambridge University Press is part of the University of Cambridge.

It furthers the University's mission by disseminating knowledge in the pursuit of education, learning, and research at the highest international levels of excellence.

www.cambridge.org
Information on this title: www.cambridge.org/9781108476508
DOI: 10.1017/9781108568562

First published 2019

Printed and bound in Great Britain by Clays Ltd, Elcograf S.p.A.

A catalogue record for this publication is available from the British Library.

Library of Congress Cataloging-in-Publication Data
Names: Guest, Deryn, author.
Title: YHWH and Israel in the Book of Judges : an object-relations analysis / Deryn Guest.
Description: Cambridge ; New York, NY : Cambridge University Press, 2018. | Series: Society for Old Testament study monographs | Includes bibliographic references.
Identifiers: LCCN 2018026585 | ISBN 9781108476508 (hardback)
Subjects: LCSH: Bible. Judges–Criticism, interpretation, etc.
Classification: LCC BS1305.52 .G84 2018 | DDC 222/.3206–dc23
LC record available at https://lccn.loc.gov/2018026585

ISBN 978-1-108-47650-8 Hardback

For Frances, whose provision of a holding environment was and is so much appreciated.

CONTENTS

ACKNOWLEDGEMENTS

I thank the College of Arts and Law at the University of Birmingham for granting study leave for one semester in order to complete this project. I was grateful for the cheery welcome from Dr Lena-Sofia Tiemeyer when forwarding my proposal to Cambridge University Press. It was good to renew the acquaintance. Thanks also to the helpful and efficient staff at the Press. Warm affection and appreciation to all my department colleagues who make the University of Birmingham such a conducive and affirming place for developing new research ideas. Your helpful and insightful responses to a seminar paper presented when thoughts for this book were only just germinating were much appreciated.

Much love and thanks to my daughter Jenny who has been 'up to her neck', as Winnicott would say, with the trials of first-time motherhood. Caspian's first three years of life coincided with the writing of this book, and his happy relationship with Jenny illustrated many of its concepts vividly and delightfully. Heartfelt thanks to Frances who patiently endured endless conversations about various aspects of object-relations theory while taking circuits of our local park and gave most generously of her time for editing and proofreading purposes.

INTRODUCTION

The relationship between YHWH and Israel as depicted in the Book of Judges is, to say the least, torrid – as passionate in rage as it is in love. The two parties are irrevocably, ardently enmeshed, even when one party abandons the other in favour of alternative deities, or when YHWH throws a tantrum and tells the objects of his obsession to go cry to these rival gods instead. As relationships go, it is a prime candidate for magazine 'problem pages'. This attachment, however, is routinely addressed within two main scholarly genres: commentaries (in an introductory subsection on 'theology of Judges' or permeating more pervasively, depending on the audience for whom the commentary is written) and broader 'Old Testament Theologies' where the rollercoaster relationship between deity and people is usually assessed across a range of canonical texts. But here lies a problem. These two genres remain embedded in a scholarly framework that has been irretrievably fractured by recent scholarship on the date of biblical texts, their genre and function, and the vexed question of their relation to history. Revisionist shifts have significance for how we read and interpret the YHWH–Israel relationship in texts like Judges. Put baldly, if the biblical narratives under consideration are late Persian/Hellenistic constructs where YHWH is present 'as a fictional character, much like the incompetent god who loses a bet to his Adversary in the book of Job' (Noll, 2013: 133–134), then using stories from Judges in theologies intended to enlighten readers about what God desires, or God's attributes, could be referencing a character who is a flawed and dysfunctional construct.

In this book I examine the YHWH–Israel relationship in the light of object relations theory.[1] Using psychology as an interdisciplinary

---

[1] 'Object relations mean interpersonal relations. The term object ... refers simply to that which will satisfy a need. More broadly, object refers to the significant person or thing that is the object or target of another's feelings or drives' (St Clair, 1986: 1).

tool is not new, but a psychologically informed approach has not yet been applied extensively to the YHWH–Israel relationship in the Book of Judges.[2] I demonstrate how key interests of traditional theologies – the character of YHWH, his relationship with Israel, covenant, the human condition – can and should be more critically explored through the psychological concepts of repression and splitting, attachment theory, and studies of the causes and effects of masochism, without losing a firm grounding in contemporary revisionist biblical studies.

As readers may have already surmised, my approach necessitates a de-privileging of YHWH's perspective. This should not immediately alienate readers disappointed with such a stance. Yes, my suggestions inevitably conflict with the confessional standpoint implicit within many, if not most, Old Testament theologies and also with 'theologies of Judges' contained within commentaries. They also conflict with the starting point of those who use psychological theory to describe the life of faith. Miner, for instance, finds great value in attachment theory, but only when it is fully engaged within a theological framework 'which assumes the existence of, and revealed nature of, God' (2007: 112)[3]. Her work concerns the spiritual lives of believers and their attachment to a deity conceived of as an omnipotent, metaphysical reality; but this is not my starting point. Nonetheless, this does not mean that a confessional approach and the approach advocated here should view each

---

[2] Psychology has informed biblical studies in various ways. Brueggemann (1995) makes reference to ego-strength and the dangers of 'false self' development in his work on Psalms of lament. Joyce (1993) reads Lamentations in terms of bereavement and reactions to the experience of dying. Kamionkowski (2003) demonstrates how Ezekiel contains indicators of psychological trauma caused by the events surrounding the Babylonian exile. She uses Freud's (1963) case of Dr Schreber and the work of Anna Freud (1942) on humiliation, shame and rage in order to unpack Ezekiel's experience of emasculation and explain why he imagines himself and his community as the wife of God. Rashkow (1993) has queried what makes a reading of a text psychoanalytic and provides engaging psychologically informed readings of Genesis. More recently, Rollins and Kille (2007) document the emerging interdisciplinary field between biblical scholarship and psychological theory, and the essays within illustrate how psychological criticism has contributed to our understanding of biblical texts and their interpreters. Studies by Lasine (2001, 2002 and 2013) encourage further investigations. There is also a growing field of trauma and memory studies that explores how psychological trauma leaves its imprint on the text.
[3] In this vein, see also the work Paul (1999) who uses object relations theory to discuss Christian conversion, or Burns-Smith (1999) who applies theological categories to psychological theory in order to demonstrate how some psychological approaches within pastoral care will be a better 'fit' with the counsellor's theological allegiances.

other with animosity. There is not only room for both within biblical studies but they could effectively complement each other. For example, I have found confessional commentaries and theologies to be profoundly insightful when it comes to exploring the character of YHWH and his relationship with Israel. It is precisely because they have faithful readers in mind that writers such as Brueggemann (2008), Webb (2012), Hamlin (1990) and Martin (2008) confront, head on, the gruesome violence in Judges, the questionable morality of some of its protagonists, the cold indifference of a deity in sending tribes to their destruction, the dismemberment and rape of woman for the purpose of getting across a pedagogical message, or the (failed) genocide of indigenous peoples. These matters become theological cruxes and while YHWH is exonerated in such studies, there is a troubled consciousness that recognises how these conundrums require serious investigation. The resolutions offered have been engaging and informative. I believe my alternative approach is equally insightful, thought-provoking and challenging for those who are practical or pastoral theologians, writers of Old Testament theology, or writers of commentaries for the faithful. If Judges promulgates a view of human–divine relationship that is damaging and distorted when read from a psychological perspective, then such practitioners will need to think about its endorsement. Rather than aligning themselves with YHWH as a default position, this book challenges those engaged in faithful hermeneutics to think again about the model of divine–human relationship they are reinforcing. I want the conversation to continue, not to end.

I appreciate, however, that the conversation might be difficult to sustain. A main assumption of theology is that the deity worshipped by Christians and Jews today is revealed in biblical texts and that his character lies beyond human comprehension and scrutiny. Robert Alter complains that 'a merely psychologizing approach cannot do justice to the imaginative and spiritual seriousness' of a biblical author, not least because, while human characters act out their parts in the foreground, in the background lie 'forces that can be neither grasped nor controlled by humankind' (1992: 22). Accordingly, 'there is little to be gained ... by conceiving of the biblical God ... as a human character—petulant, headstrong, arbitrary, impulsive, or whatever. The repeated point of the biblical writers is that we cannot make sense of God in human terms' (1992: 22–23).[4] Alter's check on

---

[4] Alter's check on investigating the character of God can also be found in Sternberg's work; the latter likens the biblical narrator to the general of an army

psychological approaches can also be found in Brueggemann's work. In his discussion of how tempting it might be to think of biblical writers projecting a YHWH to suit their own ends, he resists this way of looking at things, noting that it would mean that 'the literary character of YHWH falls victim to the projections of human urgency' (2008: 136). The reason given for why the temptation must be avoided is telling; it is because such interpretation operates 'as though there were no "real" YHWH in the narrative. It does so, moreover, without reckoning with the slippery slope that our pre-ferred YHWH may also be a projection, a point of course scored by Ludwig Feuerbach and Sigmund Freud' (2008: 136). Here, we see Brueggemann acknowledging that we do indeed create YHWH in our own image, but simultaneously distancing himself from that projection. For him, YHWH's character in biblical texts reveals something of YHWH the actual deity. His caution, if accepted, would prevent this monograph from being written.

I resist his suggestion that using psychological theories of projection puts us on a 'slippery slope'. If, brazenly, we slither down regardless, Brueggemann implies we will end up in a place of halls and mirrors where the only YHWH present is the one that we want to see, distorted by our all-too-human wishes and desires. Against this, Brueggemann's appeal to the 'real' YHWH encourages his readers to hold on to a belief that the biblical scribe is a conduit for revelation and that some biblical writers present a more authentic portrayal of this deity than others.[5] However, the elision of the

unfortunate enough to have his king enlisted in his forces. He quickly qualifies this image: the narrator's task is 'not to destroy an enemy but to redeem and establish control over his own people and ... to manipulate them into the reverential obedience that his lord exacts as his due' (1985: 154). I concur, but I cannot follow Sternberg's approach, much as I admire his close reading of biblical texts. The problem with Sternberg's analysis is that the method that results in such excellent close readings, that analyses so well the interplay of perspectives engaged by his privileged narrator, ultimately leads to a mirroring of that narrator's agenda. I thus concur with Fuchs's assessment that Sternberg's method positions the critic 'as the obedient son to the father-text (2000: 39), but for different reasons. Fuchs criticises how his investigation of the gaps in narration has an androcentric focus, considering, for example, the gaps in David, Uriah and Joab's motivations and actions and knowledge, but without any probe of what Bathsheba may think or know. I am critical of a narrative analysis that reads so astutely but so readily with the text and in so doing privileges the perspective of YHWH.

[5] For example. Brueggemann (1988) is critical of royal, statist ideology implicit within some biblical texts, seeing it as the promotion of vested interests by self-interested groups. He offsets this with the views of other biblical writers who are deemed to have more altruistic and authentic knowledge.

character of YHWH with the God of faith has boxed commentators and theologians in; compelled to align themselves, largely uncritically, with the perspective of this character, they vindicate his behaviour and, as a result, castigate the Israel represented in Judges as wayward and disloyal. When psychological theories of object relations and attachment are employed more robustly, a different view of Israel emerges as we will see.

As noted above, I do not wish to alienate those who use biblical texts as grounding for theologies; rather, I wish to open a conversation. While I no longer own any personal allegiance to YHWH of the Bible I do not doubt that biblical texts can very eloquently and profoundly point its readers in the direction of the *mysterium*. Our difference is that I do not grant YHWH a privileged special character status that is beyond human comprehension, because I focus on the biblical scribe who scripts YHWH's part. I concede that it becomes rather tedious to tag 'which is always to say the narrator's construction' every time I refer to YHWH's view. But in order to remind readers that YHWH is a constructed character replete with the scribe's projections and externalisations, there needs to be some turn of phrase that puts us at a critical distance from the elision of literary character and divinity, so that the relationship between YHWH and Israel can be assessed without any inherent adoption of the narratorial voice.

Accordingly, in order to distance this venture from what has conventionally been known as Old Testament theology, the first step is to offer a new name for this project. The use of 'Old Testament' is now more routinely replaced with 'Hebrew Bible' or 'Hebrew Scriptures'. As for 'theology' this has been recast by Clines (1995) as the study of the ideology of implied authors. The benefit of shifting to 'ideology' lies in the critical distance it creates between scholars and the texts they interpret. For example, Clines contrasts his approach with that of scholars who investigate theologies of biblical texts in order to elaborate on them for their readers, as if 'the scholarly study of the Bible has reached its goal when it has attained an "understanding" of the texts (1995: 19). Rather, argues Clines, the biblical text needs to be evaluated critically by an external yardstick that is not caught up with the ideological commitments promulgated within a text. A faithful scholar could certainly do this work so long as they were 'wide awake' to the 'designs that texts have on them' so that they did not 'find themselves succumbing to the ideology of the texts, adopting that ideology as their own, and finding it obvious and natural and common-sensical' (1995: 21). However, an external source of standards that throws the ideology of the text into stark relief helps to facilitate the wake-up required, providing 'a counterpoint' that is 'alien' to the given text. The counterpoint I use is psychological theory, which I believe enables readers to read the relationship dynamics of biblical texts in a very different light to the one usually employed.

Changing the terminology from Old Testament theology to 'ideologies of the Hebrew Bible' has at least two benefits. First, reference to 'Hebrew Bible' rather than 'Old Testament' indicates that this project makes no assumption that its texts are fulfilled in the New Testament. There is no Christocentric focus. While I would like Christian readers to engage with my proposals, I do not expect my findings to be assimilated easily or readily into a broader Christian framework of Biblical theology. So whereas Webb's (2012) commentary contains a section on 'Judges as Christian Scripture', it is not this project's remit. Others, however, may take what they find here and think through what it means for Christian faith and practice.

Second, and more significantly, the word 'ideologies' does not have the religious connotations of 'theology'. The findings of this study may well have a serious impact for the way in which Hebrew Bible texts are used to model divine–human relationships in contemporary confessional contexts, but it makes no assumption that the character of YHWH in Judges can be related to a transcendent deity. I understand why this view will be criticised by those who believe all human perspectives and stances should be put under the scrutinising eye of the inscrutable deity, but that is what existing Old Testament theology already offers.

Of course, if I embraced the terminology of 'ideologies' rather than 'theology' I would need to differentiate my approach from the interest in rhetoric that features in some narrative approaches. The narrative critic's focus on rhetorical interests is usually grounded in the politics and themes *of the text*. The danger here is that narrative criticism repeats back to us the rhetoric of the text in the 'understanding and explaining' way that Clines (1995) has rightly criticised, without recognising that a study of textual rhetoric is, itself, an 'interested' project.[6] Narrative criticism's inevitable close, detailed

---

[6] Mieke Bal (1988) has ably demonstrated how writers elevate rhetorical interests and themes that the narrator has deliberately drawn to our attention, rather than the interests that have been suppressed.

work on the text thus reflects back its politics and interests rather than evaluating whether those interests are morally dubious and what we should do about it. I am pursuing, rather, an approach that can be critical of the text, using an external discourse to highlight the text's strangeness, its questionable values and politics.

However, I am not convinced that 'ideologies of the Hebrew Bible' is a more suitable terminology. It has benefits, but the fact remains that the issues I want to address *can* be justifiably described as theological. Actually, in some ways, they are both. If we understand ideology as 'the kind of large-scale ideas that influence and determine the whole outlook of groups of people' and the 'will to power expressed in ideologies' (Clines, 1995: 11) then this project is certainly a study of ideologies, particularly in the way texts can 'give the appearance of sincerity and either moral fervour or objectivity' while actually disguising the 'issues of power, of self-identity and security, of group solidarity, of fear and desire, of need and greed' that lie beneath the surface (Clines, 1995: 24). But if we understand the close study of YHWH, his character and the way in which the scribe constructs his interaction with Israel as primary interests of theology, then this study is also theological.

An emphasis on ideologies somehow reduces the (psychological) interest I have in how biblical texts can point to the numinous as part of their engagement with profound human mysteries or experiences. Judges, no less than any other biblical text, deals with existential questions in a story world inhabited by gods, goddesses, forces and energies, often perceived as holding human inhabitants in their grip. When I refer to YHWH as the construction of the scribe I am aware that YHWH is simultaneously described by that scribe as an external force that drives events, intrudes upon human consciousness and is a stirring presence within nature, a force that works behind the scenes in a way aptly described by Alter as 'a high-voltage current' which 'can energise and transform', but also 'paralyze and destroy' (1992: 23). This *mysterium* that the narrator grapples with is an important aspect of the way he explains his experience of an uncontrollable natural world whipped about by an energy that seems to holds human destiny in its grasp. However, as I have noted, it can be too easy to then elide references to this energy with the Jewish and Christian deity and interpret the actions of the *character* YHWH as revelations of a transcendent *divinity*. As will be demonstrated in the chapters that follow, the unfortunate consequence of that elision is to privilege the words and actions of YHWH and to assume that whatever viewpoint is attributed to him is 'the' viewpoint against which all other positions must be measured. Once one takes that route, it tips the balance of the tension between human construction of a divine character and the experience of suprahuman energies far too much to one side. The speech and actions of the 'divine' character become authoritative dogma, not to be questioned, and the profundity of the text is narrowed. This results in the anxiety, ambivalence and existential discomfort of a world where supernatural energies can act unexpectedly, with capriciousness, assuaged only by making such energies part of the inscrutable ways of YHWH that mere humans cannot comprehend. But this does not maintain a balance between an ancient scribe's attempt to grapple with the *mysterium* and the way in which he constructs YHWH as a major character, replete with all the neuroses and complexes that humans project onto others, both in reality and in literary worlds. We need to use the insights of narrative critics who have provided the tools for examining characterisation, narrators and rhetoric. And we need to use the theories of psychologists, who can illustrate how notions of splitting, fragmentation, attachment and projections help us understand the dynamics of a text. But this does not mean we have to revert to a position that denudes the text entirely of its soul, reading in a solely 'academic' manner that brackets out all issues of whether or not the text has anything interesting to say about human quests for meaning, for encounters with energies that seem extrahuman. I fear that recourse only to a discussion of 'ideologies' might risk such narrowing.

Accordingly, I propose the terminology of 'God-talk' to forge a middle way that is neither caught up with Christian assumptions and allegiance to the supposed divine viewpoint within scripture, nor too rigidly bound by a non-confessional focus on ideologies that mean we focus on the text as a largely political enterprise. The phrase God-talk obviously echoes Ruether's significant book *Sexism and God-Talk* (1983), which signalled a critique of theological tradition from a feminist perspective. It is in a similar spirit of standing outside the interpellation of the biblical text that I adopt the term 'God-talk'. It recognises that the subject matter of this book *is* about theological concerns, but the more informal formulation 'God-talk' points to this being 'talk', not fundamental revealed truths. The biblical text of Judges produces its conversation about YHWH and his relationship with Israel, albeit with the ideological will to power that Clines (1995) recognises, but it is a dialogue nonetheless, a conversation that the reader hears but then responds to from their own standpoint.

My approach to the text can be likened to the position a therapist finds themselves in as they begin their work with a new client. A good therapist will listen most carefully to the presenting story, but not be sucked into alignment with it. Rather, the therapist observes the client and their own reaction to that client, alert to any feelings of countertransference. Being aware of 'how this account and this person makes me feel' grants the therapist an insight into the client's own feelings of frustration, distress, anger, happiness or whatever. Thus, if the therapist feels, say, trapped, indignant or highly constrained by the approach of the client and their storytelling, if they feel as if they are being attacked or unduly put upon, it is possible that they have an insight into the situational experiences and issues of the client. Of course, I cannot do this with the actual scribe of Judges, but my hermeneutical approach involves immersion in object relation theory alongside being aware of what this text does to me when I read it. This is a subjective move, but it is consciously so. I am fully aware that I am putting myself into an empathetic position that listens attentively to the scribe's voice, trying to be alert to the emotive content, as well as the grammar; the affect of the text as well as the rhetoric.[7] In so doing, I listen for the words that highlight possible complexes, psychodramas that lie beneath the surface account, alert to how relationships are being constructed, to the behaviours of the primary participants, to trigger events and their resolution, to the snags in the narrative, and to the key words or events that connect with the psychological literature. The relationship with the text is thus one of active listening accompanied by critical examination of the effects of the presenting story,

---

[7] Moore and Fine's explanation of the term 'affect' is helpful. 'Various distinctions have been drawn between feelings, emotions, and affects. Feelings refer to the central, subjectively experienced state (which may be blocked from consciousness); emotions, to the outwardly observable manifestations of feelings; and affects, to all the related phenomena, some of which are unconscious. The terms are often used interchangeably, however, to refer to a range from primitive to complex, cognitively differentiated psychic states. A relatively stable and long-lasting affective state, evoked and perpetuated by the continuing influence of unconscious fantasy, is called a mood' (1990: 9). Affects can be manifested in physical ways such as 'blushing, sweating, crying' (1990: 9) in response to experiences of shame, joy, fear, surprise etc. 'Affects have an important adaptive function in alerting and preparing the individual for appropriate response to his or her external and internal environment' and for making it visible to others (1990: 10).

without being pulled into its rhetoric. It quickly becomes clear that my approach differs most pointedly from the commentary tradition in this refusal to be sucked in to any alignment with the scribe and his presentation of 'YHWH's viewpoint'. Specifically, I do not have any investment in reinforcing his strategy or compulsion to 'keep YHWH good'. On the contrary, it is precisely the effort to keep YHWH good that becomes one of the most interesting features for consideration.

The idea that a scholar's observation of countertransference could be worthwhile is hinted at by Patrick Vandermeersch, who notes how religious texts can 'provoke particular reactions ... determined partly by the personality of the reader, but also partly by the text that addresses specific aspects of the reader's psychology ... Texts can evoke compassion, admiration or horror, but also irritation, an experience of absurdity or even the fear of becoming mad' (2001: 19). Vandermeersch is also right to remind us that that biblical scholars are not only engaged in the interpretation of texts in a very conscious way, but that we all have an active *unconscious* engaged in the process which inevitably affects out interpretation. Of course, as it is unconscious we are not aware of how we are manipulated to respond to storylines in particular ways, or how some story features may act as trigger points for our own psychic reactions. He notes, for example, how Wellhausen, looking ever like the objective textual critic, emended Gen. 24:67 so that Isaac makes love to Rebekkah in his father's tent rather than his mother's. Beneath this scholarly activity lurks the psychological motivation to change the text, since the latter prospect of a mother hearing her son making love was evidently unthinkable or intolerable.

Vandermeersch does not specifically raise the question of countertransference in this discussion, but it is mentioned by other contributors to the volume. Carlander's chapter on the Saul–David relationship draws on Melanie Klein's theories and confirms the value of looking at texts in terms of countertransference, suggesting that the genre of tragedy, in particular, evokes responses in the reader that are 'built on the countertransference reaction' (2001: 79). Raguse also draws on countertransference when noting how readers can be negatively affected by texts to a point when one simply wants to stop reading; i.e., 'when one gets the impression that the text is trying to do something "unpleasant" to the reader' or 'when the text tries to impose a certain role on the reader' (2001: 59). I cannot be aware of my own unconscious responses when reading

Judges, but I can note my countertransference reaction. This includes being intrigued, sometimes amused, but mostly feeling uncomfortable and rather annoyed. The scribe is not likeable. He intones with repetitive tedium the unworthiness of Israel and the wondrous patience of YHWH. The individual stories offer light relief, but the repeated message of unfaithfulness and the 'badness' of Israel wears thin very quickly. I begin to sympathise with the early historical-critical scholars who contrasted the supposed source material with the editorial hand of the Deuteronomist whose relentless aim was 'to impress upon his readers the lesson that unfaithfulness to Yahweh is always punished ... Yahweh is Israel's God; and the religion of Israel is to keep itself to him alone' (Moore, 1898: xvi). I can empathise with Wellhausen's (1885: 229–236) remarks about the pedantic editor whose rather dull, clerical work is contrasted with the supposed livelier source material. These moments of disquiet, however, become useful markers for further consideration. If I feel irritated by his heavy-handed narration, the question arises: what does this tell me about the scribe and his story? Might it hint at some kind of underlying annoyance in the scribe himself? As with therapy, it took years rather than weeks or months to locate the ulterior and deeply submerged layer in the text that would explain this and Chapter 4 is where I do the work of bringing it, finally, to the surface. It was the depth of reading in object relations theory that provided the leverage. It proved to be vitally important that this theoretical material existed outside the world of biblical studies, for its 'alien' counterpoint made sense of the affect, the readerly discomfort, and gave me the language and rationale for starting from a different place to the more usual commentary writers.

The results of this study are primarily addressed to biblical scholars, not Old Testament theologians. However, it is difficult (and not necessarily desirable) to draw a clear demarcation between the two. Commentaries on Judges can be overtly written with faithful readers in mind, containing plenty of theological claims and ponderings, yet historical-critical commentators are not averse to moments of theologising either. I have found this theological content largely instructive when identifying how the scribe's rhetoric, say in keeping YHWH 'good', has been powerfully convincing; reinforced for millennia in the history of reception. The complicity of biblical scholars is a matter I return to on several occasions, noting how it has prevented them from noticing some glaring oddities in the text, or from resisting some very dubious behaviour on the part of YHWH. When Old Testament theologians work from the groundwork of biblical texts and have as their resources scholarly commentaries that basically uphold the ideology of the scribe and privilege the perspective of YHWH, then the work of biblical scholars is caught up with the theologies that emerge. So, while I do not engage Old Testament theologians primarily or directly, I do engage with the scholars whose work on the text can inform theologies. I would like commentators on biblical texts to think more seriously about the kind of divine–human relationship their work endorses. Generally speaking, biblical scholars have been good at questioning or resisting the role and fate of women in Judges, distancing themselves from the gore and violence, and querying the ethics of genocide, but when it comes to the basic and fundamental relationship between Israel (the always wayward, rebellious, manipulative 'bad' Israel) and YHWH (the enduring, loving-while-punishing, 'good' YHWH), the appetite for questioning or resisting simply seems to fall away. I hope that this monograph makes it far more difficult for future commentaries to follow that trajectory so readily, whether or not they have faithful audiences in mind. It is in the interests of all to recognise how biblical texts, which are so culturally significant and influential, contain a template for a relationship dynamic that is contrary to wellbeing. In saying this, I am aware that biblical texts such as Judges contain one particular view of that relationship, one that could be contrasted with views portrayed elsewhere in the canon. I am also aware that the Judges portrayal is more tragic and disturbing than the depictions of the YHWH–Israel relationship available in Second Temple and early Jewish literature. I am not saying that the depiction of the YHWH–Israel relationship in Judges holds the last word, or is the most important word on the matter. It is one depiction amid a kaleidoscope of other depictions. However, this does not excuse us from doing the work on this particular text or from challenging the way biblical scholars so often endorse its portrayal of what, in my view, proves to be a dysfunctional relationship. If this monograph makes scholars think again about how the scribe constructs the character of YHWH, and how he has this character interact with a 'past' Israel, then, ultimately, this may have a knock-on effect for rethinking the representation of the YHWH–Israel relationship in other texts and, indeed, on how biblical texts are used in future Old Testament theologies. This can only be a good thing, discomforting though it may be.

My objective, then, is to provide a psychologically informed critical assessment of the way in which YHWH is projected as an ideal, loving-but-correcting, enduringly loyal parent to his hopelessly wayward, ignorant, children of Israel. The following chapters explore what is happening in that presentation through the filter of object relations theory, attachment theory and psychological discussions of masochism.

In Chapter 1, the relationship between the child/Israel and the parent/YHWH is explored through the lens the object relationship theory developed by paediatrician and psychologist Donald Woods Winnicott (1896–1971). I justify the choice of Winnicott as a primary theorist, introduce five key concepts from his work, and explain how and why his ideas have applicability to an ancient biblical text. Winnicott's work proves particularly illuminating for analysing YHWH's intrusions, subterfuge, anxieties and claims upon Israel, prompting reflection on how Judges scholars continue the scribe's investment in 'keeping YHWH good' despite his curious and dubious behaviour.

Chapter 2 turns attention specifically to the cyclical framework that characterises the Book of Judges, assessing whether this can profitably be understood, in psychological terms, as a traumatic stutter. The extent to which Janzen's (2012) work on trauma and the Deuteronomistic History could profitably be applied to Judges' cyclical framework is explored. Ultimately, the thought that we are dealing with a traumatised victim of the Babylonian exile is discounted. The pervasive humour and literary artistry of the text, and the observations of revisionist scholarship that date the text much later than previously envisaged, render the idea that an exile-induced trauma has directly affected the portrayal of the YHWH–Israel relationship unlikely. I conclude that the cyclical framework of Judges would be better illuminated through the work of attachment theorists. In this chapter the reader will find an overview of revisionist scholarship that compels a complete overhaul of previous assumptions concerning the transmission history of Judges and its genre. Once, one could talk about a lengthy transmission history for Judges, from origins in the folk stories of pre-monarchic Israel, to an early written collection in a *Retterbuch*, to Josianic and exilic redrafts. Now, shifts to late Persian or early Hellenistic dating of texts render that long line of transmission suspect. Once, commentaries were punctuated with archaeological and topographical information, implying or overtly making a connection between the stories of Judges and pre-monarchic Israelite history. Now, faith in that connection has been seriously undermined by the new archaeology that interprets the artefacts of the early Iron Age in terms of indigenous Canaanite developments, and the revisionist histories of Israel that divorce the story told in the Primary History from the realities of the kingdoms of Israel and Judah. Once, it could be assumed that the traumatic experience of the exile has left its indelible mark on biblical depictions of the YHWH–Israel relationship. Now the assumed continuity between the producers of biblical literature and an exiled community is being questioned. Once, it was largely taken for granted that religious interests and experiences drove the creation of biblical narrative, that of course 'theology' was an appropriate word to use when examining the YHWH–Israel relationship in Judges. Now, the idea that biblical narratives were originally driven by 'religious' interests is under review, and the character of YHWH is understood more as a by-product of a more philosophical wisdom-like discussion. These radical shifts within biblical studies create an opportunity for reading Judges and its YHWH–Israel relationship not as part of a layered account of a distant past but as an important feature of a largely fictional past that serves the rhetorical and psychological needs of an educated member of the intelligentsia.

Chapter 3 explores how attachment theory can illuminate what is happening in the repeated cycle where Israel serves other gods, is punished by proxy agents and cries out for help before being rescued by judges of varying quality. I apply the ground-breaking work of Ainsworth, Bowlby and more contemporary theorists such as Bartholomew, to three key passages – Judg. 2:11–23, 10:6–16 and 1 Sam. 12:7–25 – in order to analyse the ups and downs of the on–off YHWH–Israel relationship (justification for the inclusion of the latter passage is provided in Chapter 3). When considered in the light of secure, insecure and detached attachments, the YHWH–Israel relationship is cast into a quite different light than that found in theologies and commentaries. The chapter concludes that our biblical scribe repeatedly throws Israel into hostile situations, not because he is traumatised by an experience of Babylonian warfare and deportation, but in order to present the reader with a 'bad' Israel (wayward, in need of firm and repeated discipline) and a 'good' Israel (as presented in his alignment with the perspective of YHWH). The gains to be made by such splitting become clear in the following chapter on masochism.

Chapter 4 turns to one of most theoretically rich object relations theorists: William Ronald Dodds Fairbairn (1889–1964), a Scot whose delineation of endopsychic structure has been influential. His work on the internalisation of 'bad objects' and the splitting or fragmentation of the ego is applied to the portrayal of the YHWH– Israel relationship, noting particularly how Israel is split into good and bad. The 'bad' Israel is the one of 'history' who has repeatedly behaved outrageously, while the narrator himself is presented as YHWH's ideal child, loyal, obedient and submissive, delivering his verdict upon his wayward badly behaving siblings, often by putting it in the mouth of the father/YHWH, who is also split between 'good' and 'bad' aspects. This chapter uses Fairbairn's work as a spring-board for further assessment of what appears to be an on-repeat sadomasochist dance in Judges. Using contemporary theorists of masochism, the odd features of this dysfunctional relationship, its exchanges of power, its tantrums and grovellings, its splitting strat-egies and the underlying rage are illuminated in new and provocative ways.

By the time the reader arrives at the concluding chapter the overall argument is clear: read from the illuminating perspective of psycho-logical theory, the relationship of YHWH and Israel as constructed in the Book of Judges is dysfunctional. It operates as a sadomaso-chistic dance in which YHWH is kept 'safe' as the 'good parent' who punishes-because-he-loves, while the constructed Israel of the 'past' takes on the repressed 'badness' of the YHWH character. Judges scholars, confessional or not, consciously or not, have been complicit with the dance. It is time to pause the music, investigate more closely the steps of this dance, and rethink whether a biblically oriented faith can afford to continue with it.

1

PROBLEMATIC PARENTING

Donald Winnicott and the YHWH–Israel Relationship

Introduction

In this chapter I employ the work of an eminent and influential British object-relations theorist to illuminate the relationship between father/YHWH and child/Israel. My aim is not to 'analyse' biblical characters but to use the insights of object-relations theory to understand the relational dynamics of the text as constructed by the scribe responsible for the final form of Judges.[1] Concerned with how infants develop in relation with their primary caregivers and how maturation and individuation is achieved, the work of Donald Woods Winnicott sheds new light on the relationship dynamic between YHWH and Israel. I demonstrate how a fundamentally flawed relationship script is embedded in Judges' God-talk, unnoticed or suppressed by almost all existing commentators due to a built-in predisposition to privilege YHWH's perspective (which is to say, the author's construction of YHWH's perspective).[2] The consequence is a scholarly regurgitation of a damaging relational script with insufficient critical attention to the effects of this for end-users of biblical texts. This chapter's exploration of the parenting style reflected in the author's God-talk marks a significant break with that trend.

I begin with a summary of five major concepts that emerge from Winnicott's work. More detailed discussion of these ideas emerges in

---

[1] I recognise the distinction between author, implied author, narrator and implied narrator, but for the purposes of this project I use 'scribe' as a heuristic shorthand for the writer who constructed this text as it now appears in English Bibles. There is a more detailed discussion of the authorship of Judges in the next chapter.

[2] As noted in the Introduction, using such a convoluted expression would become tedious very quickly. Readers should assume henceforth that references to YHWH's perspective do not assume that he is a 'special' character or that his perspective is to be aligned with a metaphysical divinity beyond the text. It should be understood that YHWH's perspective is one constructed by the scribe.

subsequent sections, but the purpose at this point is to provide a snapshot, familiarising the reader quickly with Winnicott's terminology. The second section justifies the application of Winnicott's work to an ancient biblical text. I then justify the application of a twentieth century psychoanalyst's ideas to an ancient biblical texts before demonstrating how Winnicott's theories illuminate the Book of Judges.

Five Key Themes in Winnicott's Work

The Capacity to Be Alone

One of Winnicott's best known papers is 'The Capacity to Be Alone', first published in 1958. He believes the ability to say 'I am' is grounded in this capacity, which 'is one of the most important signs of maturity in emotional development' (1990a: 29). For adults it is a vital aspect of healthy living, and it enables the arena in which we imagine, dream and are creative. However, its healthy development depends on getting it right in childhood. The capacity emerges as the child builds up the ability to be absorbed in their own creativity while in the presence of the caregiver who might be similarly immersed in their own work. Ogden puts it well:

> the child must have the opportunity to play alone in the presence of the absent mother, and in the absence of the present mother … the mother is absent as object, but is there as the unnoticed, but present containing space in which the child is playing … The development of the capacity to be alone is a process in which the mother's role as invisible co-author of potential space is taken over by (what is becoming) the child. In this sense, when the healthy individual is alone, he is always in the presence of (the self-generated environment) mother. (2013: 56)[3]

So, in order to be able to enjoy this capacity, there are two basic building blocks. First, there needs to be a steady accretion of experiences of the reliable caregiver so that even when not in the room, the child can conjure parental presence based on those past experiences and feel secure. Second, the child needs the reliable attention of the

---

[3] Ogden, like several other theorists, uses the male pronoun when referring to the infant. I prefer to alternate between masculine and feminine pronouns, which coheres with Winnicott's own usage. He was a man before his time in such inclusive practice.

parent who holds off impingement so that the infant has the space to be and become. Impingements are disturbances that force the infant to respond and comply with an external other: 'He is wrenched from his quiescent state and forced to respond, or he is compelled to abandon his own wishes, to accept prematurely the feeble and unrealistic nature of his own demands, and to mold himself to what is provided for him' (Greenberg and Mitchell, 1983: 194). In time, all humans have to negotiate the tension between enjoying the capacity to be alone and the external demands of others, but at this early stage the infant needs the provision of a space to *be*; a reliably secure space in which she can safely relax: 'able to become unintegrated, to flounder, to be in a state in which there is no orientation, to be able to exist for a time without being either a reactor to an external impingement or an active person' (Winnicott, 1990a: 34).[4] Winnicott provides an adult example of enjoying the aftermath of satisfactory love-making, where both parties appreciate the sharing of 'solitude' while together (1990a: 31).

When not held at bay, impingements compel the child to react, which, for Winnicott, 'annihilates' being. This is a strong verb, but Winnicott's emphasis is justified. Impingements, if they recur persistently, provoke fragmentation, described by Greenberg and Mitchell as becoming 'prematurely and compulsively attuned to the claims and requests of others', losing connection with one's 'spontaneous needs and gestures, as these bear no relation to the way his mother experiences him and what she offers him' (1983: 194). When this happens, the 'source of spontaneous needs, images, and gestures, goes into hiding, avoiding at all costs the possibility of expression without being seen or responded to, the equivalence of complete psychic annihilation' (1983: 194). Furthermore, Winnicott (1990a: 46) believed nothing less than the health of the central core of the ego is at stake here, for the 'pathological alternative is a false life built on reactions to external stimuli' (1990a: 34).

Linked closely to the capacity to be alone is Winnicott's 'continuity of being'. Perhaps the desire of all beleaguered adults, continuity of being is the ability to work on one's own projects, or to relax in one's preferred way without unwarranted interference from external

---

[4] It seems paradoxical that the ability to be unintegrated is a sign of health, but as Abram (1996: 60) explains, the child who can fully relax into her mother's arms, surrendering into them with utmost trust, is the child who is developing integration and maturity.

demands. For Winnicott, it is early basis of ego-strength. If an infant is allowed to continue without 'serious interruption' she strengthens her sense of 'being real' and can begin to tolerate breaks in the continuity of being (1990a: 149). This prepares the infant for adult life where the tension between the demands of the external world and the desire for personal continuity of being has to be managed and tolerated continually. But failure to prevent impingement at the infant stage, failure to allow the child to become themselves rather than the child the parent desires, results in ego-weakening. Impingement throws the child into reactive episodes, which, if they were to recur persistently, 'sets going a pattern of fragmentation of being' (1990a: 60) between True and False Self.[5]

The True and False Self

In language that seems rather antiquated for a Judith Butler-informed scholarly context, Winnicott speaks unashamedly of a core self: we are born with an 'inherited potential which is experiencing a continuity of being, and acquiring in its own way and at its own speed a personal psychic reality and a personal body-scheme' (1990a: 46). Perhaps this could be linked to Butler's notion of identity congealing over time based on a series of performative actions, but Winnicott is far more confident in a psychic reality that may develop and shift but grounds being. However, this psychic reality is not something we can readily access because there is ultimately 'an incommunicado element ... sacred and most worthy of preservation' (Winnicott, 1990a: 187). Indeed, 'Rape, and being eaten by cannibals, these are mere bagatelles as compared with the violation of the self's core' (1990a: 187); a violation that is tantamount to a 'sin against the self' (1990a: 187).[6] This core self's communication is 'non-verbal; it is, like the music of the spheres, absolutely personal. It belongs to being alive. And in health, it is out of this that communication naturally arises' (1990a: 192).

---

[5] I follow Winnicott's practice of capitalising 'True' and 'False', as these are significant existential terms.

[6] This is why Winnicott believed silences are so important in therapy. Periods of non-communication allow 'the patient to creatively discover' rather than listen to the interrupting interpretations of an analyst. Analysts who interrupt are 'dangerous because we are too nearly in communication with the central still and silent spot of the patient's ego-organization' (1990a: 189).

The True Self is attuned to the core self, while the False Self is accommodated, in varying degrees, to the external world; although it might have a fairly close identity to one's True Self, or might allow the True Self 'a secret life', or search 'for conditions which will make it possible for the True Self to come into its own' (Winnicott, 1990a: 143). All humans negotiate between their True and False Selves since we have to comply with the polite conventions of the day. An academic, for instance, may possess a False Self that is highly successful in complying with the demands of research injunctions and producing esteemed publications. The world may applaud the success of such achievements and 'find it hard to believe in the very real distress of the individual concerned, who feels "phoney" the more he or she is successful' (1990a: 144).[7] Compliance can lead to significant accomplishments, but if the True Self and creativity is not set free, the apparently successful life can seem false, unreal, alien.

The Holding Environment

'Holding environment' refers to far more than a baby simply being held. It is a broad timeframe during which the child experiences continuity of being without undue interruptions from outside. In the first few years of life, a child's holding environment 'is in a state of continual erosion' for the mother's vital close attention inexorably tails off over a period of several months as 'the infant begins to consolidate his capacity to generate and maintain his own psychological matrix' (Ogden, 2013: 55). The 'good-enough mother' (see next section) intuitively recognises the importance of the holding environment and knows when it is time to 'let go of her identification with the infant as the infant needs to become separate' (Winnicott, 1990a: 53). During this process, the child creates an *internal* holding environment. Possessing this becomes hugely significant if, at a later stage of life, one loses the actual mother, or the person who fills in/symbolises that presence. Ogden describes the loss of such a figure as catastrophic: 'The person experiences himself as on the edge of dissolving ... the patient may report being unable to think or not knowing who he is' (2013: 59). He also notes how patients who have experienced this loss have 'a powerful need to reconstruct a holding environment' for they need to be 'contained' (2013: 60). In such circumstances, Ogden

---

[7] For more on this see Winnicott (1954).

recommends that the patient be held strongly by other humans in order to physically encompass the vulnerable person and their terror. Without this hands-on containment the patient's options are 'suicide, profound autistic withdrawal, or self-mutilation as methods of managing this state of psychological catastrophe' (2013: 60). Given this prospect, the healthy creation of the internal holding environment from infancy onward, is vitally important.

The Good-Enough Mother

Perhaps one of the most well-known Winnicottian terms, the good-enough mother is vital for creating the holding environment that provides the foundation for continuity of being and the capacity to be alone. Although Winnicott is renowned for this phrase it does not have to be the mother; he recognised that sometimes mother substitutes are necessary.[8] What is important is the reliable presence that allows for continuity of being, then an empathetic tailing off of that presence so that the child is enabled to develop self-reliance. 'Infant care', he writes, 'has as its main characteristic a steady presentation of the world to the infant ... done by continuous management by a human being *who is consistently herself*' (1990a: 87, emphasis added). At the early stage, her devotion to this act of presentation is vital and she is necessarily absorbed by it: 'soon she will be back to the office desk, or to writing novels, or to a social life ... but for the time being she is in it up to her neck' (1990a: 88). Winnicott's view of the father's role is dated but realistic for its time: the best thing fathers can do is provide an excellent, effective holding environment for the mother.

The Restitutive Gesture

The infant actually posits two mothers: the 'object-mother' and the 'environment-mother'. The former is more of a 'thing' than a human; the infant believes she conjures her (or specifically her breast), omnipotently, as and when required. Object-mother satisfies needs and can then be pushed away ruthlessly by the infant.

---

[8] His notion of the 'good-enough' mother is also a relief to those of us who are not up to motherhood ideals and I admire his consistent refusal to blame actual mothers for any failures that occur. My preferred terminology is of good-enough primary caregivers, but it is important to recognise that Winnicott is not trying to essentialise or idealise motherhood by using this phrase.

Environment-mother, in contrast, is the human that the infant comes to recognise as external, not omnipotently conjured; the one on whom the infant is dependent, the one who facilitates the infant's growth and independence. It is the environment-mother whom the infant learns to hold in his imagination when mother is physically absent, the one who makes it possible to 'be'.

The co-existence of these two mothers create ambivalence for the infant who realises that if he consumes the object-mother then his environment needs will be unsatisfied. Therefore, what arises in the infant is 'concern' for the environment-mother's survival and what Winnicott terms a 'sense of guilt' about his instinctual desires (1990a: 23). Crucial to this process is the opportunity for the infant to make a restitutive gesture that derives from the sense of guilt. Over time, the 'infant finds out that the mother survives and accepts the restitutive gesture' and thereby the infant is able to recognise and accept safely 'the total fantasy of the full instinctual impulse that was previously ruthless' (1990a: 23). What is really important here is the ability of the mother to survive the child's aggression, nay, 'extermination', for this is what enables the child to live with aggression rather than repress it. This is a process that happens again and again: '(i) instinctual experience, (ii) acceptance of responsibility which is called guilt (iii) a working through and (iv) a true restitutive gesture' (Winnicott, 1990a: 24).

These five ideas are very well known in psychological circles. When applied to the relationship dynamic between YHWH and Israel in Judges Winnicott's ideas shine a fresh and challenging stream of light on the text and on scholarly assumptions about YHWH and Israel. The initial questions are intriguing: Is YHWH the 'good-enough mother' who provides the good holding environment required for the healthy development of Israel's relationship to him and to the world, holding impingements at bay, facilitating Israel's capacity to be alone and a healthy balance between True and False Self? Or are his demands better interpreted as impingements, compelling the people of Israel's compliance, and thus leading to an unhealthy co-dependent relationship and a False Self adapted to the needs and desires of YHWH, their primary caregiver? And why does this matter? But prior to the discussion of these questions, some justification is required, to demonstrate how Winnicott's work with infants and mothers has relevance to the relationship between an Israel and YHWH in an ancient text that derives from a geographically different world and culture.

Applying Winnicott's Thought to the Book of Judges

As Gunn and Fewell note, dissuasion against using psychological tools to read biblical texts has been strong, given fears that one might be applying 'modern psychological categories on texts entirely too ancient and different from contemporary experience' (1993: 48). Accordingly, it might reasonably be asked why this twentieth-century theory concerning infants and their individuation has any relevance to an ancient text like Judges and its representation of the YHWH–Israel relationship.

There are at least three reasons why I think it not only has relevance but considerable importance for biblical studies and for end-users of biblical commentaries and theologies. First, the application of Winnicott's work revives an agenda set by Mieke Bal in 1988 but which has since lain lamentably dormant. While the analysis of themes and interests is a staple of Judges commentaries and scholarship, Bal demonstrated the shortfalls of such work. The themes usually discussed (Israelite leadership, the satirising of foreign kings, the glorification of YHWH, cultic orthodoxy, tribal unity) are surface interests, intended to be uppermost to the reader. No great prize for 'discovering' these. Bal went deeper, finding co-existing themes and interests that commentaries left unexplored – such as male fears and anxieties and the male will to power. Bal's insistence on examining repressed interests exposed fragile masculinities where ownership of women is needed to shore up masculine identity, status and honour. Informed by Freud, she analysed how the emphasis on women 'not having known a man' demonstrated how memories of a rival male could not be tolerated. Men require monopoly over women's sexual experiences; virginity offers this monopoly and 'promise of attachment' (1988: 54). But once deflowered, the woman shifts from 'an innocent and ignorant virgin' and becomes that 'other' kind of woman – the 'deadly, phallic woman' (1988: 55). Bal did not describe her work as feminist, but it contained that classic hallmark of feminist scholarship; reading against the grain in order to locate these underlying themes and interests. I continue Bal's work by exploring the God-talk in Judges with the help of the same counter-discourse of psychology that enables us to bring the ignored or repressed to the surface.

Second, biblical texts have always had profound resonance for readers, particularly readers of faith. Biblical heroes, villains, comic and shrewd plotlines all inspire recognition and have a living,

continued relevance. Not without reason are biblical figures continually redeployed in art, music, film and week after week in sermons.
Even for the non-believer, or the one who has turned away from
institutional religion and its scriptures for other forms of spirituality,
there remains something about these biblical tales that speaks profoundly about human life and all its messiness. Thus Ilona Rashkow,
while rejecting analysis of the personal psyche of the writer or his
literary character, since this is 'speculative business' (1993: 17),
believes there remains a basis for working with the characters and
plot of a text because they are sufficiently representative of human
life experiences to invite connection. It is this connection that propels
readers to continue finding resonance with characters from ancient
texts, be they in Greek myth, biblical texts, Shakespeare's plays or
ancient poems such as the Descent of Inanna. It is not surprising, for
instance, that Polden can write a profound psychotherapeutic book
on the midlife crisis by grounding her thoughts in Homer's *Odyssey*,
for the narrative sweep of the *Odyssey*

> evokes experiences of despair and of fragile hope of loneli-
> ness, insignificance and vastness: it traverses great wastes of
> the soul's internal landscape, and focuses on those intimate
> moments of connection and recognition which have the
> potential to change lives forever. As a story, the *Odyssey*
> reminds us of the potential for chaos lurking beneath our
> best-laid plans and most well-ordered existences, suggesting
> that the forces that really guide our lives may be greater, and
> stranger, than we realize. (2002: 6)

Biblical narrative can evoke similar engagement. Collicutt's discussion of how psychology can be brought to bear on the interpretation
of biblical texts notes how they are 'dominated by psychological
themes. These texts contain accounts of human behaviour and divine
behaviour described in anthropomorphic terms that proceeds
according to certain rules. Motives are attributed to the protagonists,
and inner thought processes are sometimes made explicit' (2012: 2).
As she goes on to say, reading biblical narrative can be like watching
a Greek play: populated by larger-than-life gods, goddesses, kings
and other elite characters. Such plays rehearse for the audience
significant themes such as fate, father or mother complexes; for the
audience or reader these large-scale themes have resonance. Rollins
and Kille write similarly: the Bible may not be a psychological text
but 'it speaks throughout of the trials, troubles, successes, and

victories of the self' (2007: xvii). Indeed, Lasine suggests that its stories and characters are presented to us as ancestral relatives: 'The Hebrew Bible is the "family album" of the target audiences. At various points we are urged to identify totally with them, and to relive their experiences in the present of our reading, in order not to make the mistakes they did' (2013: 54).

Critical readers, however, must create distance between their act of interpretation and the scribe's story. We may feel compelled to identify strongly with characters and storylines, but we resist in order to do our scholarly work of analysing plot, rhetoric and, in this case, the psychological drama of the YHWH–Israel relationship. Rashkow's work suggests that we could profitably undertake this scrutiny by viewing the biblical text in terms of a client's presenting narrative, which may include a 'succession of stories, occasional lyric, autobiography, and discursive monologues' (1993: 10). The interpreter takes on the role of the psychoanalyst, 'looking beyond the literal story to relate its structure and conflicts to a drama within some *theoretical* human mind, a mind ambiguously located between the fiction characters of the text and that of the reader (1993: 10).[9]

My third argument is that this chapter formalises something that is frequently happening in biblical scholarship anyway, but in an ad hoc, under-theorised and unacknowledged way. While Bar-Efrat describes the search for 'direct descriptions of internal deliberations, mental conflicts or psychological uncertainties and vacillations' as wasted because we have only 'brief glimpses of the inner lives of characters' (1989: 22), this has not prevented biblical scholars from engaging in assumptions or speculation about motives, relationships, feelings and personalities, recognising inherently that psychological matters cannot be divorced from the writing and reading project. This has been pointed out briefly by Rashkow (1993) and in greater depth by Lasine (2013). Rashkow rightly claims that we are all psychological readers whether we are conscious of it or not. Thus, when readers, ancient or modern, wonder at the description of

---

[9] Anticipating the question of how to avoid eisegesis, she points out that 'a narrative has no meaning before it is read, there can be no distinction between what is "in" a narrative and what is "in" a reader' (1993: 21). She adds: 'Meaning does not stand waiting to be uncovered behind a text, but evolves in front of it, actualized by readers and interpreters who produce new possibilities. Thus, biblical exegetes, like all readers, are in fact caught up in the very narratives we wish to explicate and play an interpretative role in the story' (1993: 22).

YHWH hardening Pharaoh's heart and sending plagues, 'Both might ask, "Did Pharaoh *really* deserve that?"' Inevitably, our reaction to these narratives is psychological. That is, in reading the Hebrew Bible, we try to shape the text until it is the kind of setting in which we can gratify our wishes and defeat our fears' (1993: 25). Lasine provides several examples of how commentators on 1 Kgs 19 attribute complexes and depression, introversion and burn-out to Elijah, demonstrating how scholarly 'psychologizing' is routinely present. Such inferences are not wrong, but they need to be examined more rigorously in the light of the diagnostic categories available to us. In Lasine's view Elijah is represented in terms consistent with a narcissistic personality, which, once grasped, illuminates Elijah's behaviour in 1 Kgs 17–2 Kgs 2 afresh. Lasine thus justifies his psychological reading of biblical characters by saying he is doing, in a more astute and informed way, something that commenters have always done. There are similar examples within Judges scholarship. Sasson, for example, has written about how YHWH places demands on a 'minor folk whose self-esteem was too fragile (or its neighbors too intimidating)', who could never satisfy the expectations placed on them, and the 'unhealthy' situation of being confronted with unpassable tests (2014: 205, 207). This comes close to the kinds of psychological inferences Lasine talks about. Sasson is not unsympathetic to Israel's plight; his translations are emotive and encourage the reader to feel the pain of their situation, but he does not engage further with the psychological aspects of the scribe's presentation, or the on-going psychological effects of presenting such a story as scripture. I therefore believe Lasine is right to bring psychological tools the act of interpretation in a far more formal, rigorous way. Posing the question more directly – what does object relations theory have to tell us about the YHWH–Israel relationship – puts us on a more conscious theoretical footing, overtly engaging tools from this field to interrogate the text.

And why Winnicott in particular? I focus on Winnicott in this chapter because his work on the child-parent dynamic and object-relations has been seminal. He was a founding figure for the issues/theories under discussion in this chapter and he remains a prominent, much-discussed figure in contemporary psychoanalytic discourse. I find his work resonant and applicable and, where necessary, I discuss how some of his key ideas have been explained and further addressed by psychological theorists.

Analysis of the Parent/YHWH–Child/Israel Relationship through a Winnicottian Lens

Israel: The Guilty Innocents

Judg. 2:10 places us in a brand new parent–child situation. Joshua has died and with him an entire generation is gathered to their ancestors. A new family of children have arrived, ignorant of YHWH and his previous works. We are thus placed at a fresh beginning for the relationship between child/Israel and parent/ YHWH whose work has to begin anew. Commentators on Judges are, however, quick to reinforce scribal accusations against this newly arrived generation. Perhaps the strongest comment comes from Hamlin who, commenting on 2:6–3:6, describes the Israelites as 'the earliest examples of a perennial problem'; they 'fit the description of the "perverse generation" (Deut 32:20), who roused God's anger by their "abominable practices"', and who 'were like the Israelites of Isaiah's time who, lacking knowledge of the LORD, were "offspring of evildoers ... who deal corruptly" (Isa 1:3–4)' (1990: 59). This is heavy load to inflict on child/Israel who has not yet even heard of YHWH and his historical deliverances, but is not untypical of the commentarial tradition which focuses *not* on whether YHWH can provide a stable holding environment in which Israel can mature and grow, but on the waywardness and rebelliousness of the child. In so doing, they follow faithfully the rhetoric of the biblical scribe and his alignment with the perspective of YHWH, which, of course, he constructs.

Judg. 2:12 criticises Israel for abandoning YHWH Elohim, implying that they forsook an existing relationship. However, the text is quite clear that there has not yet been a 'relationship'; this generation did not know of YHWH or his past deeds. The report that Israel grew up serving indigenous gods is thus entirely understandable and YHWH's indignance less so. The dissonance is clear, and when commentators, following the scribe's lead, reinforce Israel's bad behaviour, they end up in a rather contradictory place that involves accepting Israel's ignorance while still putting blame at their door. Sasson, for example, states that the reality behind 2:10's claim that they 'knew not YHWH' is that 'In fact they did, but they simply chose to ignore him' (2014: 189) but he does not justify this claim any further. Niditch says 'A new generation arises who is ominously said not to know YHWH or the deeds he did for Israel. Judg. 2:11–17 describes the *Israelites' fall from covenant faithfulness* in strongly

Deuteronomic language' (2008: 49, emphasis added). Pressler takes a similar line: 'A description of the faithfulness of Joshua and his generation precedes a notice of their deaths, which leads to the plaint that the next generation did not know Yahweh ... Knowledge of God is part of covenantal relationship. Not to know God is to *abandon that relationship* ... The generation following Joshua and his cohorts did not know God' (2002: 137, emphasis added).

Butler follows the trend with a statement that mirrors the text's dissonance: Israel 'cannot worship the God they do not know, so they forsake him' (2009: 43). But can anyone 'forsake' a person unknown to them? This question of how Israel can fall from something, or abandon someone of whom they have no experience is left hanging. These scholars appear to be following the scribal ideology which has actually set up a paradox – Israel as the *guilty innocents*. The scribe's purpose is presumably to drive home his message that leadership and collective memory is vital for the relationship between YHWH and Israel to prosper. Without it, Israel turns to deities that are readily available and knowable. But it remains a strange beginning.

Two scholars acknowledge the oddness but only to some limited extent. Lillian Klein notes how Israel is a '"victim" of its own ignorance and Yahweh's knowledge' (1989: 19) although she isn't commenting on 2:10 specifically, but on the overall ironic juxtaposition of perspectives throughout the book. When she does comment specifically on 2:10 it is only to repeat the text's incongruity without comment: 'the generation that has no contact with Yahweh has no awareness of him; it forsakes its God and adopts others' (1989: 32). Robert Polzin, distinguishing between synchronic and panchronic narratorial devices,[10] notes how 1:1–2:5 is narrated synchronically while 2:6–3:6 belongs to the panchronic narrator who 'presents his story from a psychological perspective internal to many or all of his characters' (1980: 150). Since the synchronic narration does not provide the reader with any privileged knowledge we 'experience the same shifts in thoughts and emotions that the Israelites are described as experiencing' (1980: 149) and we thus 'wonder with the Israelites themselves how and why the situation could have deteriorated so' and are compelled to ask why the Lord declares in

---

[10] In synchronic mode, the narrator relates events without displaying any 'special knowledge' or insight into what is going on and what the characters are thinking or feeling. In panchronic mode we have the omniscient narrator (Polzin, 1980: 149).

2:2 'Look what you have done!' (1980: 150). So, for a moment or two, the narrator has allowed us to share the bewilderment of Israel before he switches to panchronic narration and their condemnation. This panchronic narrator then cleverly repeats Josh 24:28–31 at Judg. 2:6 to provide a deliberate 'rewinding' to show how the tribes' military wars were *accompanied all the time by idolatrous behaviour* which accounts for their failures. Yes, it is a 'brilliant' narratorial tactic, as Polzin claims, giving the reader a lightbulb moment of realisation (1980: 125). Polzin does not, however, pay sufficient attention to the fact that the new generation that arose after the death of Joshua are said to have no knowledge of YHWH and that they are condemned for abandoning a deity that they did not know. I want to resist condemnation of an ignorant generation, and stay longer than Polzin did with Israel's bafflement.

Without doubt, this fresh generation inevitably starts off on the wrong foot, obliviously presenting overt provocation to a deity who finds their serving of other deities intolerable. Use of כעס is significant, giving us not only a strange beginning but a very ominous one. Parent/YHWH is going to make himself known to child/Israel not by the kind of attention that Winnicott advocates, i.e., Primary Maternal Preoccupation and its 'high degree of adaptation to individual infant needs' (1990b:22), but by punishment.[11] This becomes clear in the paradigmatic cycle described in Judg. 2:11–19. YHWH's parenting style is constructed to be one of didactic chastisement, using a third party to inflict pain with cruelty and for prolonged periods (eight, eighteen, twenty or forty years). This will compel his children to appeal to him for help. By using foreign enemies as his stooges, YHWH avoids applying the punishment directly, which, perhaps, prevents the punished children from

---

[11] Primary Maternal Preoccupation is described helpfully and empathetically by Ogden: 'the mother, at great emotional and physical cost to herself, absorbs the impact of time (e.g. by foregoing the time she needs for sleep, the time she needs for the emotional replenishment that is found in being with someone other than her baby, and the time she needs for making something of her own that is separate from the infant). In effect, the mother's earliest holding involves her entering into the infant's sense of time, thereby transforming for the infant the impact of the otherness of time and creating in its place the illusion of a world in which time is measured almost entirely in terms of the infant's physical and psychological rhythms. Those rhythms include the rhythms of his need for sleep and for wakefulness, of his need for engagement with others and his need for isolation, the rhythms of hunger and satiation, the rhythms of breathing and heartbeat ... [This] represents an abrogation of herself in her unconscious effort to get out of the infant's way' (2007: 78).

becoming directly alienated from him. It has certainly worked when it comes to the reception history. In his discussion of Judg. 4–5, note how Hamlin places the criticism on Jabin and Sisera rather than YHWH. Jabin and Sisera are identified as 'the Engine of Oppression'; he refers to Jabin's 'oppressive political policy', his 'Economic Strangulation', the 'sexual violation of women'. These things become the focus, not the actions of YHWH who sold Israel into their hands. The opprobrium directed at Jabin and Sisera lets YHWH completely off the hook. When Hamlin does discuss YHWH's motivations and actions it is in terms of 'tough love'. YHWH is in the right and his punishment should be seen as 'constructive'. He is the father who disciplines out of love, 'moved by their suffering' to raise up a deliverer (1990: 59). 2:16–18 affirms 'God's grace like the arms of a mother or father surrounding wayward Israel even when they continue in sin' (1990: 60). It is YHWH's patience with his recalcitrant children, his soft spot for Israel, which becomes the focus. Divine determination to remain in a relationship with Israel is seen as a comforting trait, a sign of divine loyalty. The needs of child/Israel are never put at the forefront of the discussion.[12]

But in terms of Winnicott's theories of healthy child development, this situation is far from ideal. It is a style of parenting that not only demands compliance but compels it by force. The child/Israel must conform and have no other caregiving figures. In his comments on morals and education, Winnicott argues that all children have the capacity for belief and to choose the moral good, but it is imperative that the child is allowed to develop that capacity naturally rather than have it instilled into them by a moral educator. Compliance to an authority figure may offer

---

[12] It is speculative but intriguing to ponder how far more dated biblical commentators, who align themselves so readily with the text, were living at a time when the model of divine discipline was consistent with child-rearing manuals that stressed the need to break the will of the child. Miller, for example, refers to the 'poisonous pedagogy' present in child-rearing books written between 1749 and the 1850s where breaking the will of the child in order to gain control of him is stated with a clarity that later publications would mask. Miller notes how it seems 'perfectly normal to speak of the necessity of striking and humiliating children and robbing them of their autonomy, at the same time using such high-sounding words as chastening, upbringing, and guiding onto the right path' (1987: 16). In the tradition she discusses 'it was considered obstinacy and was therefore frowned upon to have a will and mind of one's own' (1987: 43). It is very interesting to see how the child-rearing experts she discusses use biblical images of God as examples and, indeed, see themselves as participating in the omnipotence of God.

acceptance and reward but then the temptation is to construct a False Self that submits. However, 'adults only too easily mistake compliance for growth' (1990a: 201) while the child's 'true or essential self becomes hidden, and becomes deprived of living experience' (1990a: 102). As I will argue further below, the scribe's presentation of YHWH's parenting style produces the promise of an obedient, compliant child but not without that child paying a significance price. The Judges scribe projects a disciplinarian father and a split representation of Israel – the 'good' child as represented by the scribe and the interests he espouses, and the 'bad' child who is the Israel of a presumed (but invented) past.

'And They Cried Out to YHWH': Israel's Restitutive Gesture

When read in the light of Winnicott's work, Israel's crying out to YHWH could be read as the reparative gesture which maintains the relationship with the environmental parent. However, Winnicott's view is that the restitutive gesture should emerge from a tension between the expression of an aggressive id drive that wants to consume the object-mother and the contrary concern for the environment-mother's survival. The good-enough mother allows time and space for the reparative gesture to emerge. If she meets the infant's needs before he makes this gesture she smothers the need for the infant to be able to express himself, or act independently, thereby putting him back into the merged state, rather than facilitating individuation. The child needs space and time to process his own feelings and thoughts, then offering, voluntarily, the gesture that is his own, that comes from within his nascent individuality. Healthy development happens when the infant becomes able to manage this balancing act. The child thus grows into an adult who is able to manage the ambiguities in the hate/love flow of all relationships, and subsequently the tension between following one's own instinctual life and the need to satisfy the demands of a working environment. Failure to learn this at infancy, however, can lead to problems, not least an over-developed false, compliant self.

In Judges, Israel is arguably given plenty of space and time in which to arrive at that gesture. Israel is left to its own devices for varying lengths of time to discover for itself what the consequences of exploratory behaviour with other attachment figures (indigenous gods) will be. They discover that it results in invasion by hostile enemies and the inevitable return to YHWH, who responds to their cries, raises up a deliverer and restores the relationship.

However, Winnicott's model illuminates some significant problems with this pattern. First, as commentators often note, there is a question about the genuineness with which Israel cries out to YHWH; is their gesture self-serving or is there real repentance? In most commentaries, Israel's crying out is deemed mechanical, and, as a result, blame is further loaded upon Israel for their lack of authentic repentance. Scholars can be subtle or overt in their accusatory tone. Wong is fairly descriptive: 'YHWH's increasing reluctance to respond to their cries … suggests that their cries are becoming increasingly perfunctory and manipulative, until finally, they did not even bother to cry out' (2006: 185). Block, however, lays on the criticism with a trowel, utilising some particularly cutting adjectives: 'God sees past their pious words to their treacherous and parasitic hearts' (1999: 347). Both views derive from a reading position that privileges YHWH and the scribe. I want to resist this and look more closely at Israel's motivation for crying out in order to get behind the scribe's desire to present us with a 'bad' Israel and see the effects of his presentation. When we achieve that, the portrayal of Israel does not automatically prompt scholarly censure but is seen rather as the inevitable by-product of the scribal agenda.

It is clear that in most Judges narratives Israel turns to YHWH when their very survival is under threat. The situation described in Judg. 6, for example, is grim. At his evocative best, the scribe describes countless camels and a locust-like plague of Midianites and Amalekites who create famine conditions. In the face of this onslaught the Israelites are forced to take refuge in caves and the mountains. Or consider Judg. 10:8 where they have been shattered and smashed by Ammonites and are in dire straits. Had they not cried out to YHWH at these times their future looked hopeless. Commentators acknowledge this and yet still chastise Israel for having insincere or improper motivations. R.H. O'Connell, noting how the paradigmatic cycle of 2:10–3:6 does not include the 'crying out' element but refers rather to YHWH's compassion being stirred by their 'groaning', believes the scribe implies that Israel was 'motivated by the duress of oppression rather than by anything resembling a freely motivated change of religious ideology or devotion' (1996: 40). In his view, this suspicion is confirmed in 6:7–10 and in 10:6–16 where 'the sincerity of Israel's cry of repentance while they are being oppressed is called into question' (1996: 41). So, while he concedes that Israel's reparative gesture is provoked by weight of oppression, its genuineness remains questionable.

However, if we are to understand this in Winnicott's terms, a reparative gesture represents the desire to ensure the parent's survival as the child manages the tension between aggression/hate of the object-mother and the need for the environmental-mother not only to endure the aggression, but demonstrably come out of it as loving and caring as ever. The reparative gesture is about acknowledging hatred, the need to make amends and the survival of the consistently loving, reliable, primary caregiver.[13] Winnicott is absolutely clear about the importance of owning aggression if a child is to develop into a healthy adult who has learned to tolerate and manage the co-existence of love/hate within relationships.[14] For Winnicott, it is the hate that gives rise to an (un)conscious sense of guilt and capacity for concern which can subsequently be appeased by acts of constructiveness. In the constructive work (say in buying the person a present) one is 'building up a self-strength which makes possible a toleration of the destructiveness' (Winnicott, 1990b: 88). For genuine reparation to happen, the person *must* be in touch with the destructiveness.[15] Without this, acts of reparation are meaningless; they are merely distracting gesticulations.

---

[13] It seems a strong term to use for an infant but the language of 'hate' is often used in object relations theory when discussing how we learn to tolerate the love/hate aspects of relationships. Bowlby uses simpler terminology – 'getting angry with and wishing to hurt the very person who is most loved' (1979: 5). Bowlby argues that it is the fear and guilt stemming from this emotional conflict, or the inability to face it or manage it, which underlies subsequent psychological disorders. He advocates a clear channel of communication where it is ok for a child to say '"I hate you, mummy" or "Daddy you're a beast"' since 'we can show our children that we're not afraid of hatred and that we are confident it can be controlled; moreover we provide for the child the tolerant atmosphere in which self-control can grow' (1979: 12). Parental responses that punish a child for such expression, or complaints about how ungrateful he or she is, are actually controlling mechanisms; 'neither are very successful' and in fact 'exact a heavy toll in unhappiness' (1979: 12).

[14] Benjamin reinforces the point, stating that the growing child has to learn how to see the caregiver as an independent other, 'not simply as the "external world" or an adjunct of his ego' (1990: 23). Both parties need to have their irreducible otherness mutually recognised.

[15] In adult therapy this means that the client who consoles themselves with the idea that they have started therapy for some constructive outcome is employing a false contrivance that prevents contact with the urge to destroy. For therapy to work, the client must be able to get in touch with that destructive urge and the therapist must, of course, allow the client to find their aggression which seeks to 'destroy' him/her. Only in the therapist's survival does he or she become 'real' to the client, rather than a projection of the client. When that has been faced, then the client can shift towards genuine concern and reparation.

But we do not see any aggressiveness on Israel's part; the scribe describes no tantrum, no hostile rejection of the divine parent. Yes, they 'forget' and turn to local deities, but this does not appear to derive from a healthy feeling of indignation or anger on their part. Elsewhere (Psalms of Lament, Lamentations, Job and Qoheleth) the Hebrew Bible gives us an Israel that complains long and hard, but not in this text. In Judges their crying out is not from anger, but, as noted above, from a reaction to the weight of their suffering at the hands of the foreign enemies. For example, in 4:2 they cry out because of the nine hundred chariots of iron, a verse that shows O'Connell (1996) is right to say that they are motivated by duress. Schneider concurs: 'They did not consider their own actions or an absence of leadership as the cause of their distress, *but technology*' (2000: 63, emphasis added). And yet, the blame still gets heaped on Israel's shoulders. The implication is that Israel are at fault because they have not realised that it is their own apostasy that has put them in this predicament. Again the wayward child is accused; this is the default scholarly position.

However, the child/Israel is prevented from expressing anger at the external source of their predicament because of the smokescreen set up by the scribe. Looking from the perspective of the child/Israel, we could imagine considerable bafflement about why they keep getting sucked into cycles of oppression and deliverance. YHWH sent a messenger in 2:1 but he addresses the previous generation, not the one that 'grew up after them, who did not know the Lord or the work he had done for Israel' (2:10). This fresh Israel, this new born generation receives the discipline of a father/YHWH who is not direct with them; the proxy troops mask his disciplinary involvement. They thus do not cry out with real frustration at the one who is the real cause of their woe, but rather they appeal to him as the one who can save them from it. There is certainly irony here, but not the kind of irony that scholars usually note. It is an irony that puts the child/Israel in a hopeless and unsettling situation, compelled to appeal to their veiled oppressor. Psychologically it a very disturbing picture but one that is explained further in Chapter 4's discussion of the masochistic defence mechanism and its rewards.

So, the very plot of Judges means that we cannot see the healthy emergence of the reparative gesture which derives from the child's expression of anger against the caregiver. We do not see examples of the good-enough mother in action who, in Winnicott's view, must survive the attack of the infant and continue to offer a reliable,

secure holding environment (1990a). Winnicott stressed how important this is for healthy development. For example, working with
Second World War distressed evacuees, he emphasised the importance of a reliable holding environment that could withstand the
aggression of those children. This holding environment was held in
place *not by physical punishment*, but by caring, reliable, stable
boundaries that, when tested to their limits, held fast. In this he,
and his representatives in the evacuee centres, restored the original
mother–child holding environment, making good that which had
been damaged. Straker reinforces the vital importance of this toleration by the caregiver. In a most empathetic summary of Winnicott's
position she writes:

> the greatest gift a mother can give her child is the capacity to
> destroy her in phantasy while she survives in reality by
> standing her ground against the aggression expressed
> toward her. It is her survival of his aggression, real and
> imagined, that helps the child to distinguish between his
> internal world of objects and introjects and the external
> world of people and events
> For the mother to give her child this gift, she has to be able
> to withstand his or her aggression without fragmenting and
> becoming submissive or retaliating and becoming dominat-
> ing. If she is unable to stay her ground and endlessly capitu-
> lates to the demands of the child, or if she fragments in the
> face of his aggression, he is unlikely to moderate his own
> narcissism. He is likely to become tyrannical in interpersonal
> relationships and to dominate others. If she becomes retali-
> atory and dominating herself, the child is likely to become
> submissive and struggle to have a sense of self outside of a
> compliant adaptation to the other. (2015: 6)

If the relationship between YHWH and Israel is reconsidered in the
light of this theory, it is easy to detect what is needed for healthy
coexistence: YHWH has to allow himself to become the focus of
Israel's aggression and yet survive as the environment-mother, still
caring and reliably supporting his children. He would need to be
mature enough to recognise that the child will throw tantrums, push
against the boundaries, reject the parent, but that in so doing, is
merely testing that the loved parent can withstand their hate.
YHWH, however, as Lasine (2002) so rightly discerns, cannot tolerate being hated.

To some extent, the commentary tradition does recognise how YHWH provides a continuing holding environment despite Israel's turn to additional gods. This is where commentators who are writing for a believing audience seem most comfortable, extolling the deity's patient endurance and loyalty, despite Israel's provocation. What they miss is that the story world does not allow Israel to explore the love/hate tension of their feelings for YHWH because he has masked himself from being identified as the author of their oppression. The constant focus on YHWH as loving parent, who keeps faith with wayward Israel, gets in the way. Webb's (2012: 54) comment that 'Israel survives only because Yahweh does not give up on her and simply walk away' interprets divine resolve very positively but in psychological terms it could be seen as an assertion of power by the dominant party who will not let the other self-develop. Compelled by oppression to return to YHWH, Israel's cry is that of a compliant child, not the angry rebellious child. To that extent, Israel's motivations are indeed questionable but in a different way from usual scholarly interpretation. Rather than focussing on the apparent insincerity of Israel's remorse, a Winnicott-informed appraisal would look at it in terms of how an over-developed False self is being moulded by a deity jealous for his own status. And the effect of this is a child not permitted to get in touch with its own hostility or with the proper target of that hostility, without which the potential for genuine concern lies dormant. So, when commentators criticise Israel's mechanical gesture they fall entirely into the scribe's rhetoric and miss the underlying issue. They *cannot* produce a genuine reparative gesture because the narrative frame of reference does not permit an outburst against YHWH himself, whose involvement in their plight is veiled.

One might argue in response: what is the loving parent supposed to do? Let Israel abandon itself to an uncertain future with gods that would presumably not provide for them as YHWH would? Allow Israel to lose the land and their identity? A loving parent of a troubled teenager does not abandon that youth to sink or swim in a perilous milieu of predators and danger. Maybe not, but neither does the loving parent reel the child in through actions that oppress and violently circumscribe their lives until there is no choice but to comply. The healthy holding environment is not like this. In Winnicott's view of healthy child development, parents do not create a child as a potter produces a pot with a planned, known outcome to which they mould the clay. Rather they begin a 'developmental process which results in their being a lodger in the mother's body and then in her arms and then in the home ... *and what this lodger will turn out like is outside anyone's control'* (1990a: 85. emphasis added). The 'towards independence' stage that characterises the child at puberty is one where the teenager has settled into a 'pattern that is a compromise between copying the parents and defiantly establishing a personal identity' (1990a: 92). The parental role is to provide a healthy environment in which the child can mature rather than blocking that process, tolerating non-compliance as a necessary stage in that development. Winnicott puts this well: 'Shall I say that, for a child to be brought up so that he can discover the deepest part of his nature, someone has to be defied, and even at times killed, without there being a danger of a complete break in the relationship?' (1984: 52).[16] His question exemplifies the problem with the YHWH–Israel relationship: YHWH has a very clear template for the child/Israel's behaviour. The recalcitrant child's choices (other gods) are sharply and punitively rejected and their doing of what was good in their own eyes is curtailed by YHWH's manipulation of events to the extent of one tribe's near-extinction and the kidnap and rape of multiple women. It is all about compliance. And when development goes wrong then the capacity for guilt and reparation gets replaced with defence mechanisms. One of those mechanisms is the development of the False Self. Another is a masochistic defence, but discussion of this is reserved for Chapter 4.

If any hate *is* expressed, then it is YHWH's. Commenting on 2:14, Butler has YHWH 'infuriated' and resists any suggestion that righteous indignation is qualitatively different to the human experience of rage (2009: 44). YHWH burns at the nostrils on several occasions – 2:20, 3:8 and 10:7 – while in 6:39 Gideon, cautiously requesting a further sign, pleads that YHWH's nostrils will not burn as a result. Gideon seems aware that Israel has a propensity to 'push his [YHWH's] buttons' (Lasine, 2002: 47, n.27). YHWH may be credited elsewhere (Ps. 103:8, Ps. 145:8 and Exod. 34:6) with being slow to anger and full of steadfast love, but there is a volatile side to his character. David M. Gunn memorably refers to Saul's deity as 'unpredictably terrible, jealous of his own status, quick to anger and impatient of the complexities of human action and motivation'

---

[16] Of course 'killed' in Winnicottian terms refers to the *rejection* of the caregiver, the ability to express utmost anger against them in a way that necessarily tests the caregiver's love.

(1980: 131). Yet, for all the burning rage noted in Judges, YHWH refuses to let go. Winnicott's emphasis on Primary Maternal Preoccupation, so necessary for the infant's earliest months, becomes in Judges the 'divine determination' of which Webb (2012) speaks. For Winnicott, the good-enough mother will tail off her preoccupation with the child quite naturally because she inherently recognises the need for her infant to develop its capacity for being alone. Her holding environment remains, but the infant grows less and less dependent upon her. The child develops an internal working model of the reliable, loving caregiver and individuates. But YHWH's Primary Paternal Occupation consists of a determination that does not let go, that is persistently, violently, punitively, ensuring that the child provides unwavering loyalty consistent with his needs. And as Lasine argues, this 'demand for total love (Deut 6:5) is an example of enforced idealization which precludes his children from experiencing the kind of hate needed to make love authentic' (2002: 46).

To conclude this section, I underscore the absence of any overt aggression on Israel's part and put down a marker for a later consideration of its significance. Here, the focus is on Winnicott's ideas and I thus put the emphasis on the emergence of the False Self, an inability to manage the inevitable love/hate balance in future relationships and in the freedom/constraints balance of adult life, and the damage done to the ability to be unintegrated safely, or to individuate fully.

YHWH's Holding Environment, Israel's Continuity of Being and Capacity to Be Alone

In life we manage to hold a tension in play between what we want to be doing and what is expected of us from others, or between what we really think, believe and feel and the external persona that we present to others. The capacity to do this effectively has its origins in the parent's careful meeting of the infant's needs. The infant thinks it is omnipotent, conjuring the nursing breast, the change of nappy, the warm arms all at will. Of course what is actually happening is that the parent is supporting the weak ego of the infant, giving her the expectation that her needs will be reliably met. Accordingly, the infant develops faith in external reality and, as this happens again and again, she can safely let go of her imagined omnipotence, ultimately seeing it for the fantasy it had been. Once this expectation of reliability has been established the child can form relationships with objects as they are, i.e., as things independent of her will. The origins of the True Self begin, then, with Primary Maternal Preoccupation. 'Infant care has as its main characteristic a steady presentation of the world to the infant ... done by continuous management by a human being who is consistently herself' (Winnicott, 1990a: 87). In time, the child incorporates the memory of the mother and is able to go for longer and longer periods, assuming her supportive presence even when she is not there. During this crucial development, mothers often make efforts not to cause distress by being away for too long. A child slowly becomes equipped for dealing with the loss of the mother who picks up her own life again, and environmental factors such as a steady collection of mother substitutes can help, but until then the reliable support of the environment-mother who is 'consistently herself' is vital.

As noted above, the True Self can be seen in the restitutive gesture which, for Winnicott, is 'the True Self in action' (1990a: 148). However, if the mother 'substitutes her own gesture', requiring that the infant does this or that, development is thwarted. The infant 'gets seduced into compliance, a compliant False Self reacts to environmental demands and the infant 'may grow to be just like mother, nurse, aunt, brother, or whoever at the time dominates the scene' (1990a: 146). When the True Self is threated with annihilation this has its origins 'in the life of an infant whose mother was not only "not good enough" ... but was *good and bad in a tantalizingly irregular manner* ' (1990a: 147, emphasis added). The result for the child is damaging: 'Reacting to unreliability in the infant-care process constitutes a trauma, each reaction being an interruption of the infant's "going on being" and a rupture of the infant self', while on the other hand, a child with a reliable mother starts life well and 'the idea of goodness and of a reliable and personal parent or God can follow naturally' (1990a: 97).

In Judges, one might argue that YHWH is reliably present throughout the Judge cycles; turning up when cried out for, delivering Israel from oppression by raising a deliverer. Commentators emphasise an overriding, ultimate consistency in YHWH's character. Amit, for example, argues that the redactor of Judges understands God's guiding intervention in history in terms of signs. The cyclical pattern of obedience–rescue, disobedience–punishment is a sign. The actions of the judge in delivering Israel is a sign – one 'reinforcing the existence and intervention of a guiding divine providence' (1999: 27). The redactor shows how history is 'not a mere random sequence of events' but one 'rich in signs' (1999: 27) which 'convey certain messages to the reading community concerning the manner of God's providence and guidance and the behaviour expected of the people' (1999: 28).

But we need to stand outside the scribe's over-arching rhetoric. The notion of an ultimate, providential consistency and reliability only convinces if we concur that YHWH acts in appropriate ways to bring his children into covenant loyalty. But if we find his deputation of enemies to compel Israel's compliance problematic, if we think that correct oracular enquiry is not best taught by sending thousands to their death, then the overall framework of 'YHWH knows what's best for his children' is severely compromised. And once we remove ourselves from that over-arching rhetoric we see that YHWH is not, actually, consistently and reliably himself and his holding environment. This is deeply unsettling, with impingements being deliberately sent, rather than kept at bay.

Let us consider those two instances in more detail; first, the deputation of enemies to compel Israel into compliance. Recounted in variant forms, YHWH either gives Israel over to proxy forces sent to tyrannise them, sells them into the hands of enemies or his hand is against them to bring misfortune. Commentators either simply note this action without so much as a nod to the ethics involved or actively defend it. Niditch refers impassively to YHWH's use of 'subjugation as punishment' (2008: 56) while Soggin (1981: 45–46) and Boling (1975: 80) report the image of YHWH as 'divine slave trader' without further comment. Butler is straightforwardly laconic: 'Yahweh always controlled the plunderers, selling Israel to them' (2009: 45). Bowman is content to note how YHWH's willingness for punitive interaction with Israel is 'a major contention in the book of Judges' (2007: 33). O'Connell, primarily concerned with variants and plot structure, talks about 'YHWH *justly* subjugating those who served foreign Baals and Asherahs' (1996: 83, emphasis added). Webb narrates how Israel's actions, as described in 2:14–15, reap 'consequences', notes how the scribe takes 'considerable pains … to depict Yahweh's angry response as controlled and fully justified' and how the next unit (vv. 16–19) emphasizes 'Yahweh's compassion expressed in his saving them *from* "plunderers" and "enemies"' (1987: 110). He thus implicitly notes the irony of YHWH getting the credit for delivering Israel from enemies *he* sent their way, but Webb's interest in structure means that he does not raise questions about the dubiousness of the strategy. Pressler cautions the reader about victim-blaming but justifies YHWH's action: 'Divine love cannot be indifferent to sin and evil . . . God must act to stop the evil and redress the situation' (2002: 143). Webb's later commentary notes how 'Yahweh's angry response' . . . [is] entirely in keeping with warnings previously given' (2012: 144). This is consistent with Webb's introductory section on the contribution Judges offers for Old Testament theology:

> Yahweh will punish Israel for her unfaithfulness; the remaining nations will be left to be a snare to Israel, to test her, and to teach her war, but there is never any suggestion in either Deuteronomy or Judges that Yahweh will ever renege on his relationship with her . . . The alternating punishment and deliverance happen within this relationship, not in fundamental contradiction to it . . . That Israel survives the judges period at all is a miracle of divine mercy rather than something Israel herself achieves. The theology of Judges is fundamentally relationship rather than mechanistic, dynamic rather than static, and raw rather than refined. It is a theology of conflict in which both parties suffer, and in which Israel survives only because Yahweh does not give up on her and simply walk away. (2012: 54)

Webb's argument works by establishing a joint consensus that a) Israel's unfaithfulness merits punishment, b) Israel are fortunate to have a deity who punishes because this brings them back into relationship with him, c) a relationship founded on punishment and deliverance is acceptable and d) YHWH's determination to hold the relationship in place merits our applause. In other words, it works by assuming agreement that the narrator's view is the only view and the right view.

However, the fact that Webb takes up this defence signals an unstated discomfort with the behaviour of YHWH, a behaviour that readers might find disreputable if they considered the finer detail about the psychology of a punishment–deliverance cycle. Lasine (2002: 40), alert to the literature on abuse survivors, notes how theparent's/YHWH's punishing/rescuing approach 'sound[s] suspiciously like' the way abusers of women create both terror and abasing submission. It is a startling section of his paper, as is his accompanying discussion about the way abuse is masked.[17] Once

---

[17] In the context of a discussion on how battered women perceive their abuser, Judith Lewis Herman writes: 'The repeated experience of terror and reprieve . . . may

this has been observed, one can no longer think of the relationship between YHWH and Israel in the positive way that Webb recommends. It becomes clear that readers of biblical texts need the commentary tools that will enable them to think critically about the scribe's representation of the relationship, not provide a justification of the scribe's perspective.[18]

As for the second example, where YHWH's laconic response to Israel's cultic queries in 20:18 and 20:21 leads to eleven tribes setting out to avenge the Levite's woman, it is important to note the alarming death counts: 22,000 on the first occasion and 18,000 on the second. Hyperbolic numbers of course, but rhetorically effective. However, beneath the instructive discipline of the scribe's account is the disturbing indication that Israel cannot rely upon their deity's answers. This discomforting insight is pushed under the carpet by a theology that finds YHWH inscrutable; that he is a God of the Unexpected who, using highly unorthodox agents and means to accomplish his designs, demonstrates that he will simply not do what you want him to. No cultic images, priests, sacred vows or consultations will automatically ensure his favour. He will not be confined or constrained to act mechanically. He is above all cajoling, all manipulation, all human control. Polzin (1980) and O'Connell (1996) rightly demonstrate how this theme runs through the entire book. But if we see YHWH as a constructed character in the story world, then we cannot surrender to theological or metaphysical claims that YHWH is somehow 'beyond us'. We can say that supposed inscrutability is a character trait; it is simply that and we don't have to justify it. But in my view it must be criticised for there can be

---

result in a feeling of intense, almost worshipful dependence upon an all-powerful, godlike authority. The victim may live in terror of his wrath, but she may also view him as the source of strength, guidance, and life itself. The relationship may take on an extraordinary quality of specialness. Some ... voluntarily [suppress] their own doubts as a proof of loyalty and submission' (1997: 92). Lasine picks up the links between this and the repeated testing of 'special' Israel in the wilderness, arguing that YHWH behaves like an abusing but deified parent. His 'efforts to "discipline" Israel ... are perfectly suited to make his children view him in this manner: as the source of strength and life to whom they must submit and remain loyal, and whom they must worship' (2002: 40). On how abuse gets masked he cites Jennifer J. Freyd's view that children of abusing parents 'must block awareness of the betrayal, forget it, in order to ensure that [they] behave in ways that maintain the relationship on which [they] are dependent' (1996: 165).

[18] I am reminded of Fuchs' excellent discussion of how the supposed neutrality or the 'aperspectival posturing' of a scholar can actually be a contemporary re-voicing of the biblical narrator's 'claim to absolute truth' (2000: 43).

little parental consistency or reliability when acting in unanticipated ways is one of the deity's main character traits.

We are meant, of course, to view all this with humility and some humour. The omniscient narrator has given us a privileged reading position, able to see the ignorance of the characters, laugh at the ironic twists that occur, empathise with the tragi–comedy of their end and concur that God's ways are beyond human rules and norms.[19] But a psychologically informed reading resists the scribe's attempt to bring us on-side, just as a therapist may resist the story a patient initially recounts, in order to see what is going on beneath the surface. The holding environment is not healthy. Continuity of being is repeatedly interrupted as the child/Israel is brought to heel by invasive disciplinary events.

Conclusion

In this chapter, I have explored the ways in which Winnicottian theory throws new light on the presentation of the YHWH–Israel relationship, and the findings have been disturbing. The presentation of YHWH's parenting style does not correspond to 'good-enough mother'. On the contrary, he manoeuvres behind the child/Israel's back in order to compel compliance. He sends impingements in the form of brutal proxy agents to return them to his sole parenthood and then frets at their cries. He is not consistently himself; giving bad advice that sends 'thousands' to their deaths. A supposedly perennially wayward, obtuse Israel is castigated by both the scribe and the biblical commentator. But, in my view, only those who align themselves with the perspective of YHWH and the rhetoric of the scribal plot can exonerate his behaviour.

There is, however, a different way to understand the relationship dynamic between YHWH and Israel; one that accounts for the inconsistencies in the text, the subdued aggression and the flawed behaviour of deities by appealing to the psychological effects of trauma. Before progressing to the discussion of attachment theory in Chapter 3 it is necessary to consider the possibility that an exilic scribe, haunted by the injustices of recent history and marked by the experience of brutal warfare and deportation, is responsible for the dysfunctional God-talk in Judges. This is thus the focus of the next chapter.

---

[19] The terminology derives from Boling (1975) who viewed the prologue and epilogue as a tragi–comic framework wrapped around the book.

2

JUDGES' CYCLICAL FRAMEWORK AND TRAUMA THEORY

Israel's relationship with YHWH in the Book of Judges is an on–off affair marked by presence/absence, support/punishment, faithfulness/unfaithfulness and associated volatility. Its on–off character is expressed in the repeated cyclical pattern: Israel does evil in the eyes of YHWH, is given/sold into the hands of enemies, cries out to YHWH, YHWH raises a leader to resolve the crisis, the enemy is defeated and peace is regained. This formula is set out paradigmatically in 2:11–19, and repeated in modified and disintegrating forms as we move from Othniel to Samson.[1] Historical-critical scholars initially focussed attention on how pre-existing tribal folklore had been pressed into this cyclical form by an editor.[2] Narrative critics, however, with ever-increasing sophistication, have demonstrated how that supposedly earlier material is far more organically connected with the cyclical framework than previously thought. The paradigmatic exposition of 2:11–19 functions as a template, setting up expectations for each individual story which the narrator then cleverly destabilises for rhetorical effect. Almost all narrative critics assume some pre-existing material with which an editor worked, but the confidence with which one can speak of any substantial early material is decreasing as the editor's role increases in scope. Wong's comment is illustrative: Judges is the 'artful creation of a single author who, in spite of making use of diverse source materials, was nonetheless the one primarily responsible for shaping the entire book into its current form to reflect his unique ideological understanding of this period of the nation's history' (2006: 255).

---

[1] These are the broadly defining elements of the cyclical pattern. However, while 2:11–19 is paradigmatic, it is not used with verbatim repetition throughout Judges. For a detailed study of the cycle, its variations and a detailed discussion of the significance of those variations see O'Connell (1996).

[2] A more detailed discussion of this supposed source material appears later in this chapter.

I am more sceptical about the 'source material', particularly suggestions that it is to be found in the more colourful segments of
narrative within the cyclical template. In my view, the cyclical template has not been imposed on earlier source material, but is an
example of paradigmatic exposition, the ancient equivalent of bold
type used by a single author who composed both the paradigmatic
template *and* the colourful stories that illustrate it. My 1998 paper
(Guest, 1998) concluded that although the text presents itself as
history it should not be mistaken for such. At that time, I did not
question why the author felt it necessary to write so many illustrative
stories or why the message of the exposition needed to be driven
home with such repetitive force. Neither did I question why a narrator would create a supposed 'period of the judges', in which Israel
turn to other gods again and again, is subsequently made to experience harsh, hostile circumstances time and again, and why both
YHWH and Israel continually have to endure relationship breakdown. The Book of Judges is one long story of betrayal, hurt and
punishment . . . *on repeat.* The usual explanation that Judges needed
to include stories that covered the twelve tribes of Israel and allowed
for the steady deterioration of judgeship is satisfying only to an
extent. Such explanations have not taken seriously the *psychological*
function, or impact of, such repetition. Narrative approaches, while
being abundantly fruitful in illuminating the text's irony, comedy,
structural connections and sheer literary brilliance, do not shed any
light on the psyche that recurrently tells the same basic story either.
The focus on how the cyclical template is cleverly modified in order
to place emphasis on, say, gender or brutality of oppression, ignores
the questions of why Israel is propelled from one military humiliation to another, compelled to experience and re-experience the
brutalities of warfare, or how both Israel and YHWH are required
to confront the prospect of mutual abandonment over and over
again. If it can be agreed that the stories are not pre-existent tribal
folklore detailing the events of a supposed 296-year historical period,
then what psychological purpose(s) does this cycle serve?

To answer this question, it is important to bear in mind that
scribes are human beings located not only within political, social
and economic situations but within a psychological context. Biblical
scholars have been good at surmising and reconstructing the social
and historical context from which a biblical text emerges, but, until
recently, far less interested in the 'psychic context' with which it is
also inevitably marked. Recognising this does not reduce us to

'psychoanalysing' the author, against which objections have rightly been registered (Kille, 2001) but is grounded in the understanding that text production is always a 'psychological process in which unconscious, as well as conscious factors, are at work' (Rollins, 2002: 102). The examples given in Rollins and Kille (2007) provide astute reminders of this need to attend to psychological context. One of the promising avenues for exploring this further is the application of trauma theory to biblical texts.

In this chapter, I consider first how trauma theory is being applied profitably to biblical studies generally before narrowing the focus to Judges in particular. I evaluate Janzen's theory (2012) that the text, as part of the Deuteronomistic History, is marked by indicators of trauma before moving on to discuss four reasons why I resist his interpretation of Judges. The reasons concern the humour of the text, its literary genius, its possible polyphony and especially the dating of the text which I believe to be much later than is conventionally thought.

The Promise and Limitations of Trauma Studies

The Use of Trauma Theory in Biblical Studies

'Survivor literature' is the name given to work that emerges, at some point, from an overwhelming disastrous event. In biblical studies, the texts that have been most readily interpreted in the light of trauma theory include Ezekiel, Lamentations and Jeremiah, with lesser forays into other material.[3] Unsurprisingly, the trauma envisioned usually relates to the events that produced and proceeded the Babylonian exile, an event so severe that it is thought to have inescapably left its imprint upon the literature of the surviving community and their descendants.

Survivor literature is not a genre in itself, it is the name given to texts that are marked by trauma in some way. Thus, in terms of genre, the Book of Lamentations is a collection of five Psalms of Lament. But in terms of its subject matter, choice of language, God-talk and testimony to some major catastrophe Lamentations could be read as scar tissue – 'the visible trace offered by the survivor that points in the direction of the initial experience' (Garber, 2015: 28).

---

[3] For a helpful summary of the emergence and use of trauma theory within biblical studies see Garber (2015).

The books of Jeremiah and Ezekiel remain 'prophecy', but they have also been interpreted in terms of survivor literature. Kathleen O'Connor, for example, reads Jeremiah in terms of desymbolisation and resymbolisation. Desymbolisation refers to the way the trauma-tised have been plunged into a numbed or frozen state where the assumptions, institutions, ideologies and theologies have crumbled. O'Connor suggests, quite convincingly, that Jeremiah's purpose 'is to re-symbolize reality for the decimated nation' (2014: 213).

Such studies often stay within the immediate aftermath of the exile for their point of reference rather exploring how its impact may have affected generations beyond the first wave. An exception is William Morrow who deals with the effects of the trauma of Babylonian exile on second-generation survivors. His short paper, informed by the work of those who counsel victims of war, torture and political repression, illuminates how Deutero-Isaiah's message can be understood as an address to second-generation exile survivors who were suffering from collective abandonment despair, chronic shame, fragmentation, learned helplessness and at risk of turning to 'Babylonian religious practices in order to compensate for perceived inadequacies in the faith of Israel' (2004: 85).[4] In response, Isaiah offers 'a new sense of self and a new vision of Israel's God ... deliverance with more than adequate forgiveness ... a universally powerful deity ... Babylon will be defeated ... a political messiah is at hand ... The time for punishment is past, and a glorious future is promised' (2004: 85).

Trauma Theory as an Interpretative Lens for God-Talk in the Book of Judges

While it is the texts that most obviously relate to the Babylonian exile that have provided fertile material for those using trauma theory as a lens of interpretation, the Book of Judges has received some attention in this regard. Corinna Guerrero's (2013) unpub-lished paper ('Narrativizing Trauma: Tortured Minor Characters and the Writing of Judges', presented at the annual meeting of the Society of Biblical Literature, Baltimore, MD, USA) initiated dis-cussion of how the macabre stories of mutilation in Judges (the rape

---

[4] Morrow does not use the word fragmentation but it seems to be what he has in mind when discussing how 'the exilic community was in risk of losing a positive identification with Israel because it was overwhelmed with its self-knowledge as the rejected and disobedient one' (2004: 83).

and dismemberment of the Levite's woman, the disfigurement of Adoni-Bezek) can be illuminated by trauma theory, and there is the promise of a more detailed forthcoming publication from this author. But, currently, the most detailed work on Judges and trauma is in chapter 5 of David Janzen's intriguing monograph on the Deuteronomistic History, which, he has argued, bears the watermark of massive trauma. Not visible as a coherent voice, the indicators that trauma has played its part in the construction of the History are found in inconsistencies, interruptions to, or subversions of, the master narrative. While the Deuteronomistic History as a whole thus appears to tell a convincing and lucid story – i.e., 'intermarriage with Canaanites causes the worship of other gods, which results in exile' (Janzen, 2012: 22–23) – that message is repeatedly undermined, not in the way of a counter-story, but by way of anti-story eruptions – unravelling the master story's claims even as they are being made. For Janzen, the master narrative expounds two main themes. First, that apostasy leads to punishment and, ultimately, the loss of the land so that Israel's story becomes one 'great confession of Israel's guilt' and the justified destruction of Jerusalem; and second, that the leaders of Israel have led Israel into cultic disloyalty. A handful of reforming monarchs are not permitted to destabilise the overall account of kingly failures which Janzen believes is 'more detailed than generally recognized' (2012: 53). And yet 'despite the attempts of Dtr's master narrative, trauma eludes the narrative's linguistic control and challenges the very explanatory logic in which the narrative attempts to encapsulate it' (2012: 60). By the end of the History, the audience is left with an uncertain image of Jehoiachin being released from prison. Is one to imagine the promise of an eternal Davidic dynasty extending beyond Jehoiachin's exile? After all, it has not been explicitly revoked as in the case of the Elides or Saul. Does it imply that if the people would repent and return to cultic loyalty that God will bring salvation? It is possible, but no repentance is mentioned, and there is no guarantee that God would do so since Josiah's reforming acts were ignored while the sinful generations of Manasseh and Amon were left unpunished. As Janzen concludes: 'the fact that God explicitly ignores the perfect repentance of Josiah suggests further that he is not bound by the narrative's portrayal of him or of its concepts of justice, punishment, salvation, or repentance ... the usefulness of the narrative's logic for interpreting history has been gravely undermined' (2012: 211).

In Janzen's specific discussion of Judges, he first demonstrates how the master narrative themes of failed leadership and cultic disloyalty are present in this text. As other scholars have noted, there seem to be some early positive views about Judah's leadership in a book where leadership ultimately rapidly disintegrates. However, even Judah is imperfect. Drawing on Webb's (1987) analysis, Janzen reminds readers that 'Judah does not wish to fight and initially opposes the judge in 15:9–20; in chs. 17–18 it is a Levite from Judah who is involved in cultic abuses; and in ch. 20 it is Judah who goes up first to fight Benjamin ... and fails in battle' (2012: 129). The book closes with the refrain that there is no king in Israel, implying that monarchy rule might fare better, but, says Janzen, 'it is simply not clear by the end of Judges that merely changing the kind of leadership in Israel will save the nation from its worships of other gods and exile' (2012: 129). Leadership then, has no clear and consistent advocacy in this text, despite its presence as a major theme. The master narrative concerning cultic disloyalty appears to fare better. Such disloyalty clearly prompts YHWH's wrath: 'When Israel acts like the Canaanites, God will treat Israel like the Canaanites and subject them to חרם, even using Israel itself to carry out this punishment' (2012: 126). The master narrative is clear: the exile is the end result of a history of cultic disloyalty that had some of its earliest roots in this 'period of the judges': 'What has happened to the exilic community ... happened many times to Israel in the past, and for exactly the same reason' (2012: 130).

However, the indicators of trauma lie in the subversions of any easy equations or explanations that attempt to account for the exile in terms of YHWH's just punishment of a guilty generation and in the confusions, inconsistencies or gaps the text throws up. For example, repeating the death of Joshua at 2:6–10 throws into question the identity of the ch. 1 generation. Rather than closing down options via scholarly argument about source material, Janzen lets the uncertainty breathe, arguing that the temporal confusion is a sign that a trauma has left its mark on the master narrative. When we foreclose the lack of clarity by making source or redactional claims about whether Chapter 1's failures to occupy all the territories were the failures of the Joshua generation or the subsequent one, we are not allowing the text itself to stand. Read from the perspective of a traumatic event that haunts its survivors, the author is not capable of producing clear chronologies. All reduces to 'the single repetitive fate of Israel' (2012: 131) and the question of guilt and deserved punishment gets disrupted. In other words, the big event that the author is tackling is the aftermath of the destruction of Jerusalem and this is so massive, so eternally present, that it has taken over the supposed chronological history being related – it is all one huge history of trauma.

Thus, when the messenger of YHWH appears in 2:1–5 and condemns covenant-making with the Canaanites who will now remain in the land as a snare, who exactly stands accused? Does the text look back to Josh. 9, which, as Janzen notes, is the only generation in the story so far who did so, or is it the post-Joshua generation? The lack of clarity could imply that 'a generation who has not made any covenants with the Canaanites ... is charged by God with having done so and is punished for a crime of which they are innocent' (2012: 131). Maybe God is looking back to the generation of chapter 1 but it is precisely the 'absence of clarity' which denotes 'the intrusion of trauma' (2012: 132) – not as a counter voice, but as an eruption which makes the master story falter because now God's justice does not seem so clear-cut. 'This is an uncanny foreshadowing of 2 Kgs 21–25, where ... trauma will suggest that a guiltless generation is forced to suffer the siege, destruction, mass death, and forced migration of 586' (2012: 132).

Then there is the uncomfortable question of YHWH's role in Israel's fate. If the nations arc lcft on the land as a snare or a test, how far has YHWH himself facilitated apostasy? For an exilic audience, the implication is 'that God can remove the nation's ability to make a decision for vassal loyalty, and thus mocks the narrative's logic in history that explains God's justice on the basis of Israel's choices' (2012: 133). As noted in Chapter 1, I have similarly queried the sense of talking about persistent waywardness when YHWH seems to have made arrangements that seal Israel's fate.

As for understanding YHWH's continued endurance in terms of mercy, this too is problematic. I pointed out in Chapter 1 that YHWH is not consistently himself. Janzen bears this out. If YHWH can ignore the apostasy of, say, a Gideon generation, and send them a saviour, what does this say about his justice? Grace and mercy are all very well but their endowment undermines the master narrative's portrayal of 'God as the one who consistently and justly controls history' (2012: 135). And, as Janzen pointedly asks, what of the cases when God's freedom to act differently ended in punishment? Here, he turns to Judg. 10 where the Israelites *do* repent, and make a show of it, yet at that very point God becomes exasperated with them. As Janzen argues, if it has been shown that YHWH will deliver Israel when there has been no repentance on Israel's part, how odd is it that when repentance is demonstrated, the deity responds haughtily. Perhaps, suggests Janzen, such 'divine caprice' is a foreshadowing of how Josiah's 'perfect act of repentance' is also ignored (2012: 136).

But it is not just a matter of YHWH's caprice. Janzen suggests that YHWH intervenes in the Jephthah narrative in order to *protect his reputation*. Jephthah's appeal to the Ammonites is grounded in an assumption that deities grant tracts of land to their people and that Ammon should stick to what Chemosh has given them, while Israel has the land granted by YHWH. By this logic, the loss of Gilead could be interpreted as Chemosh's intervention to grant the area to Ammon. The Israelites would thus not see what has happened as the work of YHWH who is punishing their apostasy. YHWH acts, therefore, 'not because of justice ... or because of mercy ... but out of a need to demonstrate his power to the nations when Jephthah ... has signaled that a rejection of Israel will make him appear weak' (2012: 137).

More disturbing still, the traumatic eruptions into the master narrative in the Samson narrative and chs. 17–21 imply that YHWH's involvement in events indicates a *bloodthirsty interest* in slaughter: 'As YHWH becomes more distant in this story ... his interest in killing seems to increase and the interest in law and divine control of history to decrease ... God's choice of someone so asocial and violent as judge suggests minimal interest in deliverance and maximal interest in carnage' (2012: 139). Read against the backdrop of the exilic era, the implication that 'God seems to want Israel to fail and violence to be visited upon the nation' (2012: 139) is understandable.

In summary, Janzen's work interprets the repeated cycle of Judges as a succession of master narrative illustrations, subverted by inherent, undermining eruptions that expose the various ways in which YHWH cannot be relied upon to act as expected. This is not a rival source or distinctive editorial hand, it is rather, in Janzen's view, an effect of writing in the aftermath of overwhelming trauma. And the repetitiveness of the cycle makes sense when read from this perspective:

> It is not difficult to see how someone traumatized by the experiences of siege, famine, mass death, and deportation (or at least how someone from a family and community who have experienced this) would portray Israel's history as an

> unending series of such traumas, regardless of whether or
> not he or she wanted to explain them. In Judges we see the
> single time of trauma subsuming the past into the uncon-
> trollability and unknowability of 586. (2012: 143)

Ultimately, if Janzen's reading is correct, the text leaves the reader
with a host of unanswered questions and inconsistencies, begging the
question of whether Judges makes coherent sense at all, And this,
Janzen believes, is the effect of trauma, which does not provide any
convincing explanation or counter-story, just subversions that result
in ambiguity and a lack of answers.

Initially, I intended to explore further how the cyclical framework
could be functioning as a traumatic stutter. It seemed a plausible
hypothesis at first glance, certainly more plausible than redactional
arguments for inconsistencies (which Janzen discusses and discounts).
It is tempting to agree that the Judges' cycle, with its repeated focus
on suffering harsh oppression from other nations, the cries of distress,
the haunting prospect of abandonment by YHWH and the admis-
sions of guilt *could* be read in terms of survivor experience. However,
for the theory to work Janzen has to posit a narrator who was very
close to the traumatic event. Unsurprisingly, he argues that Judges
was written, as part of the Deuteronomistic History, sometime after
562 BCE either by an eye-witness survivor of the siege and forced
migrant, or a person living within an exilic community marked by its
'massive psychic trauma' (2012: 4). He does not rule out entirely the
possibility that earlier traumatic history could have left its mark in
the text; the 701 BCE Assyrian invasion could, for example, be
reflected in a Josianic edition of the History. Nonetheless, he stands
by his belief that the Babylonian exile is the more likely context for
the first draft of the Deuteronomistic History.

Janzen's argument is consistent with the fact that most of the
literature on trauma refers to the ongoing effects for a person *directly*
affected within his or her lifetime, for example, the survivors of the
Vietnam war, the Holocaust, Hiroshima or the Buffalo Creek flood
disaster. However, while Garber suggests that 'the effects of trauma
can last for years and have far-reaching implications' (2015: 27) he
does not provide any extended details. How much time can elapse
between the original trauma and the responses to it, for it still to be
considered survivor literature? Would it still be reasonable to see
Judges as marked by the trauma of the siege of Jerusalem and
deportation of citizens to Babylon if the text was written, say, in

the late Persian or early Hellenistic period? Can third, fourth or fifth generations of exile survivors be producing texts that are still disturbed significantly by the anti-narrative of trauma?

Yes, it is possible, but not without significant qualification. It is evident that the effects of a huge calamity can have an intergenerational effect, although texts written by later generations would be bearing witness not to the survival of the exile but marked by the effects, or by-products, of how the original suffering generation affected succeeding ones. Caruth moots this possibility in her discussion of how a survivor has come through an event which exceeds them – it is beyond them, it has not happened to them, they do not have mastery over it. So, 'perhaps it is not possible for the witnessing of the trauma to occur within the individual at all, that it may only be in future generations that "cure" or at least witnessing can take place' (1996: 136, n. 21). She references the work of Bergmann and Jucovny (1982), who, in their prelude to *Generations of the Holocaust*, review studies on the children of Holocaust survivors. These children were significantly affected by discovering what had happened to their parents, but also by the style of parenting they experienced. We cannot summarise these effects in terms of common denominators for much depends on the individual family dynamic. Some children felt the strain of making up for dead siblings, some felt that they were obliged to fulfil their parents' desires despite wanting different futures, some had little nurturing from parents who felt alienated from their children, preoccupied as they were with the repression of traumatic memories, some felt that they could not act out in the way that usual adolescents might express rebellion and some were weighed down by guilt, depression and physical ill-health. Dori Laub, discussing the effects on the second generation, tells how a Holocaust survivor regarded her children 'with deep disappointment as unempathic strangers because of the "otherness" she senses in them, because of their refusal to substitute for, and completely fit into, the world of parents, brothers, and children that was so abruptly destroyed' (1995: 63). Trauma thus certainly affects the next generation and is quite likely to mark subsequent generations, but not in any universalised way. Moreover, the question of how long the gap from original trauma can be for a document to merit the category 'survivor literature' remains unclear.

However, if we move beyond Janzen's work to the notion of 'chosen trauma', introduced to biblical studies by Smith-Christopher (2014), there is evidence that trauma can affect individuals and generations much further down the line. His work on Micah is informed by Vamik Volkan's suggestion that most large groups carry within them 'a shared mental representation of a traumatic past event during which the large group suffered loss and/or experienced helplessness, shame and humiliation in a conflict with another large group' (2001: 87) but has not been able adequately to deal with that loss. The next generation receive a 'deposit' of that memory in the hope that they will be 'able to mourn the loss or reverse the humiliation' and if they are unable to do this then 'they, as adults, will in turn pass the mental representation of the event to the next generation' (2001: 88). The original trauma can thus become part of the collective fabric – part of a group identity commemorated at annual events. The examples Volkan gives are the Czech remembrance of the 1620 Battle of Bí lá Hora, the Scottish memory of the 1746 Battle of Culloden, the Lakota Indian anniversary of the 1890 Battle at Wounded Knee and, in greater detail, the Serbian commemoration of the 1389 Battle of Kosovo. In this latter discussion, Volkan describes poignantly how a trauma can 'lie dormant for a long period of time', yet, given the right circumstances, 'be reactivated and exert a powerful psychological force' with devastating effect (2001: 88). Smith-Christopher (2014: 237–238) thus advises readers that the impact of events such as the Babylonian exile could arguably affect a community's self-understanding over many centuries. I was initially doubtful that a Judges constructed much later than usually thought could still carry the marks of exilic trauma, but Volkan's work on chosen trauma challenges that view. However, for this theory to be applicable, we need to be sure that there is a direct connection between the survivors of Babylonian warfare/deportation, and those who re-populated the Yehud province in the Persian period. The section 'Dating Judges: The Impact of Revisionist Theories on Existing Judges Scholarship' problematises this assumption.[5]

---

[5] Without doubt, the exile is overtly in view in Judges, not least in the Samson story which appears to tell the story of the exile in microcosm (see Brettler (2002)), but also in the exilic 'themes' that commentators have detected, such as the critical evaluation of national leadership, the question of where national identity is to be located, the devastating effects of apostasy and preoccupation with the (broken) YHWH/Israel relationship. It is possible that a collective memory (not necessarily experience) of the exile has marked the self-consciousness or self-understanding of the Judges scribe in some way, for no matter how many years later he is writing the exile does *appear* to have been a formative event. However, I emphasise 'appear' because there are significant assumptions being made about the connection between the historical deportation

The Limitations of Trauma Theory as an Interpretive Lens for the God-Talk in Judges

Four matters stand in the way of my initial thought that the repeated delivery of Israel in the hands of enemies might function as a traumatic stutter: date, humour, literary artistry and the polyphony of a dialogic text. Of these matters, date is the most complex due to the wide variety of scholarly opinions that exist. I thus leave this necessarily lengthier discussion for a dedicated section at the end of the chapter. For now, I proceed with the issues of humour, artistry and polyphony.

Humour in Judges

The comedic streak that pervades Judges seems to run entirely counter to an author and community living in the immediate after-math of the Babylonian siege and subsequent forced migration. Caruth writes of how trauma is a response to an overwhelming event that dominates the life of the individual, where the survivor does not 'possess' knowledge of the catastrophic experience so much as *is possessed by* it. The event has been so unutterably painful, shocking, harrowing, that it is, itself, somehow 'missed' only to be repeatedly re-encountered in recurring nightmares or daytime hallucinations. She thus describes traumatised people as becoming 'the symptom of a history that they cannot entirely possess' (1995: 5), the event itself being something of a void, a gap that the individual is initially numbed to, something that can never be entirely grasped, adequately spoken about or fully explained. This notion of the 'missed encounter' is explained well by Dori Laub:

> The listener to the narrative of ... massive psychic trauma, faces a unique situation. In spite of the presence of ample documents, of searing artifacts and of fragmentary memoirs of anguish, he comes to look for something that is in fact non-existent; a record that has yet to be made. Massive trauma precludes its registration; the observing and recording mechanisms of the human mind are temporarily knocked out, malfunction. The victim's narrative ... does indeed begin with someone who testifies to an absence, to an

of the sixth century BCE and the scribe responsible for writing Judges; assumptions that are discussed later in this chapter.

> event that has not yet come into existence, in spite of the
> overwhelming and compelling nature of the reality of its
> occurrence ... the trauma—as a known event and not simply
> as an overwhelming shock—has not been truly witnessed yet,
> not been taken cognizance of. The emergence of the narrative
> which is being listened to—and heard—is, therefore, the pro-
> cess and the place wherein the cognizance, the 'knowing' of
> the event is given birth to. The listener, therefore, is a party to
> the creation of knowledge *de novo*. (1992: 57)

So, the processing work is ongoing. While one can imagine that a
survivor might have experienced the worst and be able, ultimately, to
move on, Caruth discusses how work of surviving is difficult enough
and is inevitably ongoing, involving the person in 'the endless inherent necessity of repetition, which ultimately may lead to destruction'
(1996: 63). She cites the 'high suicide rates' of Holocaust survivors
and Vietnam war survivors (1996: 63) and discusses trauma's 'endless impact on a life' (1996: 7). It is her focus on the extreme
difficulties facing survivors that seems so at odds with the pervasive
humour in the Book of Judges. Furthermore, for the survivor of
trauma there is a compunction to tell one's story that coexists with
the frustrating recognition that language is simply not up to the task.
Laub states: 'There are never enough words or the right words, there
is never enough time or the right time, and never enough listening or
the right listening to articulate the story that cannot be fully captured
in thought, memory, and speech' (1995: 63).

If this is what it is to be traumatised, it is hard to imagine a
numbed, harrowed and overwhelmed survivor, or immediate des-
cendant of a survivor, having the energy and available wit to produce a book like Judges. I can understand how one might interpret
the Book of Lamentations as survivor literature; the author beats on
his chest, sending up his repeated איכה with heart-breaking pathos.
But the Book of Judges, with its genius of artistry, irony and well-
crafted comedy, makes the reader laugh. If it *is* the work of a
traumatised generation then it is not, in my view, the 562 BCE
community envisaged by Janzen. It is possible that the effects of
the exile trauma continued to inform a subsequent generation in
which Judges has its origins, but then we would be looking at a
different time and location.

Notwithstanding, there is evidence that humour can exist amid the
most harrowing of circumstances. Lipman (1991) demonstrates how

Jewish men and women told each other jokes and humorous anecdotes as part of their survival tactics during the Holocaust. Jokes were recycled, applied from a previous situation to the new, and gallows humour aided survival. He suggests that humour facilitated three important functions: resistance to the situation faced, a means of community cohesion and solidarity, and a coping mechanism that enabled people to keep going. Fry (2000: 1) also confirms the existence of 'extensive and authenticated humor literature' that derives from prison camps, places of torture, dictator-dominated societies and from locations where a natural disaster has occurred.

In Judges we certainly find jokes and parody. Jackson's examination of the Deborah/Jael narrative demonstrates examples of the comic in plot structure, irony and characterisation and she helpfully points out how such humour can be seen as 'the refuge of survivors' (2012: 114) and functions as an aid for boundary-marking. Israelite survival is what matters and, to survive, the border between Israelite and non-Israelite has to be demarcated (2012: 226).[6] The Ehud story has also long been noted for its wit; Handy's analysis demonstrating persuasively that it should be categorised as ethnic humour. It draws on two stock characters from this genre: the canny person (Ehud) and the idiot (Eglon). Add to this the toilet humour and the strong whiff of a homoerotic death scene and one can see how a story of Israelite resilience, as defined in Ehud's story, could be an entertaining weapon for a people. As Handy points out, the Moabites themselves had done very little. It was YHWH who delivered Israel into their hands. Moreover, the Moabites had to be *strengthened* by YHWH to gain just a portion of territory and, even then, Eglon could only do it with the aid of Ammonites and Amalekites. Ehud can dispatch his people with mere 'planning, trickery, puns' (1992: 237) and reliance on Moabite flabby stupidity, while YHWH, of course, is the one who makes it all happen. The joke is turned on Israel, however, when readers arrive at the story of Samson, who 'is no longer canny, but stupid and stupid enough to think himself clever' (1992: 243). The Philistines, Delilah in particular, are the

---

[6] Jackson suggests that humour can enable a group to find an '"insulation layer against the surrounding alien environment" offering warmth "when all else is cold and unfamiliar"' (2012: 228, citing Critchley, 2002: 67–68). She also notes Wylie Sypher's argument that comedy enables a person to discharge hatred of the Other 'especially when the stranger who is "different" stirs any unconscious doubt about our own beliefs … [The comedian] can point out our victim, isolate him from our sympathy, and cruelly expose him to the penalty of our ridicule' (1956: 242).

clever ones, and the situation is reversed: 'The hero is strong, handsome, virile, lusty, and dumb as a rock ... The easy external danger of the mindless Moabites faced by resolute Israelites has been replaced with clever and dangerous Philistines toying with an incompetent Israelite' (1992: 244). By this point, the humour is not so easy; it is 'laced with angst' (1992: 244). Yet it seems more likely that this narrative derives from an author writing not in the midst of trauma, but at a later stage of self-definition when the ethnic (and sexual) slur[7] offers his audience a redeeming sense of canny superiority over a dehumanised foreign nation.[8] This is written by an author confident that the enemy is actually no match for Israel.

We do not have short, pithy examples of gallows humour in Judges. We have the *permeation* of an ironical perspective, *pervasive* satire (using names, obesity and the deformities to poke fun at people and events) alongside crude scatology and *extended* narratives, such as Ehud's, that have been described as ethnic jokes.[9] Davidson (2008: 93–106) argues that we can best understand the ribald humour of Judges *overall* as an example of the 'carnivalesque-grotesque' which contains features such as dismemberment, a topsy–turvy world, disguises and masks, parody, travesty and burlesque. The vital question is whether or not a traumatised, numbed survivor could be expected to produce a substantial text of such extended, extraordinarily well-honed humour. While I have acknowledged that humour in tragic circumstances can seem jarring and incongruous and yet still exist, the well-crafted comedy of the Book of Judges does not readily sit with the image of an author's experience (or closeness to) catastrophic and overwhelming events that have left him traumatised, not if we are using the previously mentioned

---

[7] Brettler (1995), Brenner (1994), Bailey (1995), Guest (2006) note how the sexual slur works politically, reinforcing a hostile, racist presentation of the Moabites.

[8] Handy does not speculate on when these narratives were composed, who these specific 'Moabites' or 'Philistines' might be, noting only that ethnic jokes should not be thought of as history writing.

[9] Radday and Brenner (1990: 63) pick up on some of the comical names in Judges, such as 'Superblack Double-Villain' (Cushan-rishathaim), as does Mobley, who relishes the 'colorful roster of heroes and villains–Slasher, Sunny, and Scabby versus Double-Trouble, Baby bull, and Wolf' (2005: 1). Although I disagree with his suggestion that such names derive from a heroic tradition during 'ancient Israel's frontier era' (2005: 2), his work helpfully highlights the scatological nomenclature throughout Judges. Brenner (1994) provides a detailed reading of Ehud's story with attention to the way humour satirises the foreign ruler's obesity. Klein (1989) identifies several further elements of the comic in her treatment of irony in the Book of Judges. For a helpful broader discussion see Hepner (2004).

formal diagnoses of trauma. Judges reads more like serious entertainment than survivor literature, which leads me to ask whether
the inconsistences that Janzen has noted could be explained by
other means.

Literary Artistry in Judges

When discussing the testimonies written by survivors, such as those
that survived the Nazi death camps, Terrence Des Pres writes that
they are 'told in pain and often clumsily, with little thought for style
or rhetorical device' (1976: 29). This is probably why the Books of
Jeremiah and Ezekiel have been at the forefront of trauma-informed
analysis. Lamentations is more of an oddity. Its content lends itself
to analysis as survivor literature since there is a rawness about the
images of assault that pervade the Book. Yet it seems strange that
poems of such bitter, heart-wrenching, challenging, soul-searching
outbursts, which have the mark of spontaneity about them, have
been cast in such a carefully crafted aesthetic form.[10] Judges, similarly, is a work of literary cohesion. Older scholarly views that
divided the text into sources of variable date and authorship have
been undermined by the work initiated by Lilley (1967) and Gros
Louis (1974), and furthered in the work of narrative critics such
as Gooding (1982), Webb (1987), Klein (1989), Gunn (1989),
O'Connell (1996), Schneider (2000), and Wong (2006). These studies
have demonstrated how the supposed different sources of varying
provenance contain a deep, rich, intertextuality. The book is not
haphazard, strange or disorganised. It has its bizarre features, but a
tightly woven, coherent, interconnectedness marks it as a text of
aesthetic sophistication. It is hard to imagine that such a text is the
product of a highly traumatised scribe who, as trauma theory indicates, would scarcely be able to write without considerable pain and
raw-edged grief or, as Janzen argues, without incursions that make a

---

[10] Gottwald is troubled by the 'apparent contradiction between artificial literary
form and spontaneity of emotions' (1954: 24) and it does not seem quite right to him
that the emotional outbursts are cast into such a polished and disciplined form.
Westermann (1994) has questioned whether the acrostic form was added to the
laments after they had been roughly composed in the aftermath of the 587 destruction
by its survivors. The basis for this thought is twofold. First, he notes that the acrostic is
not a usual feature of the Lament and, second, because he finds it difficult to cope with
the tension between a disciplined artistic form, and the content of the poems. It is this
incongruity that prompts me, likewise, to query whether Judges can be viewed as the
work of a first- or second-generation survivor of the Babylonian exile.

text seem uneven, contradictory and uncertain. I read Judges as an intensively focussed work, entertaining in character, carefully crafted in the most marvellous ways by short- and long-range connections (see Webb, 1987); each narrative, each use of the formulaic framework is carefully managed for rhetorical effect. This sophisticated structure does not, in my view, cohere with the discussions of survivor literature found in trauma theory. Ultimately, I cannot see the Book of Judges emerging in the immediate aftermath of the siege of Jerusalem and the forced migration of parts of the Judean population to Babylon. The text is just too carefully structured, too aesthetically pleasing and too humorous to be the product of a person overwhelmed by trauma. The descriptions of traumatised individuals, especially in the work of Caruth, do not cohere with an author enjoying his craft and composing such a text.

I do concede that, amid the literary artistry and unity, there remains instability. It has been examined effectively by Exum (1990) who demonstrates how the paradigmatic cycle so clearly set out in 2:11–19 structurally dissolves even as it is repeated, just as confidence in Israel's ability to break out of the repeated pattern of behaviour fades away. Moral certitudes and notions of justice become as unstable as the text. In this regard, her paper reads as a forerunner of Janzen's work, exposing unresolved ambiguities and uncertainties in Judges. Exum notes there are questions to be asked about 'divine procedure' such as when YHWH sends Israel to their defeat twice even while his intent seems to be to hand Benjamin to them. 'What purpose does the excessive slaughter serve?' she asks (1990: 429); a discomforting question raised subsequently by Janzen who wonders if God relishes slaughter for slaughter's sake. And is YHWH motivated entirely by Israel's groans or by some ulterior, all too human motive – Exum notes how Gideon's troops are reduced in number to ensure that *they* cannot think they defeated the Midianites by their own hand. As Janzen would later ask, is YHWH motivated by threats to his reputation (2012)? Exum's paper, by focusing on the complexities of YHWH's behaviour, disrupts notions of Judges' supposed thematic coherence. However, her stated aim is to show that scholars run the risk of focussing too much on supposed stable meanings when the text itself contains far more complex messages. She doesn't go as far as saying that the text's instability is intentional, but does see it as mirroring the 'increasing corruption' and 'atmosphere of hopelessness' that emerges in the book (1990: 411). The Bible, after all, can be 'disarmingly honest' when it comes to the 'uncertain, sometimes ambivalent, nature of reality' (1990: 411). However, what is significant is that Exum does not account for such instability by recourse to the effects of trauma.

Polyphony in the Book of Judges

Polzin (1980) accounts for subversions of Judges' master narrative without recourse to trauma theory. Where Janzen sees an anti-narrative breaking through that questions whether YHWH is reliable, or why he has a tantrum of exasperation at precisely the point where the people repent, Polzin sees the unpredictability of YHWH as a deliberate rhetorical device by an author who places YHWH beyond any human control. Over against feeble attempts to guarantee divine insurance, YHWH acts in sovereign freedom. In the broader terms of Polzin's three-volume discussion of the Deuteronomistic History, we have a scribe who contrasts the voice of 'authoritarian dogmatism' as perceived in the words of Moses, and the voice of 'critical traditionalism' as contained in the words of the narrator. In Judges the voice of dogmatism is identified in 2:6–3:6 and the repeated template into which the stories are embedded, while 'critical traditionalism' is located in references to the mercy and compassion of YHWH despite Israel's repeated disobedience. Polzin's contrast of these two voices, however, goes further; both voices are shown to be subject to subversion, as the narrator uses the unpredictable to show that there is no secure ground when it comes to doctrine or theology. He leaves us with a coherent, sophisticated, cleverly written Book of Judges that deliberately uses the clash of competing voices to open up a well-managed philosophical discussion.

Susanne Gillmayr-Bucher (2009) similarly believes that any discussion of theology in Judges would be better expressed as theologies in debate within a dialogic text. She notes textual conversations about contrary matters, such as enemies not always being as dominant as they first seem, or how Israel's attitude to YHWH and cultic loyalty seems to be presented as being universally bad and yet is not always bad. She notes open-ended discussions about whether YHWH can be relied upon to answer cries of distress, or whether there is an undisputed connection between God's intervention and military success. She does not say whether the voices she discerns are the result of editorial layers, and does not mention trauma theory directly; for her the text is simply polyphonic.[11] So although the viewpoint, or the master narrative of the framework seems to be crystal clear, she argues that its subsequent enmeshment in the individual judge stories changes those stories and *is itself changed* in the process. Both she and Janzen recognise this double-voiced discourse in Judges, and both argue that there is no resultant dominant voice that brings all to a resolution. For Gillmayr-Bucher, 'the firm voice introduced in 2:11–19 fades away' (2009: 701) leaving 'no alternative (or monologic) interpretation ... in its place ... The dialogic discourse in the book of Judges remains unfinalizable' (2009: 702). However, Gillmayr-Bucher's approach does not necessitate a traumatised author living in the immediate aftermath of the Babylonian exile. She does not posit an alternative date and context for Judges, but her work implies that we have an author able to construct a vision through which one can see events of his time differently to what may have been a more mainstream view, and who uses satirical humour to makes this contrary viewpoint entertainingly appealing. Yes, the text references harsh brutal warfare which prompts cries of acute distress and this is not minimised, but it is possible to adopt a perspective on this that offsets the horror with humour and shows that for all the apparent dominance of, say, the Moabites they are actually quite stupid.

The studies of Polzin and Gillmayr-Bucher pave the way for understanding Judges as a wisdom-like text, with a scribe who is philosophical, not traumatised, writing narratives that both entertain and provoke serious debate around modes of leadership, women, ethnic boundaries and fate. In my opinion, viewing Judges as the construction of a scribe who, in wisdom-like fashion, talks aloud about conundrums, distanced by many more years that Janzen supposes, seems more likely.[12] Of course, one would then have to

---

[11] She mentions a sense of loss that pervades the contrast between Joshua's and the new generation (Gillmayr-Bucher, 2009: 690). The sense is that Israel once walked hand-in-hand with YHWH, won amazing victories, had a good leader, but now that has gone. If read in a postexilic context, this could draw attention to the broader issues of loss and discontinuity but she does not pursue this any further. Nonetheless, it interesting that she talks of loss, an issue picked up also by Hudson (1994).

[12] Biblical authors can discuss conflicting views without necessarily coming to a conclusion. Jobling suggests that the editor of Judges ponders over whether or not Israel could have discovered a form of successful government if they were not so susceptible to apostasy. How government might function is left open for the reader to consider, for the editor presents no clear and easily definable opinion and perhaps 'perceived, or sensed, that it was a contradiction that Israel should go on living

answer Janzen's question of why the Deuteronomistic History ends where it does, and why it does not go on to talk about postexilic realities, but this matter is taken up in the next section.

Dating Judges: The Impact of Revisionist Theories on Existing Judges Scholarship

Trying to pinpoint a date and context for Judges is hugely difficult, for we get entangled in wider discussions of the dating and construction of the Deuteronomistic History and more recent questioning of whether Judges is part of such a history at all.[13] There is no current scholarly consensus; radical shifts in the dating of biblical texts means that attempts to date Judges are plunged into a maelstrom of debate with little sure ground. However, this section on dating Judges cannot be avoided. The following discussion is not intended to be an exhaustive discussion of every scholar's preferred date and context for the production of the Book of Judges, but rather an explanation of why I ultimately resist the idea that the repetitive cycle in Judges is indicative of trauma.

Pre-Eighth Century BCE Material in Judges

There is an amazingly persistent scholarly assumption that Judges contains early source material. Given its lively storytelling perhaps this is not surprising. Thomas L. Thompson rightly observes how narratives in Judges are related 'with such clarity of verse that many modern historians are single mindedly attracted to these texts as it were towards historical memories of a nation's earliest beginnings', adding, perhaps with a smile, that 'this unquestionably concurs with the biblical tradition's own themes and intentionality' (1992: 355).

---

within' (1986: 45). In his work on Kings, Linville (1998: 82) concurs with Somers and Gibson (1994) that telling historical stories is a way of imposing order on chaotic experience and the historians who do this, as individuals, possess several identities which may conflict with each other. Accordingly, a corporate history account will always be an ideal construct rather than an unmediated description of the messy views held within a society, but it contains within it paradoxical themes that are not be understood as the result of 'incompletely reconciled sources, or layering of different editorial additions' (Linville, 1998: 85) but as a reflection of authorial divisions, conflicts and problems.

[13] For revisionist histories see, for example, Davies (1992, 1995a), Finkelstein and Silberman (2001), Grabbe (1997), Lemche (1988, 1994, 1998), Thompson (1992, 1999a, 1999b).

There has been a long tradition of arguing that storytelling charisma is evidence of an early core layer of folk material or the continuation of a J epic in Judges. Moore's (1898) commentary identifies material from the supposed J source (dated to the ninth century BCE) and argues that this material was combined with an E source of the eighth to seventh centuries BCE to produce what he calls the pre-Deuteronomic 'Book of the Histories of the Judges' (1898: xxxiv). Loss of scholarly confidence in the supposed ninth century J source and in the E source, however, has led to suggestions of other kinds of source material.

Boling's (1975) confidence that Judges was virtually complete by the seventh century BCE rests on speculation that there was a pre-existing 'pragmatic edition' based on a collection of local deliverer stories. He appeals to Richter's (1964) arguments for this earlier body of writing. Richter had posited a *Retterbuch* consisting of the Ehud, Deborah–Barak and Gideon-Jerubbaal stories, identifying this *Retterbuch* by the characteristic way it pressed these stories into a six-element stereotypical literary form[14]. Richter reserved judgement about where these underlining stories came from but argued that they contained close-to-the-events descriptions; i.e., the vivid, earthy language of the stories testify supposedly to their local origins near to the time they describe. He added that the lack of interest in themes of sin, punishment and repentance (the enemies were more likely scorned local foes) is indicative of non-Deuteronomic material, as is the absence of a pan-Israelite perspective. Boling was not the only one to take up Richter's claims: the *Retterbuch* features in the work of subsequent scholars.[15]

Arguments for rather vague 'containers' of judges source material can also found in Gottwald's (1979) suggestion that stories of

---

[14] That is, Israel does evil in the eyes of the Lord, is delivered into the hands of enemies, cries out to YHWH, he raises a deliverer, the enemy is subdued and peace is regained.

[15] His work informed Amit's (1999) commentary and her 2009 essay maintains her view that a version of Judges existed at the cusp of the late eighth/early seventh centuries BCE written by intellectuals responding to the fall of Israel to Assyria in 722 BCE. Her 2014 essay on how Judges has relevance for a Persian–Hellenistic audience does not undermine her confidence in that view. Guillaume (2004) engages with Richter's suggestions and claims that stories (which, for Guillaume, are largely fictitious) become the medium for interpreting the loss of the northern kingdom. Becker's (1990) discussion of redaction in Judges also dialogues with Richter's analysis and, like Richter, he argues for an original *versaffer eines Geschichtswerkes* that pressed source material into an early framework, followed by DtrN and Dtr P redactions.

military figures and leaders were preserved locally and left largely unedited by the Deuteronomist. Others speculate that oral tradition served as the 'container' for the Judge narratives. Gray, for example, proposes that the Deuteronomist had access to 'sober historical traditions conserved locally, possibly in saga form, among those who had been involved in the events' (1986: 190). Schniedewind (2004) ventures that stories of the judges circulated in the oral culture during the early Iron Age. These folk tales, as he calls them, would have existed along with early bardic material (Song of the Sea, Song of Deborah) at the time of transition from the late Bronze Canaanite city state system to the early Iron Age settlements of the Canaanite highlands, preserved, in his view, through festal practise of recitation and singing. Niditch (2008: 8) also posits oral material dating back to the pre-tenth century BCE, possibly the twelfth for the Song of Deborah. However, she is not claiming that these stories contain historical memories, interested rather in 'what sort of Israelites' the stories 'might have shaped and reflected' (2008: 9). However, she is convinced that we have in Judges 'a traditional corpus of literature that has been made and remade many times orally and in writing' (2008: 9).

Person, however, returns us firmly to written source material. He uses biblical references to the Acts of Solomon or the Books of the Annals of the Kings of Israel to suggest that these, together with 'other written sources' such as the 'sources for the prophetic stories *and the stories of the judges*', were available to the Deuteronomist at a later stage of editing (2002: 25, emphasis added). However, he is highly sceptical of any ability to guess at what might have been in these sources given the layers of editing that happened subsequently.

To summarise, scholars have produced various thoughts on the pre-existence of narratives now contained with Judges. Accordingly, a piecemeal Judges emerges, constructed of supposed fragments of early tribal folklore, saga material, possibly some written sources, pressed into an early collection or available to be used by later writers. These arguments for pre-eighth century BCE material are usually based on an assumption that the stories bear some relationship to actual events. There may not have been a 'period of the judges' as described in the final form of the text, but it is presumed that there was a Gideon-like, or a Deborah-like person acting at some point in history in ways subsequently described and celebrated in literary form. However, three challenges must be taken into consideration.

First, for such hypotheses to convince, an early Iron Age context in which these tribal figures acted would need to be feasible. But even if we imagine a much smaller scale, localised activity, archaeological evidence for the early Iron Age is not at all consistent with the portrayal of the peoples and events associated with them. The general archaeological portrait is one of loosely associated groups of people, primarily indigenous Canaanites, living in harsh times but in peaceful coexistence. Rather than engaging in skirmishes with encroaching border enemies the occupants of these settlements are fully occupied with the task of survival in difficult ecological circumstances in the late Bronze/early Iron transitional period.[16]

The second challenge emerges from Davies' (1992) robust disruption of assumptions that the biblical story world is related directly to the pre-history of the kingdoms of Israel and Judah. The latter may have left some written material, and it is possible that it was accessed by the scribes who wrote the material now in Gen.–2 Kgs., but they have created from it something that now serves their own interests. It is vital to grasp his challenge: biblical literature presents a narrative of history that is a much later Persian construct.[17] A history of the kingdoms of Israel and Judah would be something else entirely and we do not have it. At all costs, he advises us to avoid the mishmash that derives from trying to write the latter from the former. The inference is that trying to reconstruct a historical 'period of the Judges' from supposed source material within the Book of Judges not only tries to do the impossible (because even if there was some source material it is now thoroughly shaped by its new context), but

---

[16] For the view that the early Iron Age settlers were not Israelites, but indigenous Canaanites, see Thompson's (1992) detailed study which suggests that the early Iron Age highland settlers previously identified as predominantly Israelite, on the basis of their material remains, were a heterogeneous people without any obvious ethnic distinction between Israelite and Canaanite. For explanation of the settlement explosion in the highlands as an internal population shift of indigenous people see Lemche (1985, 1992), Coote and Whitelam (1987), Whitelam (1994), and Finkelstein, Mazar and Schmidt (2007). For evidence of climatic change that may have prompted this recourse to the highlands see Stiebing's (1989) discussion of growing aridity throughout the Near East, culminating in severe drought conditions which peak at c1200–1190 BCE. On the lack of evidence for warfare and contrary evidence for mutual risk-spreading communities by communities jointly eking out survival via a range of risk-spreading strategies see Hopkins (1985). For a detailed reconstruction of the early Iron Age period see Thompson (1992).

[17] Ahlström, independently of Davies, argues similarly: 'The Bible presents an ideological construction of Israel's origin as well as that of the whole world ... The Hebrew texts do not mirror any real knowledge of the empirical events of the centuries before the emergence of the monarchy. The narrative about Israel's origin is a reconstruction of the past, a past that suited their author's religious orientation and goals. In this way they "created" a prehistory' (1991:22–23).

produces something *sui generis* – 'histories' that basically maintain and rehearse the biblical schema, that make corroborative or explanatory or adjusting notes as and when necessary, that always assume that the biblical account bore, more or less directly, upon the historical period pertinent to the narrative. This hypothetical construct is described by Davies as 'the result, to be precise, of taking a literary construct and making it the object of historical investigation' (1992: 17).

Davies' work provides a timely reminder that the ideological interests in Judges need to be understood as aspects of a biblical literature that was written from a much later context, geared to very different time than the one it purports to describe. The important but unstated implication of Davies' work is that we need to switch our attention to a professional scribe who constructs Judges in a style that has panache and that entertains, but is simultaneously intellectually challenging, replete with debates about kinds of leadership, problems with unworthy leaders, relationships with 'foreigners', the permeable borders of national identity and how gods can be tricksters who intervene or play behind the scenes for good or for mischief.

The third challenge concerns the assumption that Judges' stories are so lifelike, entertaining and vivid that they must have some reality lying behind them. However, a scribe writing at a much later date can be credited with creative realism and style; one who colours his story world with verisimilitude and narrative appeal as he fills a fictional 'period' in Israel's history in order to provide a foreshadowing of the Babylonian exile. The entertaining, lifelike qualities of the Judges narratives can be explained as scribal genius and desire to provide serious entertainment. This is further discussed later. For now, I suggest that there is no pre-eighth century BCE source material deriving from folklore repositories that could have been pressed into a *Retterbuch*. It is more likely that the stories are invented *de novo* for purposes pertinent to the author's context and interests.

Eighth–Seventh Century BCE Drafts of Judges

Some argue that a version of Judges was written during the flourishing of Jerusalem and its environs from the eighth century BCE onwards. Schniedewind (2004: 64) suggests that Hezekiah, inspired by a nostalgia for the past and a yearning for a reunited kingdom, sponsored the collection and codification of texts in a like manner to his Assyrian overlords who stocked the library at Nineveh. Accordingly, a 'pre-Deuteronomic historical work' is posited for the late eighth century BCE that provides the 'framework for the writing of the biblical books of Joshua, Judges, Samuel, and Kings' (2004: 81). However, precisely what amount or kind of content is included in such a 'framework' is unclear and Schniedewind provides no further comment on how Judges might have spoken to this context.[18] Noll (2007a), while rejecting notions of a draft Deuteronomistic History being composed at this time, suggests that the books now comprising the Former Prophets may have been written in the seventh or the sixth centuries BCE. In his view, only a single copy of an early draft of Judges would have existed, written by a member of the literati for circulation among his small 'narrow group of like-minded intellectuals whose writings were not intended for mass consumption' (2007a: 336).[19] Rather, these single copy texts functioned as material for debate, a debate that had a strong *anti*-deuteronomic tone. The Deuteronomistic version of Judges, in his view, is late, probably Hellenistic. However, Noll connects himself with preceding scholarship insofar as he talks about 'old hero legends' without elaboration of where such legends may have come from (2007b: 339).

Extended arguments in favour of a Hezekian version of Judges are made by Amit (1999: 379–383) and Guillaume (2004) – the latter suggesting that Judges doubles in size under Josiah's reign, from a pre-existing Sargon-friendly collection of stories.[20] Iain Provan (1988), however, who makes a case for a Josianic draft of Samuel and Kings that favours Hezekiah, does not include Judges as part of this early version of the Deuteronomistic History; in his view it is added in the neo-Babylonian period. Ultimately, a Hezekian dating remains a minority view when compared with the number of scholars who posit a later date for the writing of Judges. A Josianic composition with subsequent exilic redaction is posited by Boling (1975), Mayes (1983) and O'Brien (1989). The details differ but as Boling's commentary has been influential his views are used for illustrative

---

[18] For further theories in favour of a Hezekian draft of the Deuteronomistic History that was later supplemented see Weippert (1972), Halpern and Vanderhooft (1991).

[19] For more detail on this small group of individuals he refers the reader to Ben Zvi (1997), Davies (1998) and his own (Noll, 2001) essay.

[20] In Guillaume's view, portions of ch. 1 and the story of Othniel are added during Manasseh's time, while new sections, including 2:1–5, 2:11–19, 6:7–10, 10:1–5 and 12:8–15, are written in the time of Josiah.

purposes. Boling was strongly influenced by Cross's arguments for a two-stage construction of the Deuteronomistic History (1973). In light of Cross's proposals, Boling assumes a substantial Josianic version of Judges that was supportive of the king's reforms, naming this a 'deuteronomic' draft which had added 2:1–5, 6:7–10, 10:11–14 and 17:1–18:31 to Richter's core collection. Although Cross did not envisage exilic expansions to the Josianic draft of Judges Boling argues that the Josianic version was followed by a 'deuteronomistic' revision in the sixth century BCE which added chs. 1 and 19–21. This 'bookending' expansion is a response to the catastrophe of the exile, but is written with a comic and hopeful eye to the future. Despite their catalogue of failures and civil war, despite the loss of monarchy, temple and land, Israel survives. There is therefore hope for the exiles if they reverse the wayward behaviour of their predecessors and live by Mosaic ideals. By suggesting such a relatively small expansion, Boling thus avoids the problematic image of traumatised exiles having the appetite for national history writing, or the equally problematic view of their overlords giving them resources and permission to construct such work.

Others, however, are doubtful that any version of Judges was written during the eighth or seventh centuries BCE. Römer (2007), who divides the construction of the Deuteronomistic History into three phases, locates the History's beginnings in the time of Josiah. Phase one covers first editions of Deuteronomy and Joshua, plus accounts of David's rise and Solomon's temple building, but he does not envisage any parts of Judges being written during this period. And while Person entertains the idea of a Josianic draft of the Deuteronomic History as vaguely possible, he limits it to the business of *collating* existing source material in a way that would 'form a more coherent narrative of Israel's history' (2002: 28) and makes a case for a Persian period version of Judges (discussed further later). Lemche is critical of the way in which scholars are dependent on the biblical text for our view of Josiah's time as a period of restoration, likening it to the way scholars used to think about the golden age of Solomon (1993: 178). Given that we have no extra biblical evidence that mentions Josiah, he wonders whether the Josiah of 2 Kgs. is a historical figure at all: 'he may be nothing more than the invention of the deuteronomistic author(s) who wrote the books of Kings' (1993: 179). In additional studies, Garbini (1988), Smith (1971) and Davies (1992) all cast doubt on any major production of biblical literature during the monarchy period. The short lifespan of the two states and

Assyria's imperial surveillance, together with the lack of concrete evidence for source material contained within later literary works, informs Davies' verdict that there is no evidence for any large-scale creative literary writing in the time of Hezekiah or Josiah. But, as discussed before, he also calls for a complete distinction between the story of Israel's history in biblical literature, and the history of the kingdoms of Israel and Judah. I concur with his judgement.

A Sixth Century BCE Draft of Judges

Here, we arrive at the time Janzen posits for his traumatised author. However, any discussion of exilic production or redaction of Judges has to include speculation about the fate of scribes deported to Babylon, conditions for the deportees and how much national history writing is likely to have been done by the first generation of exiles or by those remaining in the environs of Jerusalem. The latter possibility is one that I discount. It seems unlikely that Judges would have been written by a scribe left in Judah following the Babylonian invasion given estimations of the utter devastation in and around Jerusalem and its surrounding villages. Bright presented a picture of utter wreckage where 'all, or virtually all, of the fortified towns in Judah had been razed to the ground' (1980: 344), a view recast by Stern who, while acknowledging continued habitation, claimed this would have been on a radically reduced scale with 'barely functioning' villages (2000: 51). Additional work on the devastation of Babylon's war machine is provided by Stager (1996) and Vander-hooft (1999) who emphasise the effects for the population of Judah, and Schniedewind (2004: 145) uses the evidence for significant depopulation of the area and abandoned sites provided by Jamieson-Drake (1991) and Carter (1999) to argue that the social infrastructure required for writing was simply no longer present. However, estimations of destruction are always under revision and other scholars caution against exaggeration. Blenkinsopp, who challenges Stern's dating of some destruction layers, allows for 'the resilience of a population to restore some semblance of normality in a relatively short time' (2002a: 59). He further suggests that rural people, who would 'not have left their signature on the archaeological record' (2002b: 180–181), may well have 'retreated to one or other of the numerous places of refuge with which the country is liberally provided, to emerge once the dust had settled' (2002b: 181). However, such reassessments are not suggesting that the context would be supportive of major literary activity and it remains the case that serious disruption and devastation characterised the region no matter how quickly some measure of order was restored. I concur with Person who states, 'conditions required to support such literary activity in exilic Palestine were certainly lacking' (2002: 62 n. 109).

If any writing or major redaction of Judges was to emerge in the immediate aftermath of Babylonian invasion, scholars must look to the exiles for such productivity. However, there are divided opinions on what deportation would have meant for exiles, what conditions they faced and how possible it would have been to have access to pre-existing written records or the facilities to write new ones. Much depends on how we think deportees were treated, what resources were available to them and whether the traumas of siege warfare followed by forced resettlement would prompt scribes to write such colourful stories as are found in Judges. The debate is hampered by lack of direct evidence. Our knowledge of their fate is severely limited, reliant upon the Babylonian ration tablet, the Murashû archive and comparative analogies. The Babylonian tablet details rations granted to Jehoiachin, five princes, eight men of Judah and captured artisans (Pritchard, 1969), indicating *they* at least were catered for, but we have no records for treatment of other deportees. Coogan's (1974) discussion of the archive of a family (Murashû) trading company from Nippur, dating from 464 to 404 BCE, notes the implication that descendants of deportees were involved in commercial businesses. Römer (2007: 168), noting this, together with the presence of the 'town of the Judeans' (Al-Yâhüdu), next to Nippur, suggests that by this time, some had successful lives in Babylon and did not feel a need to repatriate to the land of their forebears. Given such limited evidence, it is difficult to say with any certainty that an exiled scribal group was suitably situated to write, or significantly revise, a national history in the immediate aftermath of exile. This has not, however, prevented the emergence of differing scholarly views.

On one hand, there are several scholars who suggest the exile was not as traumatic as we might suppose. Thompson's outline of the varying purposes of deportation notes how it could be presented to resettled populations in positive terms.[21] He states that in the

---

[21] Drawing on Oded (1979), Thompson notes how rationale for deportation can include 'punishment for resistance or rebellion ... to eliminate both actual rivals and the potential for resistance and insurrection', to create newly settle groups 'who were

Assyrian and Babylonian periods 'Deportation was not primarily a policy of punishment. The deportees ... receiv[ed] not only land and property but also support against the indigenous populations among whom they became representatives of imperial control' (1992: 415). His discussion, however, focusses on how ancient inscriptions *present* deportation rather than on the specific fate of Judaeans and there is no engagement with the social, economic and psychological effects of deportation for those subject to it. This results in a less harsh depiction of exile than the more harrowed suggestions of trauma-informed biblical scholars for whom the stresses of being deported are thought to be substantial, as discussed later.

Another who thinks the exile may not have been as traumatic as supposed is Noll. In his view, 'Life for the elites in exile was not physically oppressive ... Neo-Assyrian and Neo-Babylonian policies of deportation were not designed to inflict terror on those who were deported. Quite the contrary, the policy of deportation was pragmatic' (2013: 362). He goes on to explain that it could be a matter of removing rebellious leaders whose skills could be reused elsewhere, where they 'would constitute a minority, would not be able to organise a rebellion, and would instead devote talents to productive activities' (2013: 362). On the basis of the residential quarters in Babylon housing groups called Ashkelon and Gaza he claims that relocation did not disrupt ethnic ties.[22] He additionally draws on Lemaire's (2006) work when noting how epigraphic evidence suggests deported Judaeans 'maintained their language and identity in their new homes' (2013: 362). Garbini is even more up-beat, writing that 'life by the rivers of Babylon was not so bad after all' and he

---

dependent on and therefore loyal to Assyrian power', or can involve factors ranging from the facilitation of 'military conscription, to the control of political leaders and of the intelligentsia, the development of an economic monopoly of craftsmen and skilled laborers, the support of corvée labour and the limited slave trade' (1992: 342). It could also help with strategic 'paramilitary border settlements' (1992: 342) and the repopulation of 'abandoned or empty lands' (1992: 343). Thompson adds his personal view that it could enable 'control and sedentarization of unruly nomads, associated with the support of vassal states' (1992: 343). He also notes how deportation could be offered to a population who revolt against their leaders (2 Kgs. 18–9) where deportation is represented 'not as punitive at all but as an alternative to punishment for resistance against Assyria's power' and in such cases 'deportees not only received land and property from the Assyrians upon resettlement, but also were given support and protection against the indigenous population who, of course saw them as intruders and usurpers' (1992: 345).

[22]   Evidence for this is ultimately derived from Tadmor (1966: 102, n. 62), Zadok (1978: 61), Ephal (1978: 80) and Oded (1979: 25, n. 34).

suggests that the 'monarchy' and the 'Jewish leading class' were 'transferred more or less comfortably to Babylon' (1994: 182). However, his reference to the seven sons reportedly born to Jeconiah as being evidence for this 'not so bad' life seems somewhat questionable.

If these more positive views of deportation are accepted it becomes possible to envisage a scenario where deportees are able to revise or write material that is eventually included in the texts we now recognise as the Former Prophets. Römer (2007: 116f) and Noll (2013) both suppose that the officials numbered among the deportees may have been permitted to bring material with them which they were subsequently able to re-edit. Noll thinks it is plausible to 'imagine that the crisis of deportation to Babylon, the disruption and loss that it entailed, motivated them to raid those archives and gather as much traditional lore as possible, lest it be lost forever' (2013: 395). He posits sources from 'a royal archive, temple records, public monuments, perhaps collections of priestly literature and collections of traditional myth and folklore' (2013: 395). He then suggests that such fragment gathering 'generated a process of writing commentary on the gathered material' which became part of 'evolving texts' (2013: 395). The focus here is on material *gathering*, i.e., not writing. Römer, however, goes further than Noll and argues that a major written draft of Judges emerges at this time, incorporated during a second phase of the production of the Deuteronomistic History. Judges contributes to its major theme that Assyrian and Babylonian invaders acted as the agents of YHWH who punished Israel for apostasy with its repeated cycle functioning as a foreshadowing: 'an allusion to the end of Judah' (2007: 118). Römer (2007: 136) refers freely to the fabrication of the period of Judges, although he is not suggesting that the stories were created *de novo* during the exilic period, only the notion that these stories constructed a fictional 'period'.[23] His exilic author thus uses a pre-existing collection of judge stories that originally 'celebrated the feats of Northern legendary heroes' (2007: 137), i.e., the stories that now appear in 3:12–9:55 or possibly 3:12–12:7. While redacting these pre-existing stories, the scribe adds 2:6–12, 14–16, 18–19 and 3:7–11. This expansion 'transform[ed] the ideology of the older collection … by

---

[23] So we have not moved far from the view of Noth (1943) who viewed the 'period of the Judges' as a creation of the Deuteronomist, comprised of material salvaged from various sources.

introducing a new, overwhelming topic: the Israelites' veneration of other deities, which provokes Yahweh's anger' (2007: 137).

However, scholars who think the Judaean deportees would have been situated in a context amenable to national history writing are challenged by those who find the idea of literary production during the exile highly unlikely. Smith-Christopher suggests that life for deportees was 'no holiday' (1991: 79). This is because they may not have been slaves 'in the technical or conceptual sense' but being put to work on Babylonian labour projects was likely.[24] Schniedewind similarly suggests the deportees may have suffered a harsh existence as labourers for building programmes – a situation not at all amenable to the writing of long prose narratives. He is content to suggest small-scale redaction to Kings, updated to cover Josiah's death and the fate of the Judean monarchy; an 'appendix' that 'essentially absolves Jehoiachin from wrongdoing, justifies his surrender to the Babylonians and confirms his status as legitimate king of Judah even while dining in the palace of Babylon' (2004: 153–154). But insofar as there was a 'literature' of the exile, Schniedewind suggests this was oral – psalms and laments. Davies is probably the most outspoken critic of an exilic literary flourishing, arguing that the notion of deportees carrying with them written records that they could subsequently update is bizarre. While it was 'customary' for an imperial power to remove temple goods and archives, he suggests it would be a very strange policy to allow deported peoples continued access to their confiscated documents 'since the point of deportation is to alienate people from their homeland' (1992: 80). He criticises the guild of biblical scholarship for a 'fanciful portrait of religious fervour and furious literary creativity' given so little extra biblical evidence and going 'against everything we know or can infer about deported populations' (1992: 80). In his view, it is more likely that scribes from Jerusalem were pressed into the service of the Babylonian scribal system.

To conclude, the lack of direct evidence is the problem; the diversity of aforementioned views seems to depend largely on the individual scholar's predisposition to imagine the effects of deportation negatively or positively. Literary flourishing, however, seems

---

[24] See Becking (2009) for a discussion of how booty from conquered territories, including persons, could be understood as *ḥerem* and put to work in state-slavery projects. His discussion focusses on Moabite practice but seems applicable to Assyrian and neo-Babylon policies.

unlikely to me. Families survived and ethnic ties may have remained in place with some prospering in Babylon. Others may have been slave conscripts and yet survived and prospered. But what of the intelligentsia – and the expectations of their new overlords – is it really reasonable to imagine they bring with them national materials that they can re-edit to create a national history? Römer's case for a major draft of Judges appearing at this time does not, in my view, convincingly refute the arguments of Davies or explain how or why a deported scribe would have been permitted to work on a text concerning national history. That Judges bears the mark of an 'exilic consciousness' is not in dispute, but it does not follow that a version of Judges must have been written between deportation to Babylon and Cyrus' edict. Lemche convincingly argues that although biblical literature is 'undoubtedly dominated by the idea of exile' (2000: 132), it is a 'biblical stereotype' that has 'little to do with the historical realities in Palestine between the seventh and fifth centuries BCE' (2000: 131). Elsewhere, Lemche refers to the exile as the 'intellectual matrix' (2003: 275) for the literature of the Hebrew Bible but that literature is more concerned with establishing a future programme for the 'returnees'.[25] Thompson is also unenthusiastic about the idea of literary work undertaken by deportees. This is not so much because he thinks the conditions were unconducive but because he locates the production of biblical literature, as we have it, in the late Persian and early Hellenistic contexts. As will become clearer in later discussion, I think that biblical scholars who make much of the effects of the Babylonian exile on Judeans and the texts these exiles purportedly produced or redacted need to hear Thompson's case for a much later dating of texts. In Thompson's view, exile and its associated trauma becomes a central *literary* motif that favours the cause of resettlers who self-present as the survivors of that history and thus have a stake in the land. Accordingly, a text might exhibit foreshadowing signs of the exile to come, as Judges does, but this does not mean it was composed in its immediate aftermath or is integrally connected with the historical events of the sixth century BCE. These comments, however, raise a more profound issue: the question of continuity between the peoples and experiences of those exiled to Babylon and the biblical narrative history that now exists in Gen.–2 Kgs., an issue to which we now turn.

[25] For more on this see Lemche (1998: 86–132).

Fifth–Fourth Centuries BCE Drafts of Judges

By the time we get to the Persian period the Book of Judges has generally been thought to be largely completed, subject only to some light touch minor editing.[26] However, it necessary to rethink that view in the light of statements such as this from Carroll: 'The Hebrew Bible is the product of the second temple period ... there *may* be something to be said for the view that the Bible contains fragments of material from before the collapse of the temple in the 6th century... [but] ... the claim that the Bible *as we know it* ... comes from the Second Temple Period seems to be quite ungainsayable' (1991: 108). A footnote adds that this 'may become the consensus view' but only when 'biblical studies enters the twentieth century and gets its act together' (1991: 108 n. 3). We are over two decades on from Carroll's comment and Judges scholarship regrettably has not got its act together. Judges commentaries have not yet caught up with changing views of the Deuteronomistic and Primary History or attended closely to postulations of late Persian and early Hellenistic dates for this text.

While Davies and Thompson do not discuss the Book of Judges in any detail, the ramification of their views on the production, audience and purposes of biblical literature and its (lack of) connection to the historical kingdoms of Israel and Judah, has major significance for our understanding of Judges. In their view, the material in Gen.–2 Kgs. does not provide a window onto the history of Israel. They are not saying that source material from the kingdoms of Israel and Judah is entirely absent. Thompson discusses the antiquarian interests of scribes who collect and transmit 'fragments of memory: written and oral, chains of narrative, complex literary works, administrative records, songs, prophetic sayings, the words of

---

[26] Schniedewind (2004: 166), for example, resists any suggestions of flourishing biblical literature during the fifth to the third centuries BCE, believing this to be a time of retrenchment rather than creativity. On Judges specifically, Römer suggests small-scale expansion during his third phase of Deuteronomistic History construction dated to 539–450 BCE, namely 2:13, 17:20–23 and 3:1–6. However, as part of the book division process, he argues that Judges receives a new intro of 1:1–2:5, the insertion of the Jephthah and Samson narratives that have affinities with Greek literature, plus the epilogues of 17–21 which he sees as 'post-Deuteronomistic pieces that were added in order to create an independent book of Judges' (2007: 138). This meant that the story of Samuel, who was the twelfth judge, was dislodged, cut off from the core narratives of Judges by the intervening expansions.

philosophers, lists and stories' (1992: 421), some of which may well have had historical referents (1992: 366). But he then refers to the 'formative process by which "Israel" was created out of such fragments that survived the political and historical disasters of the Assyrian and Neo-Babylonian periods' (1992: 384). This process is initiated by those presenting themselves as 'returnees' who have created 'a literature aimed at self-understanding in terms of a surviving remnant' (1992: 421). But he is quite clear: 'whatever people were being transported and returned to *Palestine* they were certainly not Israelites' (1992: 418, emphasis original). He is actually rather elusive about the ancestral homeland(s) of the people retransported to Yehud by Persian decree, but is convinced that this was no 'restoration' to homeland. Rather, he posits the 'creation of a new people with a new cult' who, in 'the development of a written tradition came to understand themselves as the population of long lost Israel returning to "Eretz Israel" from bitter exile after having been delivered from Babylon by their savior and master Cyrus' (1992: 418). For Thompson, the exile is a central *literary* motif in biblical literature whereby the immigrant population can present themselves as the surviving remnant, regardless of 'whether or not one's ancestors had originally come from Babylon, Nineveh and Egypt or had always been in Palestine. To identify with the true Israel was to assert one's roots in exile and through it in the lost glory of the Davidic empire, in the conquest with Joshua ...' (1992: 422).

Davies also requires us to rethink notions of continuity between exiles from Judah and 'returnees'. He reserves judgement on where these resettled peoples originally came from; the 'returnees' could have been descendants of a Judean deportation or they could be from parts of the Persian Empire occupied by people originally from disparate locations.[27] Yet he is clear about the artificiality of a 'returnee' narrative that masks this people's recent, imperially directed immigration into the land by appeal to a history of great ancestors who once lived in the great kingdoms of David, Solomon and so forth. Like Thompson, Davies suggests that biblical literature has some limited continuity with the history of the kingdoms of Israel and Judah since it probably incorporates some of their archive material, but this gets bound up in a new history 'which explained

---

[27] No doubt, he argues, both Persians and immigrants want to justify the land grab: prior occupancy was what the Persians told them and 'they may have believed it themselves, and it may have been true' (Davies, 1992: 117).

their own post-"exilic" society and the rights and privileges of the immigrant élite within that society' (1992: 87).

It seems to me that the uncertainty about the returnees' ethnic connection with deportees from Judah matters most for those who need to explain how material from that kingdom was available for scribes who later composed biblical texts; i.e., it is important if we are invested in having source material so that texts can be dated nearer to the 'events' they describe. Other scholars, predominantly in the revisionist camp, are less concerned with ensuring ethnic connection because they are more convinced that biblical 'history' has a high fictional content and do not need to justify the existence of previous drafts or substantial source material. However, no one is talking of complete invention. Davies, as noted before, writes of 'some archive material' (1992: 87), while Thompson refers to 'fragments of memory: written and oral, chains of narrative, complex literary works, administrative records, songs, prophetic sayings, the words of philosophers, lists and stories' (1992: 421). Noll similarly suggests that the deportees 'preserved some ancient writings that would become the nucleus around which the biblical anthology grew' (2013: 363).

The implications of this section for our understanding of Judges are several. First that Judges may be a redacted text but not necessarily over centuries; a much shorter period of time could be envisaged. Second, Judges may have been composed by a member of the intelligentsia using some popular name or memory of a legendary exploit that was used as a foothold for inventing a narrative around such names *de novo*. Third, the portrayal of a history of Israelite waywardness and cultic disloyalty may be part of a necessary storyline to justify the presence of the 'new' Israel as constituted by the 'returnees'. To that end, Noth and subsequent scholars were partly correct (the text is part of a wider rationale and theological justification for the exile), but what has changed is that we now see a Persian period interest in presenting a historical narrative that deliberately provokes a past trauma in order to present the authors as its healers. Accordingly, familiar motifs such as 'divine control of Israel's destiny by Yahweh, of Yahweh's jealous anger at Israel's unfaithfulness and the ever recurrent need for reform' might be the result of 'didactic and moralizing theological reflections on the traditions sometimes haphazardly gathered from the past ... [but] ideologically they belong to the Persian period circles which developed the collections of sayings and oracles in the prophetic works' (Thompson,

1992: 383). In presenting a catastrophic narrative of Israelite unfaith-fulness in order to present a future community with whom one could identify as the surviving remnant, Judges thus invites readers to take on both identities – the Israel of the past and the Israel of the future. In so doing, the identity of Israel is, in psychological terms, split (an intriguing development addressed further in Chapter 4).

One of the objections to the above scenario is the pessimistic tone of the Deuteronomistic History which ends on a bleak note. If authors, or redactors, knew of the return under Persian hegemony, it seems odd that the Deuteronomistic History makes no mention of this. It is more likely that the history, including Judges, was written in the immediate aftermath of the exile, when the future looked uncertain. However, Linville rightly points out that Noth's dating of 560 BCE for a bleakly pessimistic history doesn't make sense. Why would one write if Israel's days were ended and God had forsaken her? It makes better sense to presume it is written to bequeath a future for which it supplies a programme.[28]

Person's work offers some idea as to how Judges might contribute to that programme. His 'Deuteronomic school' consists of scribes who 'produced the first complete Deuteronomic History from Moses to the exilic period' (2002: 28). They returned to Yehud in the time of Zerubbabel, and were prepared to work with the Persian-supported administration in Jerusalem.[29] The primary message for the post-exilic audience was that restoration follows repentance and the advice on how to 'remain and flourish in the land' would have been relevant for that time (2002: 55). The whole sorry saga of the 'judges era', as presented in the Book of Judges, becomes a commentary on Zerubbabel:

> until Zerubbabel becomes a proper Davidic king who can govern over all the people, insuring that they strictly obey the law, there will remain a certain amount of apostasy with the likely consequence of divine punishment ... Zerubba-bel's becoming king according to the Lord's plan would at

[28] Linville notes how this view was proposed by Danell in 1946 and found support in Wolff (1975) who argued that the representation of Israel in exile was only a phase of the recurrent and ongoing cycle of apostasy, judgement, repentance and salvation.

[29] Ultimately, their hopes for a restored Davidic king did not cohere with Persian plans for the new temple community. He speculates that Ezra's law book that 'was an attempt by the Persian authorities to reassert some control over the Jerusalem political and religious establishment in face of antagonism caused by the increasing disenfran-chised Deuteronomic school' (2002: 59).

least begin to break this cycle and therefore, the critique of the period of the judges also applies to some degree to the period of the reconstruction of the temple. (2002: 109)

There is some subsequent redaction. Person locates Judg. 3:1–6 and its prohibition of intermarriage during the time of Ezra, but the main creation of the text belongs to Persian I (450–332 BCE).

The hypothesis of literary flourishing during the Persian period is supported by Garbini. In his view it is the relative calm of this period – a time of '*pax iranica*' – that facilitated a 'golden age' of Hebrew literature (1994: 188). On a more practical level, Davies' argument that the rebuilding of the temple and its economic use as a tax-raising centre would require a 'fairly large scribal class' (1998:67) is worth noting. In his view, an impetus to produce a national ideology is understandable at this time. He gives a broad-brush picture of scribes operating with Persian patronage and writing a national history that supported the claims of 'returnees' to the land. These scribes may have had access to surviving relics from Palestine ('pieces of written or of oral material—for example, stories about kings, warriors and holy men, songs cultic and non-cultic' [1992: 94]) but the extensive literary flourishing is of the *Persian* era, with additional work in the Hellenistic period. Moreover, it is most important to note Davies' vital comment that those earlier pieces of source material would have not been the relics of the 'ancient Israel' we are familiar with from the Hebrew Bible, because this Israel is an ideological construct of biblical writers. The relics would have emerged from the actual 'old kingdoms of Israel and Judah' and 'about which we know fairly little' (1992: 95).[30]

A Persian date would also be consistent with Thompson's view that the biblical literature presents the 'returnees' as 'the population of long lost Israel returning to "Eretz Israel" from bitter exile after having been delivered from *Babylon* by their savior and master Cyrus' (1992: 418). The importance of such a narrative for those who settle in land that others already occupy is obvious and, strategically, casting the returnees as the 'victims of Assyrian and Babylonian deportation practices' (1992: 417) is a clever move. But, as

---

[30] Davies strongly emphasises the distinction between 'the historical Israel (and Judah)' and the 'society which created the biblical Israel. This latter society is born only in the Persian period, and in that sense the biblical literature, as opposed to the relics which it incorporated and re-formed and re-contextualised, is a product of what we call the Second Temple Period' (1992: 95).

Thompson points out, 'the perspective of the tradition suggests we are involved with an entity that is both intellectually and literarily an entirely new creation beginning in the late Persian period's transforming revisions and collections of tradition' (1992: 354).

Certainly, the book contains themes or discussions that would have resonance for a Persian period readership. Amit's (2014) discussion notes how Judges' negative presentation of northern tribes would have resonance for the conflict between the Yehud and Samaritan communities. Also, its negative depiction of Shechem would be helpful considering how 'the population of the north built a temple near Shechem on Mount Gerizim ... In other words, the tone of the criticism of Shechem in the book of Judges has a supportive audience in the late Persian period' (2014: 109). She notes the emphasis on religious sin that is quickly punished by hostile enemies, and the interest in theocracy – both issues that were favoured by the chronicler. The anti-Saul polemic is echoed in Persian period texts such as Chronicles Hag 2:20–23, Zech 3:8, 4 and 6:12, and Ruth 4:17 and 22 and in the legitimisation of certain foreign women (Jael) which has some resonance with the book of Ruth and the 'Chronicler's attitude to non-Israelite women' (2014: 114). Gerstenberger (2011) also identifies a resonance between themes of Judges and the Persian situation. He believes that the stories of Samson, Micah and the Levite and his abused woman 'answer questions pertaining to the Persian period' (2011: 284), i.e., postexilic concerns with centralisation, holiness and authentic YHWH worship. His brief comments culminate in the opinion that the 'final or near-final form' of Judges 'was read in light of their own situation by the postexilic community of Yahweh' (2011: 284–285). Like Amit, he remains committed to conventional views that the Book of Judges contains pre-monarchic material and a pre-exilic schema into which it was pressed.

Ultimately, my view is that a late Persian context makes sense – but, unlike Amit and Gerstenberger and scholars previously discussed, I am not convinced by speculation about pre-exilic and exilic drafts of texts, none of which actually exist in any shape or form. A rationale for the text's themes can be found in the needs of the ones 'returning' to Yehud, presenting themselves as purified heirs to a previous 'bad' Israel. Thompson and the revisionists have their critics, but I believe the momentum and argument is with them.[31]

---

[31] For critical responses to the revisionists see, for example, Provan (1995), Japhet (1998), Halpern (1999), Dever (1999, 2001), Long, Baker and Wenham (2002).

However, the discussion is not yet over for there is a small but growing number of scholars who suggest that the Hellenistic age is an even better fit for literature like the Book of Judges.

Third Century BCE Drafts of Judges

If the scholars mentioned earlier found themes that were resonant to a Persian period, other scholars have been noting reverberations with the Hellenistic age. Similarities between the Samson story and the tasks of Hercules, or between the abduction of the Shiloh girls and the rape of the Sabine women have long been noted.[32] Gnuse thus stands in good company when he sees these narratives as late 'abrupt' insertions to the Book of Judges inspired by the scribe's new familiarity with Greek material. While there is no direct literary connection with the work of Livy (59 BCE–17 CE) and Plutarch (46–120 CE), he notes, convincingly, a significant number of continuities that warrant the hypothesis that earlier forms of these stories were known to Livy, Plutarch and the editor of Judges. Gnuse thus concludes the 'most likely' time that allows for this editor to be familiar with the Greek versions 'would have been the late Persian or Hellenistic era' (2007: 240).

Gerhard Larsson's essay on Hellenistic influences on biblical narrative argues that the Hellenistic age was one where literature could flourish. He cites the Egyptian, Babylonian and Greek histories produced by Manetho, Berossos and Erstosthenes as examples and, while reluctant to claim any overt borrowing, he considers it 'likely' that such works stimulated an interest in writing national history. Moreover, their availability to Israelite historiographers can be reasonably assumed given 'frequent communications between Jerusalem and the strong Jewish communities in Babylon and Alexandria' (2004: 307). Certainly there are differences between these works and the biblical literature; he refers to the 'richer content', the 'fascinating narratives' and the more overt 'tendencies' of biblical texts (2004: 310), together with the greater emphasis on the covenant relationship between Israel and YHWH. Nonetheless, he believes it makes more sense to think of biblical historiography being *written* in the same period rather than the redaction of pre-existing large-scale material that dates back to the sixth or fifth centuries. As he states, it is asking

---

[32] See, for example, Margalith (1966, 1986a, 1986b, 1987).

rather too much to suppose similar biblical narratives existed 'hundreds of years before such works were established for the surrounding and more powerful people, and without external or internal evidence during the "silent" fifth, fourth and partly third centuries' (2004: 309). He concludes that while previous decades may have been a time for gathering material for antiquarian interests, the Hellenistic age would have been a time of *writing*, not just putting final touches to previous drafts written centuries before. The impact of this shift would be that it moves our scribe even further away from the exile and its traumatic effects. We are now centuries away from the 560 BCE Deuteronomist envisaged by Noth and the views of other scholars such as Janzen. We are in a 330s context, just prior to the Ptolemaic era.

Positing a Hellenistic context for the substantial writing of Judges does at least get around Thomas Bolin's objection to placing biblical material too readily into the Persian period. It is far too convenient, in his view, to abandon the exile as a period ripe for the flourishing of biblical texts, only to take the next available time slot available. He is thus sceptical of any convenient re-dating of texts from the exilic to the Persian period, arguing that this 'is not the place to look for the writing of the biblical texts', but rather only the 'collection and development' of material that had been going on from 539 BCE onwards (1996: 15, 15). The writing and subsequent editing, however, belongs to the Hellenistic period.[33] His argument is based on the results of his examination of Nehemiah and Ezra for indicators of pre-existing, known biblical traditions. Finding only scattered and fragmented references to traditions referred to in the Hebrew Bible he surmises that by '350–300 there is no biblical corpus which resembles the size of the present day HB [Hebrew Bible]' (1996: 12). Having come to this conclusion, he paints the following scenario: an antiquarian scribe draws on recently collected material in his composition of newly forged 'collective self-identity in the present . . . to outline a clear destiny for the future by constructing a common past—a past arranged around the motif of former glory lost through a divinely commanded fall from grace' (1996: 13). This newly written tradition is *presented* 'as the ancient, sacred and normative texts which have always been the birthright of the people' (1996: 12),

---

[33] A footnote qualifies this position, noting that some material may have long roots that 'reach back into the Iron Age', but he is dealing with 'the earliest point at which these traditions begin to be collected' (Bolin, 1996: 13, n. 36).

but what the scribe has actually produced is an 'aetiology' in order 'to supply an identity which explains the circumstances of life for the Hellenistic-era inhabitants of Palestine' (1996: 14).

Bolin's proposal for a Hellenistic time of writing of biblical 'history' inevitably affects how we perceive the emotive content of a book like Judges. Bolin does not present us with traumatised biblical author coming to terms with national destruction, nor a subsequent generation still working through the immediate theological and psychological effects of deportation. They are not even repatriated exiles, for Bolin shares Thompson's view that they may be 'new settlers charted with a mission to create a past shared identity where none theretofore existed' (1996: 13). Bolin's scribes are settler descendants concerned with identity and boundary maintenance, going about their work with antiquarian diligence and creative drive. If his suggestions are accepted they would undermine any understanding of the repetitive cycle in Judges as a traumatic stutter and, inevitably, call for a radical reinterpretation of the genre of Judges. If we can no longer view the text as history, if it is not a traumatic response to national disaster nor a theological explanation of that disaster in some kind of larger 'salvation history', then what is it? Perhaps, as mooted in the section above on polyphony, it is better understood as a wisdom-like discussion paper.

This is a possibility that Jobling seems to entertain in his assessment of leadership options presented in Judg.–1 Sam. 12. In his view, the scribe had no clear and easily definable opinion on how the community should be governed and opens up a debate on leadership without coming to a specific conclusion. The discussion, he says, is 'a classic example of talking around a contradiction' (1986: 46). Jobling does not overtly claim that the genre of this work is wisdom literature but his insights give us a more philosophical scribe rather than one bent on propagandist agenda for Davidic monarchy rule; one who conjures options and plays with them, identifying benefits and flaws in judgeship, kingship and theocracy in a 'very complex' discussion that allows for contradictory viewpoints.

If Jobling gives us scope to imagine a more philosophical scribe, Noll gives us both a philosophical and inventive one, able to engage in creative fiction for the purposes of prompting discussion. Commenting on the book of Kings, he writes:

> If the ancient scribe knew he was inventing a tale, a name, a date, or a chronology, or if that scribe was revising a

received tale, altering its content or narrative context, there is no reason to think he also believed he had described a real past by doing so, or that he expected his reader to believe this was a description of a real past. The category of fiction was not unknown to the ancients. (2007b: 54–55)

For Noll, readers of Hebrew narratives would have understood that while a narrative describes a past and may indeed contain nuggets of tradition form a historical past, it 'was not really about the past' (2007b: 56). In words that resonate with Jobling's, Noll argues that the stories about prophets in Kings function on a rather 'cynical level, which is not far removed from the worldview of Qoheleth: they narrate various hypothetical situations, sometimes juxtaposing alternate possibilities, that can arise when people are in relationship with a distance, cold, and unreliable god—and they never really arrive at a conclusion' (2007b: 61).

If this sounds rather like the work of Greek historiographers then it should come as no surprise. Ever since Van Seters' (1983) study that compared the Deuteronomist's work with that of the fifth century Herodotus there has been a significant rise in scholars who are now seriously looking at the possibility that the Hebrew writers of material within the so-called 'Deuteronomistic History' had access to the work of the Greeks. Van Seters does not go so far as to say that Deuteronomy was dependent upon Herodotus' model of writing but neither does he rule out mutual influence. Critical of this hesitancy, found also in Mandell and Freedman (1993), Jan-Wim Wesselius makes a bold case for the direct dependence of the Primary History on the *Histories* of Herodotus written between c445 and 425 BCE. He argues that once we have recognised this then its inconsistences and discontinuities can be understood as deliberately stylistic, meant to give the impression that it has been constructed from a variety of documents. Given the need to posit ready availability of Herodotus's work to non-Greek Jewish readers, he suggests 425–300 BCE as the time frame for the production of Primary History. The 'view' of the Primary History is that of 'a learned Jew of late Persian or early Hellenistic times on the history of his people' (2002: 5), 'a highly talented author who most likely lived and worked among the intelligentsia of Nehemiah's Jerusalem, in the second half of the fifth century BCE' (2002: 163). The 'history' he constructs is meant 'to assist in restructuring Jewish religious life in Jerusalem and also, probably at a somewhat slower pace, in diaspora communities such as those of Elephantine and Nippur (2002: 71). It is an intriguing suggestion, but the parallels between the Primary History and Herodotus' work fade away when we move into the material of Judges–Kings, only the abrupt ending is similar (a fact not lost on Wesselius who suggests that it ends there in order to give the *impression* of being written during the exile by an anonymous author). Ultimately, Wesselius' portrait of a biblical scribe borrowing so directly from Herodotus has not met with plaudits. Reviewers tend to welcome the originality of the theory but are ultimately sceptical.[34] I return, then, to the view espoused by Noll, that biblical texts formerly deemed 'historical' to lesser or greater extents, are better understood as stories exchanged by the intelligentsia: philosophical, wisdom-like ponderings, written at a time conducive to such writings, i.e., when Greek literature was becoming known and read.

One of the reasons Lemche shifts to a Hellenistic period for biblical material composition is that, compared with the Persian period, it gives sufficient time for the Greek writers to become 'known and extensively read' (1993: 184). Materially 'the Persian conquest seems to have brought little positive to Palestinian society in general' (1993: 184) and he would like to see the results of more archaeological studies of Persian period conditions before he would consider the composition of 'great literature' in Palestine of this time (1993: 185), together with more information about Persian administration of the Yehud province. Lemche himself speculates that the Persians may have been largely disinterested in what went on in such areas. He claims that 'the revitalization of the ancient Near East only became a fact after the Greek take-over ... city life vastly expanded after the conquest of Alexander' (1993: 186). It is at this point that Lemche gets 'a glimpse of a society in which great literature may have been composed, kept and loved' (1993: 186).[35] Yes, biblical literature is different, Lemche (2000: 138–139) touches on this when he concludes that although late,

---

[34] Davies claims that the comparison between Herodotus and the Deuteronomy is welcome but Wesselius's specific argument is rejected, given that the similarities are 'trivial and unsurprising', while the differences are 'so great as to make literary dependence out of the question' (2004: 806). L. H. Feldman (2004) similarly welcomes the fresh ideas in Wesselius' monograph but ultimately is left unconvinced.

[35] Anticipating objections that the Hebrew of the Deuteronomistic History is classical as opposed to the later Hebraic texts such as Ecclesiastes, he postulates that we might be dealing with differences of location, maybe also differences of time, but this might not be as lengthy as once thought. As for differences between Septuagint and Hebrew manuscripts, he argues that the Septuagint originates in Egypt. Hebrew literature may have originated in Mesopotamia. Perhaps if Hebrew texts were translated into

with ties to classical literature, biblical texts remain quite distinctive. The way in which they directly link causality to the acts of YHWH and distinguish those who love/forsake YHWH rather than dividing people into good and bad categories are some of the ways in which he thinks biblical literature stands out. Yet, the suggestion that biblical scribes were working in the same milieu as classical authors, influenced by the Greek material that had reached them, puts the field of biblical studies into a radical new context.

Conclusion

The revisionist scholarship of Noll, Lemche, Thompson and Davies attract criticism but has to be taken seriously. The old assumptions about Judges' transmission history no longer hold. Specifically, the case for Judges being part of a Deuteronomistic History written in the immediate aftermath of the exile would have to be argued rigorously and convincingly rather than assumed. One has to posit a deportation policy that not only allowed but facilitated the transportation of both scribes *and* extant written material in order that they may work on it in their new location. But this runs counter to the views of scholars who posit a far more painful experience of loss, grief and trauma. Personally, I would welcome studies that use contemporary analogies and refugee studies in order to help elucidate the emotional, psychological and physical costs of siege warfare and subsequent deportation and how such experiences are made manifest in their literary outputs. I do not think, however, such work would necessarily help us to understand the transmission and 'message' of the Book of Judges.

The previous discussion has demonstrated how difficult it is to date the Book of Judges with any certainty. The previous consensus on pre-exilic material with Hezekian or exilic major redrafts continues to be widely assumed but it no longer convinces. It has not been the purpose of this chapter to provide a detailed defence of a Persian or Hellenistic date of writing for Judges, but rather to demonstrate why the notion of a traumatised survivor of the Babylonian siege is difficult to maintain given such possibilities. The humour that permeates Judges, the narrative artistry with which it is put together and the polyphony of a dialogic text all suggest that it

Greek by Jews living in Alexandria who were more familiar with the Greek language then they may not have been much older than those translations.

is more of a wisdom text than a piece of historiography. Positing a date in the late Persian or early Hellenistic period supports that suggestion. The book presents a story world populated by suprahuman characters and cosmic phenomena intervening on behalf of Israel. Its philosophical musing explores how the human world is a playground for the gods whose sway over human autonomy affects human destines, and how expectations can therefore be overturned by unlikely means. Unlike Noll (2013), who sees the capricious deity of Samuel as merely a plot necessity, I believe biblical writers were very interested in the whims of deities and fate. Their stories reflect considered pondering of how and why the world cannot be reduced to guaranteed effects of human striving. This does not mean that I see YHWH as a transcendent deity. I do not 'believe' in him and I don't privilege YHWH's perspective; he remains a constructed character, one that represents a scribe's worldview that is alive to the effects of gods operating behind the scenes. While this scribe may have been supremely conscious of the fact that he constructs images of YHWH as he writes, I think it is likely that he thought the images corresponded to some extent with life as he experienced it. If life could be unexpected, capricious and could deal a good or a bad hand without any obvious connection to a good or bad life, it is not surprising that the deity has a constellation of traits that range from steadfast love to abuse. In other words, I don't see Judges purely in terms of a political programme for a late Persian community justifying its existence in Yehud. Yes, it may be that, but it is also something far more. Trauma theory, however, while it might have much to offer biblical studies, is limited in its application to the Book of Judges. Here is a more peaceful time in which a scribe creates a fictional period of the judges to enable the philosophical pondering of fate, justice, the flaws of human male leadership and the irony of life.

So I return to the initial question of this chapter: why does the author propel Israel from one military humiliation to another, compel them to experience and re-experience the brutalities of warfare, requiring both Israel and YHWH to confront the prospect of mutual abandonment over and over again? And to answer this question I turn away from trauma theory and towards attachment theory. The application of attachment theory to the Book of Judges has the great advantage of focussing on the psychological dimension of the text without necessitating the hypothesis of sudden, overwhelming trauma.

3

YHWH AND ISRAEL IN THE 'STRANGE SITUATION': ATTACHMENT THEORY AND GOD-TALK

Introduction

Having resisted the idea that Judges is the product of a traumatised scribe, this chapter analyses three key passages, using attachment theory as a lens for interpreting the on–off relationship between YHWH and Israel. Staying with the overall framework of object relations theory, I turn to the research of Mary Ainsworth and her team, the delineation of attachment and loss in John Bowlby's now classic trilogy and more recent exponents of attachment theorists.[1] Their work helps explain the cycle of betrayal, punishment and rescue that characterises Judges.

The chapter falls into two main sections: the first provides an overview of attachment theory, noting some of its key concepts, while the second contains an analysis of three biblical passages. Section one opens with a brief summary of the pioneering work of the American–Canadian development psychologist Mary Ainsworth and her co-contributors (Ainsworth, 1963, 1964, 1967; Ainsworth and Wittig, 1969; Ainsworth, Bell and Stayton, 1971; Ainsworth et al., 1978). It is important to consider this material, as it provided the fertile ground from which Bowlby developed his material on attachment and loss (first published in 1969, 1973, and 1980) (Bowlby, 1997, 1978, 1980b). Bowlby analyses, in detail, the rationale for attachment, how it is manifested and the effect of different kinds of attachment for the people involved. I am particularly interested in his astute understanding of how relationships contain elements that are antithetical to attachment, his views on how and why such

---

[1] Attachment theory investigates patterns and workings of human relationships not only between child and caregiver but between adults. Holmes describes it as 'not so much a single theory as an overall framework for thinking about relationships, or, more accurately, about those aspects of relationships that are shaped by threat and the need for security' (1997: 231).

elements exist and his assessment of the damage that can be inflicted by the antithetical behaviour on both parties in the relationship. The discussion then shifts to more recent work on attachment categories and internalised models of relating – secure, anxious and avoidant – in order to explore how these models are forged early in life from the interplay between infants and primary caregivers and played out in subsequent adult relationships.

I find their work highly conducive for analysing God-talk in Judges. It enables a robust and thoroughgoing theorisation of the generalised statements about YHWH's attachment to Israel often made in commentaries and in Old Testament theologies. For example, in his *Old Testament Theology* Brueggemann writes: 'whereas YHWH governs all peoples in a public way, YHWH's *attachment* to Israel is of a different sort, an *attachment* bespeaking intimacy, peculiar passion, and entitlement for Israel that are not extended to other peoples who are also YHWH's subjects' (2008: 82, emphases added). He also nods to YHWH's '*profound attachment* to the oldest son, Israel', but also 'to the king' (2008: 115, emphasis added). John Oswalt, commenting on Isa. 49:15, writes 'God uses the strongest images of *personal attachment* to protest that he has not forgotten or forsaken Zion' and goes on to reinforce how 'God's attachment is more than a mother's. The prophet asks us to think of a mother's attachment and then go one step farther. *That* is what God's attachment to us is' (1998: 305). The use of this psychologically charged word is, however, left under-theorised. In a short section on God's anger in Judges, Sasson notes only how 'a rather intimate drama is repeatedly played out, with all sides expressing a desire for *abiding attachment*' (2014: 204 emphasis added). Posing the question more directly – what does attachment theory have to tell us about the YHWH–Israel relationship? – puts us in different territory. References to attachment are put on a more conscious, formal footing, used directly to interrogate the text.

I am conscious of the cautions noted by Collicutt (2012), particularly concerning anachronism and ethnocentrism, and am well aware that my approach involves using theories that derive from a very different geographical and cultural gulf time to the biblical passages under consideration. It is very important to be wary of universalisation in particular. However, attachment theory addresses the human condition in a very fundamental way. It does not seem unreasonable to suppose that the human need for a secure base, protection and reliable relationships with primary others has been long standing and crosses cultural divides. No doubt there are variables in how it is experienced and provided from culture to culture, but I believe there is enough common ground to warrant the use of theory written from the mid-twentieth century onwards for the interpretation of ancient texts.

In section two, I turn to the text. Informed by the work of attachment theorists, I argue that the repeated cycle of Judges, with its ever downward spiral, enables the scribe to play out fantasies of abandonment and rescue in a one-sided, conflicted relationship. The analysis is focussed on three key passages: Judg. 2:11–23, 10:6–16 and 1 Sam. 12:7–25. It may seem odd to introduce the latter chapter in a monograph focussed on Judges but the cycle of apostasy, repentance and rescue does not end its plunging trajectory in the story of Samson. On the contrary, the pattern continues not only to the first twelve chapters of Samuel but beyond, as argued by Jobling (1998: 43–53, 2003) who makes the case for an extended book of Judges consisting of Judg. 2:11–1 Sam. 12:7–25,[2] but in a subsequent paper argues further that the histories of the north and south monarchies are presented as being stuck in a 'cyclicality from which there is no obvious egress' and that the story of Jehu 'is cast precisely as a judge-cycle' (2003: 56). The theology of the overall cycle remains one of 'salvation through punishment' (2003: 58) with the same 'obsession': leaders and what to think about them. Biblical book divisions, and commentaries based on those divisions, can thus limit a discussion that merits a wider perspective. Hertzberg suggests that 1 Sam. 12 provides 'the theological light in which the period of the judges should be seen' (1964: 97), but I would qualify that statement – it provides *a* theological interpretation of the judges through the perspective of a character whose motives are questionable. I include 1 Sam. 12:7–25 because it overtly recalls characters and situations described in Judges and because it places the reader back in a scenario reminiscent of Judg. 10:6–16, not so much providing a bookend for that narrative, but offering an important codicil to it. In terms of illustrating further the attachment issues between YHWH and Israel it is an important passage to include.

I conclude the chapter with a discussion of the implications of the analysis. If it turns out that the pattern of relating described in Judges and 1 Sam. 12 is best described as a variant of the insecure

---

[2] He divides this material into two disproportionate halves: Judg. 2:11–1 Sam. 7 and 1 Sam. 8–12. In his view, the overall aim of these blocks of material is 'to present judgeship as a divine dispensation and as in some sense an ideal, and to explain how it gave way to kinship' (Jobling, 1998: 43).

category, should the reception history's reinforcement of 'keeping YHWH good' be sustained? What is the import of this finding for ethical, responsible interpretation of texts and the future of the commentary genre?

Attachment Theory: Definitions, Key Theorists and Concepts

Mary Ainsworth and the 'Strange Situation'

Ainsworth is well-known for her Ugandan study of infant–mother attachment within the Ganda tribe and her subsequent comparison of those findings with a longitudinal study of 26 mother–infant relationships in Baltimore, undertaken in 1964. The Ganda tribe observations highlighted three key elements of attachment behaviour: 'the use of the mother as a secure base from which to explore; distress in brief, everyday separations from the mother; and fear when encountering a stranger' (Ainsworth et al., 1978: viii). These elements did not emerge so forcefully in the Baltimore project. Speculating that they might emerge more forcefully if the American children were observed in an unfamiliar situation rather than a home study, the 'strange situation' experiment was devised.

The 'strange situation' involved a child being introduced to an 'unfamiliar but otherwise unalarming playroom' in the company of his or her primary caregiver (Ainsworth et al., 1978: xi). The room was equipped with many toys intended to encourage play. Then an additional 'tactful' adult person entered, while the mother left for a few minutes before returning again. The experiment allowed the observers to analyse the responses of children, both to the exit of the caregiver and to her re-entry moments later. After this episode there was a further surprise for the child as the caregiver would again depart, leaving the child alone in the unfamiliar but toy-laden room. Then the stranger would re-enter, before finally the caregiver came back into the room.[3] It was the infant's heightened responses to the returning mother that contributed most to Ainsworth's development of attachment categories. On the basis of their observations, she and her team classified the responses into three groups. The *securely attached* child typically demonstrated distress at separation from her attachment figure, sought comfort upon their return and received

---

[3] For more detail on the method involved in the 'strange situation' see chapter 2 of Ainsworth et al. (1978).

it. The *ambivalently attached* child also demonstrated distress when the attachment figure disappeared but was not easily comforted upon her return, exhibiting signs of wanting to punish the mother. The *avoidant* child was not, at face value, unduly distressed by the temporary loss of the attachment figure, nor did he seek comfort on her return, preferring to focus on other objects such as toys.

This terminology has informed all subsequent attachment theory and has stood the test of time, albeit with some nuancing by more recent studies. What is interesting about Ainsworth's pioneering work is the attention given not only to the children observed, but to the primary caregiver's interaction with the child. Children grouped into the three categories are likely to have received certain kinds of mothering that creates those attachments. I return to this in the discussion of subsequent scholarly work on attachment.

Key Elements of Attachment Behaviour in the Work of John Bowlby

Although strongly informed by Ainsworth and her team's research, John Bowlby's work is probably better known. The first volume of his trilogy on attachment and loss has the most significance for this study. Originally published in 1969, this book honours Ainsworth's findings and takes her work further, demonstrating how early experiences of primary caregiving create confidence, or lack of it, in a person's own sense of autonomy and self-expression, and how an unreliable attachment figure can create fearful adults (Bowlby, 1997). In this discussion I focus on the three key emphases in his work that have most relevance for the study of the YHWH–Israel relationship in section two.

Proximity Maintenance

Bowlby discusses a range of animal experiments that showed how attachment could be formed even if the figure did not provide food or other kinds of maternal care, indeed, even if the animals were punished by the attachment figure. Studies on children indicate likewise – attachment can be formed without any physical satisfactions being provided. If attachment is not the result of the child's need to secure its food supply and care, then what is the rationale for attachment? He suggests it drives from the child's need for 'protection from predators' (1997: 244) and also that proximity can help the infant 'learn activities and other things useful for its survival' (1997: 225). Bowlby concludes that a child's need for attachment figures is primarily aroused by the human need for protection and security. At their healthiest, early attachment relationships function similarly to Winnicott's notion of the slowly diminishing holding environment provided by the good-enough mother. Bowlby similarly envisages a symbiotic relationship between mother and child, one of 'dynamic equilibrium' (1997: 236), wherein proximity and protection is provided alongside nourishment and growth. In this reciprocal relationship the child, feeling safe and secure, can engage in creative exploration and play.

During the course of a day the child and caregiver might be in one another's company or somewhat apart, engaged with each other directly or not, but distance between them is unlikely to 'ever exceed a certain maximum. Whenever it does so, either one or other member of the pair is likely soon to act in such a way that distance is reduced. On some occasions it is mother who takes the initiative – she calls, or goes to see where the child has got to; on others the child may take the initiative either by scampering back to mother or by crying' (Bowlby, 1997: 236). Distance between mother and child is monitored by both parties with a view to ensuring the healthy experience of mutual equilibrium.

Effects of Parental Separation

Bowlby notes how studies on children separated from their family setting coalesce around predictable responses: phase one consists of protest, phase two is despair and phase three is characterised by detachment. It should be understood, however, that although talk of phases gives the impression of distinct responses, 'in reality each merges into the next' (1997: 27). The protest phase 'may begin immediately or may be delayed; it lasts from a few hours to a week or more' and a child's protest may well include 'the full exercise of his limited resources ... [he may] cry loudly, shake his cot, throw himself about ... look eagerly toward any sight or sound which might prove to be his missing mother' 1997: 27). The motivation for this protest activity lies in the acute distress experienced at the thought of a lost mother and the desire for reunion. Phase two is less energetic. In despair the 'behaviour suggests increasing hopelessness ... he may cry monotonously or intermittently. He is withdrawn and inactive, makes no demands on people in the environment, and appears to be in a state of deep mourning' (1997: 27). It is important to note that the quietness of this phase does not 'indicate diminution of distress' (1997: 27).

The detached phase is the response observed in a child whose mother has returned. One might expect a happy state of affairs. However, underlying trouble is seen in the child's reaction to the mother, from whom 'he may remain remote and apathetic; instead of tears there is a listless turning away. He seems to have lost all interest in her' (1997: 28). In situations where a child has to contend with a prolonged residential stay in a hospital, nurses provide some substitutionary cover, but while the child may form some attachment to these figures, the fact that they are transient 'repeats for him the experience of the original loss' and ultimately he 'will stop altogether attaching himself to anyone ... [and] become preoccupied with material things such as sweets, toys, and food' (1997: 28). When visited 'he will appear cheerful and adapted ... apparently easy and unafraid of anyone. But his sociability is superficial: he appears no longer to care for anyone' (1997: 28). Some critics asked whether the strange environment might account for such behaviour but Bowlby cites studies that reinforce his view that while 'a strange environment is of consequence' it is parental absence that is key (1997: 31).

Antithetical Attachment Behaviour

Bowlby suggests that relationship dynamics between child and caregiver are marked by pro-attachment and antithetical attachment behaviours on both sides. The child's pro-attachment behaviour is evident in tactile connection to their caregiver but also in their crying. Crying is an obvious 'signalling behaviour' (1997: 244), usually effective for indicating that mutual recognition and attachment is desired. If a caregiver shows signs of not maintaining appropriate proximity then the child will make efforts to recover it, while if a mother remains in proximity this means that 'her child can relax his own efforts' (1997: 260). Attachment behaviour may also be prompted by the mother holding a different child.

Child behaviour that is antithetic to attachment includes precarious exploration. Bowlby recognises that sometimes a child endangers themselves, as when playing by an open fire. He recommends some measure of policing in these cases: 'a firm yet friendly intervention' (1979: 13), but notably *not* any form of punishment that 'can create in anxiety and hatred evils far greater than those it is intended to cure' (1979: 14). Punishment and parental complaints of a child's ingratitude are identified as controlling mechanisms – ultimately unhelpful, unsuccessful and likely to 'exact a heavy toll in unhappiness' (1979: 12). For Bowlby, the firm but friendly intervention is ideally a way of demonstrating to the child how violent or jealous reactions 'can be curbed by peaceful means and that there is no need to resort to those drastic methods of condemnation and punishment which, when copied by a child, are apt to become distorted by his own primitive imagination into pathological guilt and ruthless self-punishment' (1979: 14). Bowlby, like Winnicott, is aware that parents cannot be perfect, but recommends that they endeavour to tolerate their own ambivalent feelings for the child and model a healthy way forward.

Bowlby identifies the pro-attachment behaviour of the primary caregiver as a mother's 'retrieving' behaviour, which is aimed at proximity maintenance. The child may be outdoors or with others, and the mother may be engaged with matters uppermost to her own life, but she remains in retrieval mode, 'likely to keep a watchful eye on him and to be alert to any cry, ready to act at shortest notice' (1997: 240). He refers to Ainsworth's views on what contributes to secure attachment: '1. frequent and sustained physical contact ... together with mother's ability to soothe a distressed baby by holding him' 2. 'sensitivity to her baby's signals, and especially her ability to time her interactions in harmony with his rhythms' 3. A regulated environment wherein the 'baby can derive a sense of consequence of his own actions' and 4. 'the mutual delight that a mother and infant find in each other's company' (1997: 346). Behaviour that is antithetic to attachment includes all contrary behaviours to those noted above, i.e., malattunement to a child's needs, expectation that a child would conform to the caregiver's timetable and demands, and neglect of the child.

Attachment in children is usually related to the mother's sensitivity to the infant's signals and the quality of interaction. Bowlby points out how a pattern quickly gets established. By the end of the first year, 'whatever the child provides in the way of behaviour, mother has come to expect and to respond to in a typical way' and vice versa. 'Each has shaped the other' (1997: 333). A measure for attachment 'is whether or not he protests when his mother leaves him for a brief time and how strongly he does so' (1997: 333) but Bowlby qualifies this, noting Ainsworth's research with the Ganda, and how a securely attached child could be the one happy to explore. An accurate assessment of the state of affairs may therefore be likely when observing a fatigued child, or one in pain, since this 'is often especially revealing' (1997: 335). A psychologically healthy child will seek out mother.

Overall, he describes how during the course of a day, mother and child might be in one another's company or somewhat apart, engaged with each other directly or not, but the distance between them is unlikely to ever exceed a certain maximum. Proximity maintenance is the key thing and what matters is response rate and depth of healthy interaction. Contentment is found whenever the careful dance of support and trust is at its sensitively managed best, but 'whenever interaction results in persistent conflict each party is likely on occasion to exhibit intense anxiety or unhappiness, especially when the other is rejecting' (1997: 242).

Subsequent Scholarship on Attachment Categories and Internalised Working Models

Contemporary attachment theorists have developed three basic categories which have their origins in Ainsworth's 'strange situation' experiment. The precise terminology varies depending on the theorist but includes: a) secure, b) anxious, ambivalent or preoccupied, and c) an avoidant group that is further subdivided into detached/dismissing and fearful/avoidant.[4] Kim Bartholomew, who uses the work of both Ainsworth and Bowlby to inform her work on contemporary adult attachments, argues that what produces these different attachment styles is the nature of the caregiver's response to signals from her child. A securely attached child is one whose caregiver has been sensitive to their signals and reliably present, and one who mirrored mutual love and delight which enables the child to see herself as an acceptable child, worthy of such love. In the future, this child will be comfortable with the balance between intimacy and autonomy and like to engage in 'secure and fulfilling adult relationships' (1990: 163).

---

[4] Hazan and Shaver (1994: 16) note how several studies in varying countries have replicated Ainsworth's finding that around 55% of adults in any study will be secure, 25% avoidant and 20% anxious/ambivalent, although there can be blurred edges around these categories (see Bartholomew and Horowitz, 1991: 241). That said, the attachment categories of infancy are not written in stone. Hazan and Shaver note how an 'average person participates in several important friendships and love relationships, each of which provides an opportunity to revise mental models of self and others' (1987: 522).

However, experiences of a caregiving figure who has not responded consistently or reliably or in a timely and sensitive way is likely to produce an anxiously attached person who loses confidence in the dependability of their partner. Rather than possessing a positive self-image, this person is likely to conclude that they themselves are unworthy. Bartholomew explains and notes the unfortunate consequences: the child who has experienced 'inconsistent and insensitive parenting, especially if accompanied by messages of parental devotion, may conclude that their own unworthiness explains any lack of love on the caregiver's part. The result is ... an insatiable desire to gain others' approval and a deep-seated feeling of unworthiness' (1990: 163).

There is a common element in both secure and anxiously attached people: they perceive Others as basically good and trustworthy (regardless of the likelihood that inconsistent caregiving has been received by the anxiously attached person). The securely attached are confident in their own basic goodness and, because they have received sufficiently reliable and nurturing care, their internalised model of this care enables them to trust that they will find it elsewhere. The anxiously attached tend to blame themselves for any shortcomings in the caregiver, but thereby retain the goodness or basic trustworthiness of the Other. However, when we shift to the avoidant category, Others are seen as unreliable and rejecting while self-image differs depending on whether we are dealing with the subcategory of avoidant–dismissive or avoidant–fearful. The avoidant–dismissive group includes those who can maintain 'positive self-image in the face of rejection by attachment figures', by distancing themselves and nurturing a 'model of the self as fully adequate and hence invulnerable to negative feelings' (Bartholomew, 1990: 164). The pay-off for those in this category is that they 'have attained autonomy and a sense of self-worth at the expense of intimacy' (Bartholomew, 1990: 165). Those who have an avoidant–fearful style of attachment, however, regard themselves as unlovable and are anxious about the possibility of rejection. Likely to suffer from low self-esteem, Bartholomew notes how they will attempt to prevent such rejection by avoiding 'social situations and close relationships in which they perceive themselves as vulnerable to rejection' with the unfortunate results that they miss out on future relationships which might 'serve to modify early attachment representations' (1990: 164). In both cases, however, the Other is problematic, untrustworthy, and perceived as rejecting.

Bowlby argues that we all create internalised working models based on our early experiences in infancy. There is not just one model: a person could have a range of attachment figures (for example, grandparents, siblings and peers) who offer different styles of attachment, although Bowlby does emphasise the significance of the *primary* caregiver in his work. But, more complexly, it may also be the case that a child develops more than one inner model of himself and his attachment figure, one that is dominant but unconscious and another which is conscious but not necessarily the driver of relationship patterns. For example, when a child's experiences of his mother differ from the latter's pronouncements of love, it puts the child in a dilemma: 'Is he to accept the picture as he sees it himself? Or ... the one his parent insists is true?' (Bowlby, 1978: 362). If the child recognises the validity of his own experiences and resists the caregiver's claims, then 'the rupture between him and his parent(s) is bound to be serious and may well prove unbridgeable' (1978: 362). The situation is exacerbated if the parent's view is validated by other people, which may lead to the child's counter-understanding being attributed to his 'disturbed condition' or deemed 'unintelligible' (1978: 363). If the child attempts to resolve the problem by trying to integrate the contradiction or 'oscillates uneasily' between perspectives, then the

> maturing child continues to accept his parent's version of the family scene, either without apparent reservations or else with them. When this is so, the child, even though fully adult, is still accepting his mother's picture of herself as a devoted and self-sacrificing woman when to an outsider she may appear demanding and possessive, and is still accepting her picture of himself as selfish and given to unreasonable tempers when to an outsider he may appear pathetically compliant. (1978: 363)

Should the child seek to challenge the caregiver's version this may result in threats in order that the caregiver's viewpoint remains the dominant one. Yet, if the child exhibits fear that the caregiver will carry out the threat 'she may disclaim ever having made them' (1978: 364). A child in this situation is between a rock and a hard place; either he stays true to his own instincts, is duly punished/rejected and potentially loses the caregiver's love and affection, or he suppresses those instincts in favour of retaining the caregiver's love and acceptance, but in so doing loses himself. This latter option damages the True Self (a concept discussed in Chapter 1). However, as Bowlby recognises, it might seem the lesser of two evils: 'Exposed to all these pressures, it is not surprising that he despairs of establishing his own construction of events and instead complies weakly with his mother's, or even assertively endorses it' (1978: 364). The possibility of the Self fragmenting in the face of such pressures is a matter I will turn to in the next chapter when discussing the work of Fairbairn.

Applying Attachment Theory to the God-Talk in Judg. 2:11–20, 10:6–16 and 1 Sam. 12:7–25

I find it quite difficult to see YHWH as an attachment figure, despite the fact that commentary writers and theologies are able to recognise him as such very readily, attributing to him love and fixation on Israel and divine determination to stay in the relationship, while also recognising that he is vulnerable to rejection and experiences pain, anger, grief and irritation. Commentary writers thus have no reservations about acknowledging YHWH's attachment needs (i.e., requiring Israel's absolute loyalty), even while YHWH, as the divine character, is usually granted special status. He becomes the secure father figure whose disciplinary actions are instructive, for Israel's good. There is less willingness to conceive of YHWH as a bad parent, overly intrusive, insisting on conformity and accordingly prompting in his people an insecure mode of attachment.

One reason why it is difficult to see YHWH as having attachment needs is that he is never positioned as a child. He is always the caregiver par excellence, the supra alpha parent who has no parentage himself. If attachment theory helps us to see how cycles develop, i.e., where an anxious ambivalently attached person who becomes a mother may prompt attachment issues in her children, then the cycle stops at YHWH. He is First Parent. But acknowledging this is to believe the hype. Although it is too long-winded for me to say it, every mention of YHWH in this book implies 'YHWH as constructed and scripted by the scribe'. He, along with scribes of other texts that have been canonised, gives the deity a history, memories of previous actions and words, that construct his personality and character in varied ways. It is not that the scribe is faithfully recording observations and recognition of the paternal power of YHWH who exists beyond them and whose traits he faithfully records, it is rather that he actively constructs those traits, perhaps based on his lived experience of existing in a world where fate seems unpredictable, impossible to control. Brueggemann notes how YHWH has a 'wild dimension' (2000: 28) but while he acknowledges that YHWH can act capriciously, he puts this wild side into a revelatory ongoing drama of YHWH's growth and history. My methodological assumptions mean that YHWH is not let off the hook so easily. And although I know virtually nothing about this scribe, he must have been located within a family marked inevitably by attachment cycles of behaviour. He *presents* us with a divine figure whose character is to be above and beyond humanity, and yet as a human construct YHWH inescapably has human qualities including an array of foibles that a scribe cannot erase from his presentation because he cannot escape from what it is to be human. Yes, he can *imagine* what it is like to be non-human, but he cannot step outside his human boundaries. Notably, he writes into his text a deity whose parenting is wrapped up in coercive insistence: it is a choice of conformity or being 'swept aside'. It is worth noting that again – conformity or doom. This arguably tells us more about the scribe's desire for power and the placation of fateful power than any divine revelation of what God might be like. 'Past' Israel is used as a rhetorical device, a scapegoat, a whipping boy, for a scribe who wants to portray a history of failure, punishment and exile in order to highlight the alternative required for his own times: a conforming, repentant and loyal Israel who will assent to the programme of governance advocated by YHWH's faithful representatives.

In the three sections that follow, I follow through on these thoughts. I have selected passages where the relationship between YHWH and Israel is clearly in focus in order to demonstrate how an analysis informed by attachment theory creates a fresh interpretation of each text. For each passage translated I have used the same English verb for a repeated Hebrew verb so that similar language across the texts is easily recognisable. Terminology that is significant from an attachment theory perspective crops up again and again across all three texts: serving/not serving, abandoning, anger, doing evil, delivering/saving, other gods and crying out. To avoid repetition I provide a detailed discussion of each feature when it first crops up, and in the second and third text discuss only how the feature is modified or extended.

Judg. 2:11–23

11.   And the sons of Israel did evil in the eyes of YHWH and served the Baalim,

12.   and abandoned YHWH, the god of their fathers who brought them out of the land of Egypt, and went after other

gods – from the gods of the people who were surrounding them, and they bowed to them and they angered YHWH.

13. And they abandoned YHWH and served Baal and the Ashtaroth.

14. And YHWH's nostril burned against Israel and he gave them into the hand of plunderers, and they plundered them, and he sold them into the hand of their surrounding enemies, and they were continually unable to stand in the presence of their enemies.

15. Whichever way they turned, the hand of YHWH was against them for evil, according to what YHWH had said and according to what YHWH had sworn to them, and he put them into a much hemmed-in situation.[5]

16. But YHWH raised judges and they saved them from the hand of those plundering them.

17. But they did not even listen to their judges since they lusted after other gods and bowed down to them. They turned quickly from the way which their fathers walked in order to hear the commands of YHWH, and did not do the same.

18. But when YHWH raised judges for them, YHWH was with the judge and he delivered them from the hand of their enemies all the days of the judge, because YHWH rued their groaning caused by those squeezing and inundating them.[6]

19. And when the judge died, they turned back and bowed themselves down to them even more than their fathers, following after other gods, to serve them and to bow

[5] The vocalisation of וַיָּצֶר is odd. Boling (1975:73–4) reads the root צוּר with the LXX and OL and translates the last three words as 'they were besieged'. Niditch has 'And they were in very sore straits' (2008: 46), which is preferable as it signals the connotations of צרר, i.e., being in cramped, narrowed circumstances. Sasson translates as: 'They therefore suffered terribly' (2014: 185), which picks up the connotations of the verb's use in 2 Sam. 13:2 where it describes the state Amnon got himself into over Tamar, i.e., Amnon was 'so vexed' (King James Version), or 'so distressed' (Jewish Publication Society Bible), or 'so tormented' (New Revised Standard). However, in his subsequent commentary, Sasson notes that the terminology 'connotes distress that comes from being restricted in avenues or choices' (2014: 192). I resist the emendation to the third person plural for retaining the third person singular means that the deity's involvement in this scenario comes more to the fore. Soggin does likewise, translating 'thus he afflicted them greatly' (1981: 37).

[6] I selected 'squeezing' because of the evocative way it conveys the constraint and confinement that seems to characterise this passage. The verb דָּחַק is used in Joel 2:8 to describe the swarming of locusts through the defences, so 'inundating' seemed an apt translation. The intent is to conjure an image of being confronted by enemies breaking through on all sides, as one might feel if attacked by a swarm of insects.

themselves down to them. And they did not drop their practices or their stubborn ways.

20.   And YHWH's nostril burned against Israel and he said 'because this *goy* has ignored my covenant which I commanded their fathers and not listened to my voice[7]

21.   I will no longer dispossess a man from their presence i.e. from the *goyim* who Joshua left when he died,

22.   in order to test Israel as to whether they will keep the way of YHWH, to walk in them according to how their fathers kept (them), or not'.

23.   So YHWH left the *goyim*, not quickly driving them out, and he did not give them into the hands of Joshua.

From an attachment theory perspective, the aspects of the narrative most relevant to our discussion include the behaviour antithetical to attachment noted for both Israel and YHWH – the former's serving, bowing down and lusting after other gods and concomitant abandonment of YHWH, the latter's fury, use of his hand, the terminology of restriction, and the divine test. I also discuss the pro-attachment references to crying out and deliverance. The analysis of all three passages organises such issues into three headings: attachment and abandonment, attachment and affect, and attachment and game play.[8]

Attachment and Abandonment

When reading the above passage, nothing stands out more than the language of abandonment. Abandonment is already implied in the references to Israel's serving of other gods, but the scribe goes out of his way to reinforce the fact that they thereby abandoned YHWH. There are several other examples of behaviour contrary to attachment in Judges, such as Israel's willingness to look to their own strength, or towards human leadership rather than YHWH's, but abandonment, or 'forsaking' remains the action that provokes YHWH into antithetic actions of his own. The studies of Ainsworth and Bowlby have a strong interest in the effects of abandonment, but

---

[7] I have left 'goy' as a transliteration in order to highlight how Israel is now being referred to with a term that is used elsewhere to describe non-Israelite nations (as it is in the following verse). Sasson (2014: 193) is right to note the scorn that underlies the use of this term, for while goy can be used more positively, here it is pejorative.

[8] For a definition of 'affect' see Introduction, footnote 7.

it is the primary caregiver's neglect of the child that is usually in focus, not the child's abandoning of the caregiver.[9] They do, however, discuss a child's exploratory activities, which can sometimes put the child in jeopardy and require the intervention of the caregiver. Bowlby's examples include the penchant of the child to wander off limits, perhaps to test boundaries, to act on their own autonomy, but in so doing getting involved in adventures that might put them in danger. As noted above, proximity maintenance is a key aspect of attachment for both child and parent, and in Judges we see Israel's wandering off from 'the way' (v. 22) until YHWH acts; there is no scampering back that characterises usual child–caregiver relations until their wandering is punished by the proxy agents.

As the story world plunges Israel from one crisis to the next, the reader is not given much time to ponder Israel's exploratory behaviour, other than to note it always ends in apostasy. But it is worth pausing. Scholars have been interested in how these gap periods between each judge story function. Thus, for Buber (1967) and Jobling (1986, 1998) specifically, but also for commentators more generally, one of the main thematic interests of Judges is the vexed question of how Israel is best governed. The gap periods suggest times of direct theocratic oversight, but such oversight is clearly never effective because Israel ends up serving other deities – an action that prompts the next cycle of judgeship. Kingship, hinted at in the minor judges whose sons ruled after them, and raised more prominently in chs. 17–21, is the alternative that would grant continuity of leadership and, so long as the king was YHWH's man, this could be an acceptable way forward. I concur; this issue of leadership is a major theme, but beneath the surface lies a deeper, more psychological question that pertains to the relationship dynamic between Israel and YHWH: what is the nature of their attachment? What are the end-boundaries of proximity? By what measures is proximity maintained? How far can Israel's exploration be tolerated? Is it thinkable that YHWH could actually be abandoned? I cannot provide a fully rounded answer to these questions until further aspects of the passage have been discussed below. However, it is

---

[9] That said, an apparent abandonment of the caregiver can be seen in the behaviour of the children who did not rush to welcome the return of their mother, but, instead, occupied themselves with the toys in the room and ignored her. However, this should not be understood as abandonment; it is the child's way of coping with their distressed feelings.

worth noting here the effects of abandonment identified by recent attachment theorists. Humans have an inbuilt 'attachment system' which can be 'activated', and, upon activation, Hazan and Shaver note an urge to 'seek proximity to the attachment figures' regardless of whether or not this is a sensible thing to do (1994: 14). They note the universalisation of this tendency: 'Even though there is tremendous cultural variation in associated rituals and customs, the human response to the breaking of an attachment bond hardly varies ... [and] is not essentially different from the way infants and children respond' (1994: 14). It includes:

> intense separation-protest behavior. Individuals report feeling agitated, anxious, and preoccupied with thoughts of the lost partner, coupled with a compulsion to search for him or her, as though trying to undo the loss even if it is consciously known to be irreversible. Eventually, with the realization that the loss cannot be recovered, there comes a period of deep sadness, during which intense activity and rumination give way to depression and despair ... Gradually, the sadness subsides, and most people achieve an adaptive degree of emotional detachment from the lost partner and return to ordinary living. (1994: 14)

In Judges, both parties appear to have their 'attachment system' on high alert. YHWH's determination to intervene is usually interpreted as the manifestation of his steadfast love for Israel. After all, it is Israel's 'groaning' that induces him to send deliverance. But psychologically, it signals anxiety-led protest behaviour. The one thing guaranteed to prompt YHWH's compulsion to re-establish proximity is Israel's abandonment. No surprise then that the Judges formula shifts in quick succession from abandonment to being sold into the hands of plunderers – oppression that prompts Israel to send out cries to YHWH and recreate the bond.

We never really learn why the other gods are so successful in winning Israel's service; why they are so enticing. Robinson and Sasson suggest they may have found these gods better at delivering crop and herd successes – but both commentators proceed to undermine that possibility by declaring such gods mere fertility idols (Robinson, 1993: 70) or 'patently false' (Sasson, 2014: 194), thereby robbing them of any serious threat to YHWH's power and ownership of Israel. However, Sasson may well be on the mark when he suggests that gods 'eagerly championed those venerating them and fought battles for their favorites, with perhaps a better success rate than the Hebrew God' while 'their record for capriciousness or whimsy did not differ much from that of the Hebrew God' (2014: 195). This reminder that there is something to be gained by Israel's switch of allegiance is helpful. Mostly though, because commentators tend to align themselves with YHWH's perspective, there is little speculation on why Israel decides to serve competitor deities – a disinterest that mirrors the scribe's lack of explanation. We never find out how Israel would get along with these alternative caregivers because it is not in the scribe's interest to dwell on such things. He closes down any insight into what might happen if Israel had been permitted to find alternative security and also, more interestingly, what would happen to YHWH if, in fact, he was completely abandoned. It is simply asserted that this is a terrible turn of events. The people are to blame of course; Israel is always in the wrong. Had Israel remained faithful, the contented symbiosis of a healthy, operative holding environment could have continued.

My question is whether the implied golden period of coexistence could ever have been one of genuine contentedness. It is implied that this is what we should think, but any reader of Winnicott's work would be highly suspicious of the fact that Israel's capacity to be alone and their continuity of being is sharply curtailed as soon as they do something that threatens YHWH's sole right to their service.

The pertinent factor is that YHWH intervenes, and intervenes in ways that keep the relationship active, even if torridly so. As noted in Chapter 1, there is a will to keep a relationship; an unwillingness to let go in this punishment–reward cycle. It is the manner in which YHWH holds on to Israel that gives rise to concern. The kind of proximity envisaged by YHWH is one that requires Israel's pathological accommodation. This is a term used by Brandchaft to describe what happens 'when a child is required pre-emptively to adhere to the needs of its primary objects at the expense of its own psychological distinctness' (2007: 667). He compares this with wholesome, healthy accommodation, which includes 'respect for the legitimate needs of one's partner' (2007: 670), for in secure attachment the child's distinctiveness is not over-shrouded by the caregiver's influence. In a telling comment, Brandchaft describes how pathological attachment is contrarily grounded in the caregiver's own insecurities. The anxious caregiver 'will direct the child, thus beginning the extinction of any center of initiative in the child. The obsessive caregiver will keep scrutinizing the child for flaws and defects, and they then become enmeshed into a ritualistic system of "fixing". The center of the development stage is shifted from the child's vitalizing expressions to the caregiver's deadening, impinging, frightened, or abusive mismatch' (2007: 674). While Judg. 2:11–23 speaks about Israel's abandonment and casts the blame there, and while commentators write positively about divine determination to keep in a relationship with Israel, attachment theory flips the reader's attention to the insecurities and needs of *YHWH* and his desperation to retain proximity and loyalty by means not conducive to the child's wellbeing.

Attachment and Affect

Commentaries widely note how Israel's service to other gods is the key insult to YHWH. The very notion of alternative attachment figures is something that utterly infuriates YHWH. Unfaithfulness is completely unacceptable. All the actions YHWH engages in are grounded in fury. This pivotal affect pervades all three passages and from this plunge into wrath come the trials that beset Israel. As noted in Chapter 1, I can only go so far with commentators who view this as a firm and loving intervention. The descriptions of intervention are far *too* firm; it is violent, brutal and merciless in its years of duration. The grammar of this passage gives a strong sense of constriction. The enemies are surrounding (v. 14), the hand of YHWH prevents Israel's ability to go out, they are in dire straits/ cramped (v. 15), and they are crowded upon by their oppressors who swarm against them (v. 18). This is the result of YHWH's protest behaviour. Using his proxy agents and his hand to restrict their movements and hem them in, Israel is boxed into a corner until compelled to cry out.

From a psychological perspective, anger is a typical result of frustrated attachment needs. Understood as protest behaviour designed to re-establish attachment, anger is the 'attachment regulator' that 'is triggered when there is threat of separation and, in what is essentially a negative reinforcement schedule, has the function of ensuring that the attachment bond remains intact' (Holmes, 2001: 13). Holmes goes on to write about his work with couples where there has been infidelity, and describes how male clients may be given anger management classes. YHWH certainly has problems with infidelity. Although we are not yet at the vehement, highly charged, prophetic indictment of Israel as a rebellious and adulterous whore, v. 17 uses the verb זנה of Israel's serving of other deities. Pressler picks up this language of adultery and suggests that we are dealing here with a hurt lover. YHWH's response in this passage is not that of a 'coldhearted … distant, dispassionate God. Rather, the speech is the passionate, pointed response of a lover whose love is betrayed one too many times. God will not again rescue the people who have repeatedly violated the relationship' (2002: 198).[10] However, while it is tempting to see here a foreshadowing of pornoprophetic texts where YHWH's jealousy is emblazoned across the page in furious rhetoric, Pressler introduces an image of wife/Israel that isn't overtly present in this passage or in Judges generally. So while attachment theory could be employed to understand the pathology of the cuckolded husband in other texts, this is not the focus here.[11] I acknowledge that the use of זנה presents the image of a slighted YHWH, but in my view the scribe has chosen to depict disloyalty in highly charged sexual terms, engaging in deliberate and provocative language in order to stress the affront caused to YHWH. The scribe has latched on to hyperbolic way of describing their behaviour that grabs the attention and denigrates Israel still further by the use of sexual slurs. Thinking this through in terms of attachment theory, I return to Brueggemann's

---

[10] Pressler is not alone in this. For Sasson, YHWH's anger and jealously is incited primarily by Israel's worship of other gods and he refers to Israel indulging 'its lust for the gods of its neighbors' (2014: 194). Sasson also notes how 'Israel's incapacity to bridle its passion for other gods is declared in carnal terms' (2014: 193).

[11] Future studies could fruitfully investigate the connections between the husband–wife biblical metaphor and attachment theory. One of the arguments of Davis, Ace and Andra's (2000) paper is that an insecure style of attachment, particularly an anxious one, can be a predictor of the psychological (and actual) maltreatment of partners. Citing the work of Bowlby (1980a) and Bartholomew, Henderson and Dutton (2001), the authors claim that 'fears of abandonment typify the highly anxious dimension of attachment insecurity. Fears of abandonment and threats to an established relationship thus can trigger rage, attacks, and, when the partner has left, stalking to re-establish contact' (2000: 412). Aggressive performances are part and parcel of the 'protest behaviour' repertoire, designed to affect the attachment figure and bring them back into the relationship. Dutton, Ace and Andra, for example, make the connection between 'intimacy anger', 'insecure attachment' and domestic abuse, arguing that forms of insecure attachment, notably the 'fearful' kind, lend themselves to jealousy and abusiveness. Such work could add a further dimension to studies of the pornoprophetic texts, as it is possible that the abuse heaped upon woman Israel is grounded in attachment problems. As Dutton et al. go on to say: 'The anxiously attached man, unaware that his dysphoria is intimacy produced, attributes it to the real or perceived actions of his partner and retaliates with abusiveness. The dominance/isolation factor can be viewed as an overgeneralized attempt to diminish anxiety about abandonment. The yoked dysphoric modes – anger and anxiety – thus may have a common origin in insecure attachment and operate to generate both abusing and controlling behaviors' (1994: 1382).

references to YHWH's attachment to Israel as his 'treasured *posses-sion*', which Israel becomes 'not simply by divine designation, but by vigorous, intense, intentional adherence to YHWH's commands given in the Torah of Sinai' (2008: 82). These are strong words from Brueggemann. There is an uncompromising resoluteness about this that Brueggemann views positively but which would cause dismay to attachment theorists. Dutton et al. found that it was the fearfully attached who 'experience high degrees of both chronic anxiety . . . and anger' (1994: 1379) and contend 'that anger accompanies anxious attachment' (1994: 1380). But what is really interesting is how fear-fully attached men project blame onto the devalued attachment object. Israel may not yet have been metaphorically transformed into a whoring woman that we meet in Jer. 2:20–3:5 and Ezek. 16 and 23, but the fury of YHWH in the three passages discussed in this chapter certainly casts blame on to an apostate, wayward Israel, who not only bears the brunt of the scribe's antipathy but centuries of reception history. A commentary informed by attachment theory might more fruitfully redirect the spotlight on the character of YHWH rather than continuing to heap blame on apostate Israel.

Turning attention to Israel, the affect that is prominent in this passage is their groaning. Both Ainsworth and Bowlby include audible signalling in their description of protest behaviour, noting that its aim is to reinstate proximity to their caregiver when in trouble. Ainsworth's observations of the Ganda tribe included notes on how attachment is commonly demonstrated by an infant's crying and the prompts for such crying can include the mother leaving the location or the child being hurt or frightened. Crying is singularly useful because of its known effects in terms of producing a reaction. When a child cries helplessly, as Bowlby notes, it 'is never easily ignored' (1997: 204). What we have in the above passage, however, is groaning; a groaning that results from enemy oppression that is described in terms of being constricted, hemmed in, squeezed. This is not in the same league as the child who sends out a cry in order to reinstate proximity maintenance with the mother, having temporar-ily lost her through some exploratory excursion or falling over. It is more like a scenario where the mother has picked up warning sounds that indicate the child has got into real trouble and who reacts accordingly. What is different, of course, is that this child – Israel – is groaning from an oppression that their caregiver organised. Unsurprisingly, neither Bowlby nor Ainsworth addresses or envis-ages this kind of 'strange situation'!

Attachment and Game Play

Rather like the testing of Job, YHWH sets up an experiment. Will Israel freely choose to serve YHWH when there is the option of turning to rival gods deliberately left, by YHWH, in their proximity? Playing psychological games in this way is a common feature of attachment dynamics. Modern examples of attachment games between adult partners include the silent treatment, sending a text that mirrors precisely the unsatisfactory shortness of the one received, threatening to leave, and manipulative though largely empty threats of self-harm. Attachment games basically involve a range of protest behaviour and in Holmes's view 'couples are attracted to one another if there is some kind of "fit" between their own inner world and that of the other. Each must consciously or unconsciously know the steps of the other's dance' (2001: 15).[12] Then there are adult trade games, whereby one may be willing to surrender some wishes and desires in order to gain a more secure footing for the relationship, for example, trading consensual but unwanted sex for relationship stability. On the other hand, an avoidant adult may let go of their desire to be close in order to create a distance that won't put them in danger of their partner's rejection. They trade intimacy needs for security.

When considering YHWH's test of Israel's faithfulness, the more broadly focussed work of Brueggemann (1997) and Levenson (1994) is helpful. Levenson points out that the presence of other, alluring deities enables a real testing of fidelity to a suzerain. In an opposite argument to Sasson, for whom the other gods are nothing, Levenson rightly says they have to offer a real viable option from which YHWH can woo Israel, an option that Israel chooses to surrender; otherwise what has YHWH won? In terms of Judges, this means that other gods have to be present; it is a test, just as Job has to have his wealth and comfort taken away. Both Israel and Job must actively make a decision whether or not to continue with YHWH. YHWH *is*, then, vulnerable to rejection and presumably *can* be abandoned. However, the choice before Israel is Hobson's choice, because if they do abandon him they face disaster. We do not arrive at that point in

---

[12] People often locate a partner who co-responds to their internal working model's pattern but hopes that it can be transcended. The '"trigger" points ... for rows, disappointment or misery arise at these nodal connections between one person's set of painful assumptions and the other's' (Holmes, 2001: 15). This insight raises interesting questions about the YHWH–Israel pairing. The scribe, it seems, has constructed a deity whose steps fit his needs; a matter that is discussed further in Chapter 4.

Judges, because YHWH responds to their cries before they are utterly destroyed; but the fate of an Israel who did not cry out would be doom, as is made clear in 1 Sam. 12:25. Levenson is clear: 'for all the language of choice that characterizes covenant texts, the Hebrew Bible never regards the choice to decline covenant as legitimate ... In fact, the wrong choice results in nothing short of death' (1994: 141).[13] To hold this threat at bay, what is required by YHWH is the continual surrender of autonomy. Brueggemann also writes with unreserved clarity about the cost of joining forces with YHWH: 'None of the partners is finally permitted autonomy ... Yahweh's self-regard is massive, savage, and seemingly insatiable' (1997: 556). Ultimately, however, both scholars find ways of accommodating such a deity and it is interesting to see how Levenson and Brueggemann return to the description of Israel as God's 'treasured possession'. They use this to demonstrate that Israel has something to gain from the surrender: a God who is interested in them, nay *treasures* them and holds back chaos on their behalf. I have much to say about this 'treasuring' aspect of the relationship but have to defer that conversation until Chapter 4 when the master–slave dialectic is explored in detail. For now, I suggest that the test YHWH puts in place bespeaks his own protest behaviour. It is a divine tit-for-tat riposte, grounded in anger, which is never a good starting place for wise decision-making. This game play, however, appears to be beset by anxiety: *would* Israel serve him by choice? But ultimately, the test is flawed. If Israel has no genuine choice, then whatever service they offer is almost meaningless. YHWH is thus hoist with his own petard because the game play cannot bring him the satisfaction that he craves. Unable to tolerate the possibility that Israel would abandon him for good, he always intervenes and the test is rendered redundant. Attachment theory illuminates the problem: YHWH is presented as a deity who does not surrender control in the way that a healthy mother gives up her omnipotence to give exploratory space for the developing child. His is not the reaction of a mother who safeguards the child from dangerous forays near, for example, a busy main road. The only danger that can come to Israel is from YHWH himself. His is the reaction of a deity with unmet attachment needs, but he does not have the skills of resolving this other

---

[13] At this point Levenson cites Deut. 30:19–20 and notes that Israel's 'would-be suzerain has already stacked the deck ... Israel will live only if she freely makes the *right* choice. Covenant is an offer that the vassal cannot refuse, especially if the suzerain is omnipotent' (1994: 142).

than through reassertion of his own omnipotence time and time again, largely achieved by this large-scale game play.

Judg. 10:6–16

6.   And the sons of Israel continued to do evil in the eyes of YHWH and served the Baalim and the Ashtaroth and the gods of Aram and the gods of Sidon and the gods of Moab and the gods of the sons of Ammon and the gods of the Philistines, and they abandoned YHWH and did not serve him.

7.   And YHWH's nostril burned against Israel and he sold them into the hand of the Philistines and into the hand of the sons of Ammon.

8.   And they shattered and smashed the sons of Israel, all the sons of Israel who were in Transjordan, in the land of the Amorites, in Gilead, for eighteen years.[14]

9.   And the sons of Ammon crossed over the Jordan to fight against Judah and Benjamin and against the sons of Ephraim, and Israel was in a much hemmed-in situation.

10.   And the sons of Israel cried out to YHWH saying 'we have sinned against you because we abandoned our God and served the Baalim'.

11.   But YHWH said to the sons of Israel: 'Did I not from Egypt and from the Amorites and from the sons of Ammon and from the Philistines

12.   and from the Sidonites and Amalekites, and Maon when they squeezed you … ? And you cried out to me and I delivered you?[15]

13.   But *you*, you abandoned me and served the other gods, so accordingly I will no longer save you.

14.   Go! Cry out to the gods who you have chosen, and let them save you in the time of your constraints'.

---

[14] The Hebrew refers to 'that year' and also adds the number eighteen. I have suggested a duration of eighteen years rather than *the* eighteenth year since duration of oppression is the norm in the book as a whole. The translation 'shattered and smashed' is an attempt to reproduce the alliterative and onomatopoeic effect of רעץ and רצץ although 'ground into the earth' might convey more of the second verb's meaning. Butler also achieves a similar effect but chooses 'extinguished and exterminated' (2009: 266).

[15] I translate v. 11–12 as a deliberate anacoluthon meant to represent an exasperated YHWH. The translation of לחץ as 'squeeze' is consistent with the translation of Judg. 2:18. It contributes to the hemmed-in qualities of the two passages.

15.   But the sons of Israel said to YHWH 'we have sinned. *You do to us according to all the good in your eyes, but please –* deliver us!'

16.   And they removed the foreign gods from among them and served YHWH. And his soul was irritated by the malady/ mischief of Israel.[16]

This passage repeats key themes addressed in the first passage with further references to abandonment, serving/not serving, rival gods and burning of nostrils, but the relationship between YHWH and Israel comes into sharper focus, enlivened by the scribal incorporation of direct speech from YHWH and Israel. In the intervening chapters, themes struck in Judg. 2:11–23 are developed in a worsening trajectory until the reader arrives at this crucial passage where the relationship between the two attached parties hits a crisis point.

Attachment and Abandonment

Abandonment again works two ways in this passage, but there are significant developments. The eyes widen as the list of Israel's service to other gods goes on and on. By now the reader expects reference to Baalim and Ashtaroth, but not the seemingly interminable parataxis of one set of gods after another. V. 6 bookends this long list of rival gods with references to Israel's serving and not serving YHWH, interpreting this shift of allegiance in terms of desertion. The broadening of Israel's service to no fewer than seven alternatives enables the scribe to bring the relationship to exploding point as Israel's expanded abandonment of YHWH results in his own tit-for-tat threat of abandonment. The reader is expected to react with dismay and commentators generally oblige. In this analysis, however, I am not obliged to explain or exonerate YHWH's threat of abandonment in terms of his enduring love for Israel. Considered in the light of attachment theory, other interpretational options come to light.

In a discussion of coping strategies adopted by children reared by a disciplinarian, Bowlby notes how a child might believe they can

---

[16] I can think of no English word that captures the dual sense of עמל. It can mean misery or trouble in a range of instances but, depending on context, can also mean mischief. The context here does not help; YHWH could be irritated by their mischief or affected by their malady. I explain why I use mischief/malady in order to express the dual connotations of the Hebrew in the discussion of the passage.

only attain the caregiver's comfort and approval 'if certain rules are kept. Provided the rules have been moderate and sanctions mild and predictable, a person can still come confidently to believe that support will always be available when needed. But when rules have been very strict and difficult to keep, and when sanctions on breaking them have been severe and especially when they have included threats to withdraw support, confidence is likely to wilt' (1978: 242–243). He particularly draws attention to the damaging effects of any sanction that includes a threat of abandonment. If such sanctions are 'used repeatedly, or even only occasionally but with intensity ... [they] can have calamitous effects on a developing personality ... because they cast grave doubt on whether an attachment figure will be available when needed, such threats can greatly increase a person's fear that he will be abandoned, and thereby greatly increase also his susceptibility to respond to other situations fearfully' (1978: 243).

Reading Bowlby alongside the story world of Judges prompts the disturbing recognition that a biblical text, used within faith communities as revelation of God's attributes and engagement with his people, promotes to its readers an attachment recognisable as insecure. Bowlby (1978: 242–243) talks about the unhealthy effects of being confronted with strict, difficult-to-keep rules. The instructions by which Israel must live are certainly strict: Israel is ordered to destroy or live separately from the surrounding culture, eschew local deities, and put all energies into the service of this one, possessive father/deity. Bowlby (1978) also mentions the damaging effects of sanctions that are overly severe and the threats to Israel are indeed dire. Against this, the cost of compliance is also significant: a 'voluntary' surrender of autonomy and concomitant emergence of the False, compliant, Self who can reap the rewards of being 'good' but simultaneously reap the consequences of damage to the True Self. Effects of this were discussed in Chapter 1 but it is worth noting Ogden's warning: 'The isolation of the True Self inevitably leads to feelings of emptiness, futility and deadness' (2013: 53). Or Greenberg and Mitchell's caution that if and when the True Self goes into hiding this is 'the equivalence of complete psychic annihilation' (1983: 194).

The scribe has thus conjured a story world that, probably unconsciously, describes an unhealthy relationship between his two main protagonists. Rather than promoting a healthy pattern of secure attachment, with YHWH providing the kind of holding environment that allows for continuity of being, healthy development and individuation, Judges sets before us a model of anxious/ambivalent attachment with its concomitant potential for negative effects. That said, the 20% or so of people so categorised do manage and may find themselves in adult relationships that can provide a more secure base, whereby the previous attachment style is revised. But while all human beings have this kind of development available, what we are presented with in Judges is a more fixed scriptural model, proffered to faithful readers as an insight into their deity's parental assumptions and commitments. If the template presented is one that is likely to promote an anxious style of attachment, then that is a matter of concern for anyone using the Judges as revelatory for contemporary faith.

The need for secure attachment is thwarted on both sides due to abandonment issues, but commentators have consistently taken the perspective of YHWH, the hurt but loyal father figure. In light of the discussion above, these commentators could be viewed as the supporters of the inconsistent caregiver who insists that he *is* loving, reliable, etc., despite the child's experiences to the contrary. While commentators express some sympathy for the child/Israel's position, it ends up being undercut by their ultimate siding with the scribe's representation. Martin, for example, sees YHWH as a loving parent whose anger should be understood as an inherent aspect of his intense and enduring love. He interprets YHWH's refusal to save the Israelites in 10:13–14 as an emergency disciplinary threat, not as a real possibility. His justification for this view lies in his privileging of the statement in 2:1 that YHWH will never break his covenant. So, rather than a scene in which YHWH is inconsistently himself, Martin can argue that YHWH's angry declaration that he will not save them bespeaks only an *inner* tension between anger and compassion (2008: 226), as YHWH does battle with his love and infuriation. In other words, YHWH didn't really mean what he said. Martin thus finds a way to explain YHWH's conduct in consistent terms, so that his behaviour is not deemed capricious. It is interesting to see how Martin, in this section of his work, makes informal psychological diagnoses based on what he reads, referring to YHWH's 'internal conflict' (2008: 220), and reading the terminology of 10:16 to 'indicate a draining, depleting, diminishing, exhausting compassion' (2008: 221). This supposed inner tension within YHWH is also called upon to exonerate his sending tribes to their death in 20:18. Martin suggests it might be a 'reflection of his own prolonged inner conflict . . . Yahweh is turning the tables on Israel and forcing them to experience the same kind of conflicted situation which he is suffering' (2008: 225). But this is tentative psychoanalysing not grounded in any actual psychological theory. It is Martin doing what many other commentators do: engaging emotionally and empathetically with the characters of the story world. It is not necessarily 'wrong' to do this, but to psychoanalyse without using the formal theoretical tools of psychology is to risk reading always with the grain of the text and in accordance with one's own faith commitments. It is not surprising, therefore, that throughout his work Martin finds ways of explaining YHWH in consistent terms so that his behaviour is not seen to be capricious.

In terms of attachment theory, an actual relationship founded on the kind of one-sided symbiosis we see in Judges could never work. Whether we look at this in Winnicott's terms, where the compliant False Self will never be engaged genuinely with commandeering parents, or in Bowlby's terms, where attachment behaviour turns pathological, the relationship will inevitably flounder. While it is disconcerting to think that the God-talk of a biblical text projects a dysfunctional relationship, this is something that must be acknowledged and taken up in the work of practical and pastoral theologians. Bowlby is clear: what a child needs is security and reliability; a primary caregiver who is consistently herself. What we have in YHWH's threatened abandonment is a retaliatory argument that prompts anxiety and an even more grovelling approach as the False Self of Israel is deployed to ensure his continued presence.

Attachment and Affect

The entire passage is permeated by affect. Again the Hebrew idiom of nostrils burning is used to describe YHWH's anger. 'Yahweh's anger blazed against Israel' translates Butler (2009: 253), while Sasson has 'incensed against Israel, the LORD turned them over' (2014: 115), but the stakes are raised further. YHWH doubles the enemy and the descriptions of their force go up a notch. As is so often the case, it is a commentator writing for a believing audience who seems most aware of the relationship breakdown. Martin, who ultimately exonerates YHWH's behaviour while unpacking the strong emotional tenor of this passage, notes YHWH's 'vehement' response to his feelings of rejection and points readers to new verbs used to describe the brutality of Israel's oppression (2008: 201). While there have been forceful descriptions of previous oppression such as 4:3's being 'squeezed' (לחץ) with force (בחזקה), in Martin's view nothing

compares with the 'severity of "shatter" (רעץ) and "crush" (רצץ), words
that signify near total destruction' (2008: 202). However, these strong,
evocative enemy actions noted by Martin have their origins in
YHWH's decision to sell Israel; an action grounded in affronted
feelings and fury. While we may tell ourselves that it is never a good
idea to act out of anger, calling upon the old adage to sleep on it before
making a response, commentators do not seem to notice or criticise
how YHWH's actions stem from his burning nose. We are not
expected to read against the grain when it comes to the character
of YHWH.

In addition, YHWH reacts with a spluttering, outraged speech
when they inevitably cry out, and confronts them with a threat of his
own abandonment. Several commentators note how YHWH cannot
get his words out. Sasson, for example, describes YHWH's outburst
as 'mercilessly critical, with a fractured syntax (anacoluthon) that
effectively approximates bursts of anger' he issues a 'bill of separation' (2014: 412).[17] In the translation above I have not followed the
lead of translators or commentators who suggest YHWH has a
change of heart because he is grieved by their suffering.[18] It is true
that קצר can imply emotional grief or suffering. It is a verb used
elsewhere to describe harvesting or cutting down, and can carry
Niditch's idea of YHWH being 'cut to the quick' (2008: 120). Its
connotations of cutting short can also, however, be interpreted as
being impatient, or annoyed. Accordingly, some commentators
interpret 10:16 in terms of YHWH's irritation or impatience. Sasson,
for example, translates קצר נפש as 'the spirit/throat constricts' and
argues that it is nothing to do with being grieved but 'connotes lack
of patience or displeasure', noting how Samson is said to be 'wearied
to death' in a further use of this idiom (2014: 414). The thing that
arouses YHWH's impatience is Israel's עמל O'Connell (1996: 190
n. 265) thus argues that it is Israel's suffering that provokes
YHWH's reaction. However, given that YHWH has sent the oppression to make them suffer, it seems odd that he finds himself distressed

---

[17] It would not be the only example of such a grammatical device. Brueggemann
notes how a lamenting psalmist can be unable to complete a sentence owing to the
emotional tide of feelings. Ps. 6:3 'My soul also is struck with terror, While you,
O Lord – how long?' (1997: 319). There will be a further use of anacoluthon in 1
Sam. 12.
[18] The King James Version has 'his soul was grieved for the misery of Israel', Good
News Bible similarly states that God becomes 'troubled over Israel's distress' while the
New Revised Standard Version translates 'he could no longer bear to see Israel suffer'.

by it. Another explanation is that this is the response of a guilty parent. Niditch thus suggests that in 10:16 we have an 'emotional, empathetic, *and perhaps guilty deity*' (2008: 121, my emphasis). Pressler similarly suggests YHWH is split by the plight he himself has put them in: 'God's heart is torn by the competing demands of judgment and mercy, but mercy finally prevails' (2002: 198). But there are commentators who take a different line, suggesting that it is Israel's inauthentic repentance and whingeing that constitute the עמל YHWH finds so exasperating.[19] Polzin thinks the עמל YHWH is so annoyed by is 'Israel's impertinent, even presumptuous request' which ends 'do whatever you want, only save us immediately!' (1980: 178): a none-too-subtle attempt to make God work for them.

Ultimately it is one big hissy fit on YHWH's side, but his reaction is seemingly justified by that eye-watering number of gods being serviced by his unfaithful people. Whatever line commentators take, this passage is a crucial scene in the book as a whole. Webb puts it well: 'the relationship ... has reached a major point of crisis, with a complete breakdown of it looking like a very real possibility ... The relationship has come to a shuddering halt. If he does not relent, Israel has no future. All is lost' (2012: 303–304). However, what is often left without comment is that it is not only Israel who has no future, it is YHWH who risks losing one too.[20]

Attachment and Game Play

Unsurprisingly, given Bowlby's view that exposure to serious peril provokes highly visible attachment behaviour, we see a marked development in Israel's behaviour. Faced with the severity of the new oppression, they not only cry out but make a confession of sinning by abandoning YHWH and serving the Baalim. When that does not work they redouble their efforts at assuaging his anger by

[19] Contra Hamlin (1990: 111–112), Wong, for example, argues that Israel are making 'a show of repentance' and that it is only after they have 'grovelled further' that YHWH, 'exasperated by their misery, finally gave in' (2006: 184). Pressler concurs that the second confession is inauthentic: 'the second outcry appears as self-serving and utilitarian as the first' (2002: 198), implying that YHWH is fed up with their whingeing.

[20] Sasson is an exception. Likening Israel's fate to that of Sisyphus, destined to continued, painful efforts to maintain a foothold in the land, he notes how YHWH, too, is caught up with a difficult Sisyphean challenge since he is bound to punish and also bound to forgive. He has no alternative if his 'reputation lies in Israel's success' (2014: 14).

repeating their confession, putting away the offending gods and asking YHWH to do what is good in his eyes, just so long as it involves deliverance. As discussed in Chapter 1, this behaviour is often interpreted as self-serving game play rather than earnest and sincere repentance. However, from a psychological perspective, we could bear in mind the 'strange situation' experiment and ask ourselves whether signs of distress, when faced with severe oppression and unpredictability, are any less genuine for being self-serving, or are any less worthy for demonstrating some sign of initiative and life? In both Ainsworth's study and the story world of Judges, an experiment is going on: how will the child's attachment to their primary caregiver be manifested when they are put under stress? The two experiments, however, have notable differences. Ainsworth's experiment was real, it put actual children into a scenario that caused temporary distress, but it was a short test and the child was given the substitute adult presence and toys to play with. The children did become upset but they remained at all times within a safe environment. The biblical text, by contrast, is only literary, but the experiment is far crueller with much longer periods of oppression (eight, eighteen, twenty or forty years), the barbarity of warfare (recall the chariots of iron), the threat of extinction related in ch. 6 when the Midianites and Amalekites create famine conditions, and, most notably, with the caregiver himself responsible for the alarming situation. Israel does not have to bear with the strange situation for just a few moments, but until they can bear it no longer and wail in desperation. If we imagine for a moment how this would look in a family analogy, it exposes the edginess of the game play that has resulted from YHWH's protest behaviour. The family scenario would be one where a parent has, behind the scenes, put violent, enduring pressure on the child but waits until the child is in so much distress that it begs for help before stepping in. And does this repeatedly. For some commentators this is 'tough love', but if this is the only way by which the child can be kept in relationship with the parent, what is the cost to the child, what kind of relationship would this be and what kind of child does it produce? Yes, the tales of Judges are just that, tales. The events are not real, no one actually gets hurt. In fact, we are asked to view YHWH as the parent who lovingly saves Israel from itself through whatever means necessary, but the attachment model it provoked will hardly be secure.

As for the game playing from Israel's side, I return to the prompt for YHWH's fury and neediness throughout Judges. In 10:6–16,

Israel are accused of serving not just one or two other gods. 10:6 contains an array of foreign deities: Baal and Ashtaroth are accompanied by the gods of Aram, Sidon, Moab, Ammon and the Philistines. The list is 'a veritable "who's who" of Israel's enemies in the book of Judges and the larger tradition' (Niditch, 2008: 122). The hyperbole underscores what the key problem is: jealousy. YHWH deals with their switch of allegiance by threatening to leave them knee-deep in the oppression he has sent. The implication is that they would not survive. But for the first time, we read that Israel removes the foreign deities that were among them. This is the shift that either allows YHWH to save face and give in to their cries or to express his further exasperation at the transparently calculated nature of their act. Either way, Israel clearly recognised the salient thing: they had to get rid of the rivals and serve YHWH alone. I will return to the question of whether we have a show of repentance that is intended to bend YHWH to their needs when discussing the next passage, since very similar game-play tactics crop up in 1 Sam. 12.

1 Sam. 12:7–25

7.   And now, stand up! So that I can judge you in the presence of YHWH, with reference to all the righteous acts of YHWH which he performed for you and your fathers.

8.   So, Jacob entered Egypt and your fathers cried out to YHWH, and YHWH sent Moses and Aaron and they brought your fathers out from Egypt and settled them in this place.

9.   But they forgot the Lord their God and he sold them into the hand of Sisera, captain of the army of Hazor, and into the hand of the Philistines, and into the hand of the king of Moab, and they fought with them.

10. And they cried out to YHWH saying 'we have sinned because we abandoned YHWH and served the Baalim and the Ashtaroth, but rescue us from the hand of our enemies so that we can serve you!'

11. And YHWH sent Jerubbaal and Bedan[21] and Jephthah and Samuel and he delivered you from the hand of your surrounding enemies so that you could live securely.

---

[21] The reference to Bedan has long vexed scholars. Some scholars such as Alter (2013) and McCarthy (1978) let it stand, suggesting that Samuel refers to a judge not mentioned in Judges, probably deriving from an old tradition. Some suppose textual

12. But you saw that Nahash, king of the Ammonites came out against you, and you said to me 'No! A king will rule over us'. But YHWH your God was your king.

13. And now – look! – the king who you chose, who you requested – yes look! – YHWH gave a king to you.[22]

error and emend to Barak, following the LXX and Peshitta (see, for example, Day (1993), Klein (2000), Smith (1899), and Tsumura (2007: 323)). The emendment does have its merits; as Day argues, the relevant letters 'are frequently confused in Hebrew' and 'the support of the LXX is particularly significant, since it is now generally recognized that this version often preserves the original text of Samuel better than the MT, which is frequently corrupt' (1993: 263). However, the fact remains that we have to posit a quite careless scribe who would have rendered a name familiar in Judges to one that is entirely unfamiliar. McCarter (1980: 211) is right: Bedan is the *lectio difficilior* and he accordingly lets it stand, but not without expressing some sympathy for Zakovitch's (1972) proposal that Bedan was part of Jephthah's double-name, as with Gideon-Jerubbaal. Yet it would be odd to list someone by the very part of the double-name that is not mentioned in Judges. Moreover, if Judges is largely a fictional story world, then the attempt to argue that a person was known externally as having two names does not convince. The story world *is* the world. Fokkelman (1993) revives an old suggestion that we should read Abdon instead of Bedan. This was posited by Ewald (1865) (but known also by Clericus [1708]), and championed by Jacobson (1992), but I am unconvinced. The Hebrew letters are not as close as the emendation proposed for Barak, and Abdon was a minor character who does not readily fit the sequence described in this verse. Indeed, Fokkelmann seems motivated to make this emendation on the basis that it provides additional reference to the root עבד that crops up in this chapter. Ultimately, there is no scholarly consensus and while the possibility of a grammatical error is certainly possible, with Barak being the most likely original, it remains difficult to imagine the name of a major Judges character being misrepresented in this way. I thus return to the text and follow my original reaction when translating, which was to exclaim 'Bedan? Who on earth is Bedan?' If I stay with this question and entertain the possibility that it is the intended reaction, then the inclusion of an unfamiliar and unexpected name could be read as a deliberate ploy, promoting the reader to query (further) Samuel's version of events. Miscall (1986: 74) has suggested something similar. He notes how Samuel has modified the account in Judg. 10:10–16 by having Israel coyly say that they can only serve YHWH if he first rescues them. He suggests that the inclusion of an unexpected reference to Bedan 'signals the alteration' that has just happened. My interpretation differs. It is consistent with the idea that Bedan is placed as a 'heads-up' narrative interruption, but I see it as a scribal tactic used deliberately to destabilise Samuel's speech, subverting the rather pompous self-importance that his character adopts. Happily, this verse does not figure strongly in the interpretation, so my translation choice is not crucial to what follows.

[22] Smith describes this as an 'overfull' verse (1899: 87) but if one views Samuel as one involved in an intense drama, his repeated invocation of 'you' and his disparaging views of their actions – *you* chose, *you* requested (i.e., not me), then the scribe has ably characterised Samuel's indignant reproof which comes directly after his alternative version of events, concerning the Nahash incident. Unlike the account that appears earlier in 1 Samuel, when the people requested a king *before* Nahash appeared on the horizon, Samuel has relocated their demand for a king at the moment of attack.

14.   If you fear YHWH and serve him and listen to his voice and do not flout Yahweh,[23] then, for you and the king who rules over you (after the Lord your God) …[24]

15.   But if you do not listen to the voice of YHWH and flout Yahweh, then what will happen is that the hand of YHWH will be upon you and upon your fathers.

16.   So then you, stand up! See the great thing which YHWH will do before your eyes!

17.   Is it not the wheat harvest at the moment? I will call to YHWH and he will provide thunder and rain, then you will know and see the magnitude of evil which you did in his eyes by asking for a king over you.

18.   And Samuel called out to YHWH, and YHWH provided thunder and rain on that day and all the people were terrified of YHWH and Samuel.

19.   And the people said to Samuel 'mediate on behalf of your servants with YHWH your God, so that we may not die because we added on to all our sins this evil of requesting a king over us'.

20.   And Samuel said to the people 'Do not fear! It is you, you who have done all this evil; however, do not turn aside from following YHWH and serve YHWH with all your heart

21.   and do not turn aside on account of going after the insubstantial (ones),[25] which do not benefit and do not deliver, for they are insubstantial,

[23] The Hebrew literally refers to rebellion against the mouth of YHWH and I wanted to get the sense of behaviour that would constitute a slap in the face for YHWH. 'Flout', in my view, delivers this sense.

[24] My translation ends deliberately with an ellipsis even though the gap left in this text is described by Smith as 'unconscionably long' (1899: 88). Indeed, the missing apodosis usually proves impossible to leave unattended. Klein, for example, adds 'then *you will truly be followers of* Yahweh your God' (2000: 110), Tsumura similarly has 'both you and the king who rules over you *will be following* the Lord your God' (2007: 321). Hertzberg adds 'it will be well' (1964: 96) while McCarter inserts 'then he will rescue you' (1980: 209). McCarter, however, does acknowledge Driver's (1890) view that we have here an aposiopesis. Narrative critics are more open to the possibility of a deliberate aposiopesis than historical critics and Fokkelman finds no reason to fill in the gap. In his view, Samuel 'cannot bring himself to say the main clause': 'The ellipsis signifies his mood. In his grimness he cannot and does not want to put into words that this obstinate people will prosper if they keep to the rules of the game … let alone he hold out the prospect of blessing' (1993: 521). I concur.

[25] I like *The Message* translation: 'Don't chase after ghost-gods. There's nothing to them. They can't help you. They're nothing but ghost-gods!' It gets across the sense of

22.   then YHWH will not abandon his people because of his Great Name; YHWH has determined[26] to make you a people for him.
23.   Moreover, as for me, it would be profane for me to sin against YHWH by desisting from mediating between you, and I will instruct you in the good and right paths.
24.   So then, fear YHWH! Serve him in truth and with all your heart and – see! – the great things which he has done for you.
25.   But if you really do evil, then you and your king also will be swept away.

In this passage we have a retrospective, abbreviated overview of the how the relationship between Israel and YHWH floundered during the time of the judges, presented largely from the perspective of its last judge: Samuel. Our scribe creates a lively scene, interjecting his own direct voice only minimally as he scripts an exchange between Samuel and the people and has the deity present.[27] Narrative critics rightly draw our attention to the different points of view present in the passage. It is worth noting Fokkelman's caution that 'Samuel's point of view does not coincide with the people's point of view does not coincide with God's point of view does not coincide with the narrator's point of view' (1993: 488).

Attention to the exchange of perspectives is important for Sternberg. He argues that a biblical narrator is no didactic instructor, but rather can be pictured as a tightrope walker 'suspended between heaven and earth' (1985: 483), trying to balance an authoritarian deity whose will and punishments can seem harsh on the one side, and the audience who may be alienated by this deity's behaviour on the other. The narrator's task is to bring readers round to his point of view without alienating them. To achieve this, the narrator permits his readers various opportunities to be annoyed. Illustrating this with an analysis of King Saul's story, Sternberg notes how the narrator pulls the reader towards Saul and then away, towards and away, allowing us to sympathise, then not, until finally we are persuaded

insubstantial-ness very well, but introduces the term 'ghost' which is not within the semantic range of this noun so I prefer to leave it as 'insubstantial ones'.

[26] Usually translated as 'pleased' this Hiphil verb can suggest persistence or determination.

[27] Fokkelman draws attention to 12:7 which he translates as 'I want to confront you in law with all the redemptive acts of the Lord, in the presence of the Lord' (1993: 507) and the fact that the deity grants Samuel's request for a sign.

that the narrator is right, Saul deserves what he gets. Crucially, we think that we have come to this conclusion ourselves; that it has not been imposed on us. It is a piece of narrative genius that operates by 'subtle persuasive art rather than blunt ideological fiat' (1985: 484). The narrator gets the reader on side by giving them a vicarious presence in the text so that the reader can vent some of their frustrations via the character of Samuel. Thus, when God rejects Saul, Samuel is said to burn with anger and cries to the Lord all night, thereby functioning as the reader's representative. In doing this, the narrator takes a significant but 'calculated risk' that the reader will not side too strongly with Saul; he has to take this chance to avoid reducing his narrative to 'ideological simplifications of didacticism and melodrama' (1985: 493). Ultimately, the tightrope walking pays off. The narrator and God stand side by side and the reader is with them: Saul deserves his punishment and God's rejection of Saul is just.

I summarise this to demonstrate how Sternberg's reading enables the reader to acknowledge multiple perspectives and also expose problems with YHWH's behaviour. I admire Sternberg's work and the work of narrative critics generally, but I cannot concur with Sternberg's explanation of Samuel's role. Samuel is not my representative, not in the Saul narrative and certainly not in 1 Sam. 12; he is self-interested, self-righteous, pugnacious and at times repellent. I am not alone in this view. Polzin's (1989) reading of 1 Samuel prompts readers to interpret Samuel's take on events with a very strong hermeneutic of suspicion. His detection of a Bakhtinian double-accented chapter means that the narrator is everywhere even while his direct presence is so minimal, using a style of narration that undercuts Samuel at every turn by characterising him as self-serving and manipulative, desirous of power while presenting himself as innocent of such desires. If I have no empathy with Samuel then those readerly opportunities to vent disappear. Moreover, Sternberg's approach can never, methodologically, unlock the issues pertinent to this study, because he necessarily reads so closely with the text, following the narratorial lead too docilely, and in his admiration of the narrator's rhetorical style, he closes down a reader's critical assessment of YHWH. The narrator ultimately exonerates YHWH and so does Sternberg. The doubts that we have in YHWH's goodness are allowed, but only temporarily. Sternberg's logic rules out the other possibility: that YHWH is not good.

My approach, however, listens attentively to the presenting story *not* for the purposes of following its rhetoric and explaining it, but in order to detect the psychological drama that underlies and motivates such rhetoric. My method reads with the grain *in order to read against it.* In foregrounding the YHWH–Israel relationship, focusing directly on it, the issue of leadership is greyed out in favour of seeing how the attachment issues discussed above are developed and what new features come to light. I am interested in how the scribe constructs Samuel's assessment of the relationship, particularly the new information on why YHWH is unwilling to let Israel go. Although the perspective is Samuel's, our now rather shadowy scribe is very present, not only in describing events, but creating questions in the reader's mind about Samuel's motives, and clarifying that the 'choice' Israel has is one of absolute faithfulness or doom.

Attachment and Abandonment

The new factor that occurs in this passage is the explanation given of why YHWH could not abandon Israel. In Judg. 2:18, the scribe indicated that YHWH kept the relationship together because he was affected by Israel's groaning. נחם could mean that he felt compassion or pity, or, as I translated it, that he rued their groaning; apparently experiencing a pang of conscience for being the one who sent the enemies who exacted this distress. In either option the pertinent point remains: YHWH acts to maintain the relationship because he is affected by their signalling behaviour. By Judg. 10:10–16, YHWH is far less inclined to respond favourably to their cries. Their signalling behaviour provokes the opposite: a stinging rebuff and a narratorial description of YHWH's irritation. It is pertinent to note that when Otto Fenichel discusses abandonment, he suggests that an angry response to abandonment 'is strongest precisely in those people for whom to be loved is more important than to love ... those people to whom loss of love really is the worst that can befall them – to whom it means ... *a severe impairment of their self-regard'* (1953: 350, emphasis added). Perhaps Judg. 10:10–16 reflects this, confirming that YHWH's attachment to Israel has just as much to do with his own self-interest and concern for reputation than it has with Israel's cries and groaning. When we arrive at 1 Sam. 12:22, Samuel clarifies that the reason why Israel will never be abandoned is because there is indeed too much at stake for YHWH: he will not forsake Israel because of his 'great name'. This claim is put in the mouth of Samuel whose perspective is not to be elided with that of the narrating scribe, but concern for YHWH's reputation so pervades Judges and the Hebrew Bible more generally that Samuel's claim rings true.

At first glance it is not entirely clear what Samuel means by this. It implies that YHWH's reputation would take a knock if he abandoned Israel. But in what specific way? Because he has been shown to lack commitment to his people? Because he is exposed as capricious, endowing specialness only to whisk it away again, thereby rendering the gift of specialness somewhat arbitrary? Most commentators just acknowledge and skip over the reference without any detailed comment, although McCarter (1980: 217) draws on Ezek. 20:9 to explain that what is at stake is the defilement of YHWH's name among the nations, i.e., that it is about damage limitation concerning his public reputation, and McCarter is happy to leave it at that. There is a much fuller discussion of reputation concerns in Glatt-Gilad's (2002) discussion of a large variety of biblical texts concerning YHWH's need to protect his reputation. Glatt-Gilad does not include 1 Sam. 12:22 in his paper, but his observations are applicable to it. The damage that would be done to YHWH's reputation needs to be understood in an ancient military context where 'name' is caught up with military prowess. If he abandons Israel to their fate, allowing the proxy agents that are rounded up in Judges to destroy them completely, then his ability to deliver is called into question. He cannot afford to let the surrounding nations, or indeed Israel, entertain the mistaken belief that he is ineffectual. If he has special responsibility for Israel as his treasured possession, he must be seen to be powerful on their behalf. He is thus caught on the horns of a dilemma. His jealousy and honour requires that he punishes Israel for serving rival gods, but his manipulation of enemy nations to administer the punishment means that they might think they (and of course their gods) are more powerful. In such a situation YHWH's 'great name' would be inevitably tarnished. Commenting on Deut. 32, Glatt-Gilad rightly outlines the logic: 'God must spare Israel on the brink of destruction so as to forestall the foolish enemy from claiming credit for her total destruction ... The enemy's misunderstanding of the source of Israel's sorry state requires Yahweh to fight on Israel's behalf ... Israel's enemies ... become Yahweh's enemies ... and Israel is preserved, though badly battered' (2002: 7). It is an apt summary of the situation pertaining in Judges and supplies the rationale behind Samuel's assertion that YHWH will not abandon Israel.

Glatt-Gilad's outline of the reasoning for the 'fascinating' representation of 'an omnipotent God being effectively limited in his course of action due to potentially negative fallout' (2002: 64) is helpful, but studies of both masculinity and attachment theory could add further dimensions. In terms of masculinity, Samuel's claim needs to be read against the cultural understandings of masculinity in which the scribe is embedded. Honour/shame is the primary binary for masculinities in the ancient world and its codes inform the characterisation of YHWH just as much as any other male literary character.[28] We miss this when we locate studies of YHWH's nature within the field of Old Testament theology, which conventionally reads with the grain of the text and grants YHWH an honoured status. Within the theology framework, YHWH's acts of deliverance are understood as indicators of his steadfast love. Through the lens of masculinity studies, however, they bespeak an alpha male's need for honour and recognition. As divine warrior, YHWH must ensure that he gets the credit for Israel's victories. It is thus YHWH, not Gideon, who will strike down every Midianite (6:16, 7:22) and he ensures that his recognition does not get redirected by instructing Gideon to cut the size of his army (7:2). It is YHWH, not Barak, who decimates the army of Jabin and Sisera. Foreign enemies are given lease to oppress, they do not achieve it for themselves, and YHWH easily routs them when they have served their purpose.

But as with most traits of hegemonic masculinity (an idealised fantasy that men can never live up to), the preservation of honour has its costs. Success in warfare is a means of demonstrating strength, domination and superiority over other men. Honour is won, not granted, and it must be secured continually. Moreover, the codes of honour/shame mean that YHWH is not only a fiercely jealous deity but also a very vulnerable one. 10:6–16, with its reference to YHWH's burst of indignant anger, reveals a deity whose 'words smack of wounded feelings and resentments' (Niditch, 2008: 124). But more than that, there is an unwillingness to let go of a relationship that is predicated on his terms. Again, in theological sources, this is viewed as a positive divine attribute, but masculinity studies take a far less pious view of the situation. Honour, as Clines (forthcoming) points out, is 'a competitive matter ... constantly

---

[28] See Clines' (forthcoming) assessment of divine masculinity in the Bible, particularly his focus on the language of divine violence and killing, honour and holiness and his discussion of the ethical issues raised by the image of the divine warrior. I concur with Clines that YHWH is 'caught up in the quest for honour, striving to maintain the status he holds' (*Play the Man: The Masculine Imperative in the Bible*). (www .academia.edu/14079928/The_Most_High_Male_Divine_Masculinity_in_the_Bible).

open to challenge, and a man with honour always has to be prepared to defend it'. YHWH has traditionally been immune from such studies due to the assumption that his character within the text is intrinsically connected with a metaphysical reality beyond it. Once that privilege is stripped away, the embeddedness of the character within the very human cultural codes of the ancient world can clearly be seen. Clines compels us to see the extent to which YHWH is a gendered character who is just as obsessed with the quest for honour as any other and that, beneath the bluster, is a masculinity that is vulnerable, and that needs others to provide the recognition and status. And this is where psychological theory provides a very useful adjunct to masculinity studies.

Lasine (2002) furthers existing work on YHWH's capricious and arguably abusive relationship with Israel by using psychological literature on narcissism, splitting, parental ambivalence, child abuse and trauma to illuminate the dynamics of YHWH's relationship with Israel.[29] Lasine paints a picture of divine aloofness and an unsettling parental gaze, suggesting that if Israel ever looked into their father's eyes they might not be able to 'rely upon Yahweh to return their gaze with the smiling face of an adoring parent' (2002: 37 n. 3). In fact, rather than Israel basking in the parent/YHWH's approving eyes, it is YHWH who seeks the adulation. Deities need human allegiance, exaltation and recognition to ensure alpha male status. And this particular alpha male is a jealous deity who tolerates no rival for human males' loyalties. Israel is not allowed any deity/parent substitutes. Rather than see this as an element of the 'glorification of YHWH' theme that commentators often note, the work of Lasine suggests that the deity suffers from pathological narcissism. Drawing on the work of Lowen (1997) and Kernberg (1985) he suggests that Israel exists as YHWH's mirror: there to provide loyalty, submission and veneration.[30] But as he goes on to point

---

[29] He engages specifically with Blumenthal (1993a, 1993b), Brueggemann (2000) and Noll (1999).

[30] Lasine argues YHWH's parenting as modelled on a royal paradigm. Drawing on biblical literature that extends beyond the Book of Judges, he notes the dominance of the 'Yhwh is king' motif. He is a royal divine parent, and treats his special children with 'all the ambivalence, suspicion, rivalry and strings-attached love which characterize the attitude of a king when he views members of the royal family as competing to succeed – or overthrow – him' (2002: 38). And this royal divine parent 'can be an abusive narcissist, who may seek the loyalty and submission he needs from his children by breaking their spirit, by burdening them with feelings of guilt and inadequacy, or by keeping them cravenly dependent upon him' (2002: 39).

out, YHWH does not have it all his own way: 'narcissists are never self-sufficient, no matter how much they might claim to be. Viewing Yahweh as a narcissist highlights his need for others, even when He trumpets that He alone is God and there is no other. And it is precisely in his behavior as father that Yahweh most clearly displays this neediness' (2002: 48). Returning to Samuel's claim, that YHWH cannot abandon Israel due to his 'great name', I suggest that YHWH's concern for reputation bespeaks his attachment needs, activated by Israel's abandonment of him. He is not simply a male writ large, he is a psyche writ large.

Attachment and Affect

This passage is so permeated with affect that commentators are unable to resist engaging in their own psychological pondering. Narrative critics seem especially attuned to the emotional tenor of the scribe's narration. Fokkelman is one of the best examples, suggesting that the scribe presents us with a 'sour' prophet in a 'bad temper' (1993: 485, 521) who gives the people a dressing-down 'dripping with emotions: anger and grief, which together form the deadly chemistry of resentment; there is self-pity, and there is repression as soon as his sons are brought up' (1993: 496). He actually uses the phrase 'psychological probe' to describe the scribe's exposé of Samuel as one who 'reveals . . . the need for being appreciated' which 'reveals inner weakness' (1993: 497). Samuel's inability to complete his sentence is further interpreted by Fokkelman as a signifier of his dark mood: 'In his grimness he cannot and does not want to put into words that this obstinate people will prosper if they keep to the rules of the game . . . let alone he hold out the prospect of blessing' (1993: 521). Fokkelman's commentary is just as engaging as the text and it is his forays into the realm of affect and psychological motivation that bring the text to life. He limits himself, however, to the task of providing exquisite detailed narrative analysis combined with an insightful assessment of characterisation and narratorial rhetoric. He thus recreates the text of 1 Sam. 12 in all its richness, attentive to the effects of the unspoken psychological drama that is going on, but without any direct analysis of the text from the perspective of psychological theory. Jobling also supplies a splendid literary analysis. His focus is on politics but he too lingers around the edges of psychological assessment, focussing more on the character of YHWH than Samuel and arguing that YHWH, who grants the people a king even while presenting that request as a personal rejection, is depicted as being 'torn in two' (1998: 62). His comment on 1 Sam. 8, for example, reads that YHWH

> wants to see the people's request as a *direct* uncomplicated rejection of himself. So he stumbles over his words. Worse, having gotten into this fix he stubbornly insists that the people must have their way even when they cease to want it. YHWH passes from confusion to petulance and punitiveness. He is punishing the people for reminding him of words of his own that he wanted to forget! (1998: 62)

Jobling quickly clarifies that 'this "divine" dilemma is happening, of course, in the mind of the Deuteronomic historians' (1998: 62), and it is an inevitable one given what the scribe is facing, i.e. the incoherence of divine permission for 'a form of government of which he disapproves' (1998: 62). In this way of thinking, then, YHWH's behaviour is a by-product of a clever and intricate scribal discussion.

Both Fokkelman and Jobling show how the characterisation of Samuel and YHWH gives us three-dimensional, very 'human' dramatis personae, replete with flaws, vulnerabilities and insecurities, both of them susceptible to heavily personalised interpretation of events, both brought to apoplectic stuttering. This is quite close to an assessment of characters as psychologically compromised by their own self-interests and complexes, but this is as far as both scholars go. Methodologically, narrative readings may interact with psychological concepts but it is not in the remit; critics are not expected to apply them in any detailed or rigorous fashion. If, however, 1 Sam. 12 is read with attachment theory at the forefront, the descriptions of affect take on fresh resonance, not least in the way Samuel presents and responds to the people's request for a king.

I raise a hurrah for the assertiveness of Israel as described by Samuel. The declaration he puts in their mouth, 'No, we will have a king', brings colour and a fresh element of independent spirit to Israel. What interests me, however, is the heavy handed way in which this self-assertion is quickly closed down. The people have requested a king. Samuel has been told by YHWH to grant their request. Yet, Samuel, using lawsuit terminology, brings Israel to heel by employing no fewer than three strategies.

First, he is creative with his narration of events, relocating their request to a point in the story where the reader might have expected them to cry out, i.e., at the point of oppression by Nahash. In so doing, Samuel presents their 'No, we will have a king' as a deterioration from their crying-out submission to YHWH. Brueggemann catches the spirit of Samuel's presentation of events, referring to their 'no!' as a 'brazen request' issued as 'Israel dramatically departed from its long-established and reliable way with Yahweh' (1990: 92). My counter hurrah is a response to the fact that Israel is, for once, depicted as reacting in a more self-directing way and I am glad of the sign of life. Fokkelman (1993: 515) suggests that their declaration has the air of 'chutzpa' about it and I get the feeling that he too appreciates their boldness. However, while the scribe allows the people their say, giving voice to their need to get themselves free of the enmeshed cycle in which they find themselves, he then lets Samuel be economical with the truth and represent their request in this more negative way.

Second, Samuel effectively cancels out any independence or autonomy for this people by effectively hamstringing their king. This is noted by a range of commentators, but Brueggemann again provides a perceptive summary: Samuel 'denies kingship any theological significance. Theologically these verses nullify the institution of kingship! In the insistent categories of covenant, kingship is an institution that makes no difference, simply does not exist, and is not acknowledged. All that counts is the torah' (1990: 93). So, while the people say 'No!' Samuel's response is that their 'no' makes no difference to the state of affairs since the king will remain subject to the covenant just as the people. As Brueggemann later adds: 'The relentless rhetoric of chapter 12 has rendered the king genuinely irrelevant to the life of Israel ... the king can matter in the life of Israel only by being obedient' (1990: 94).

The third way in which Israel's spark of initiative is blown out is via the heavy-handed display of power – thunder and rain at harvest time. Any agricultural society appreciates the potential catastrophe this could bring, but above that, it is the supernatural force of the demonstration that is relevant, and the way it terrifies the people. Fokkelman puts it well when he notes how Samuel's negative view of their request is 'hammered into the people with cosmic violence' (1993: 526). Divine determination is again the name of the game as the voice of YHWH – the thunder – reinforces Samuel's presentation of the situation. The initiative of Israel is thus heavily curtailed[31] and,

---

[31] It is not just that enemy nations squeeze, cramp and put Israel in dire straits, they are also hemmed in from the impingements of Samuel and YHWH. The imagery of curtailment has these wider horizons.

unsurprisingly, their reaction is one of terror, confession of sin and preparedness to give up their request for a king (which puts Samuel in a tricky situation, as YHWH told him to grant this). Throughout, Samuel manipulates Israel into a readiness to acknowledge their faults. He can now inform them that their role is to listen, fear, serve and not rebel; and they are prepared to hear it.

To conclude, the affect visible in this passage, overall, is significant. Indignance, terror and bad temper – the passage is full of emotive life. I am reminded of that Bowlby is very clear about one thing; attachment patterns of behaviour involve demonstrations of affect. Interaction between the attachment figure and the respondent 'is accompanied by the *strongest* of feelings and emotions, happy or the reverse . . . whenever interaction results in persistent conflict each party is likely on occasion to exhibit intense anxiety or unhappiness, especially when the other is rejecting' (1997: 242, emphasis added).

Attachment and Game Play

V. 11 stands out most clearly when read from the perspective of attachment theory. Samuel refers to the capacity for Israel to live *securely* בטח – a desire their request for a king implies. Having connotations of safety, refuge, feelings of trust and assurance, it is an adroit choice of language. In attachment terms, the noun smacks of Winnicott's blessed images of continuity of being, of mutually shared company, free from impingements. Given the repeated periods of oppression, the prospect of living בטח would appeal strongly. In Samuel's rhetoric, they are wrong to be looking to human leaders or other gods for such bliss. The haven of security is the result of YHWH's deliverance. As Eslinger astutely observes, 'The attainment of such a state of peaceful security, courtesy of Yahweh, is the goal of Israelite existence; there is nothing more to be achieved. Subsequently, Israel is expected to act in accordance with the wishes of Yahweh, who has fulfilled his covenantal commitment by giving them this secure refuge' (1985: 400). The ideal that Samuel holds out is, however, part of an attachment game. Shift away from complete loyalty to YHWH and he will ensure that all security is lost; enemies with brutal chariots of iron or swarming enemies that hem in on all sides will be the order of the day. It is YHWH's way or doom. Samuel's other, more obvious, piece of attachment game play is his heavy-handed reinforcement that doom is a real possibility. His dramatic show of power, calling up the growling thundery voice of YHWH with accompanying rain, terrifies Israel. Green, who overall has a more positive evaluation of Samuel than Eslinger, Polzin, Jobling and Fokkelman, recognises the foolishness of his game. It is 'helpful only to scare the people back towards the reactive mode with God against which all participants need to struggle' (2003: 191). For 'reactive mode', I read insecure attachment. Samuel holds out the desirable ideal of security, of living בטח, but promptly terrifies Israel into adopting the price it involves.

However, things are not entirely clear cut. YHWH does not have it all his own way, for Israel has its own attachment ploy. Although v. 10's description of Israel's confession to YHWH comes from the mouth of Samuel and is thus not an infallible interpretation, it can be interpreted in terms of attachment game play on Israel's side. If YHWH can be beset by reputation concerns, they have an ace up their sleeves. How can his reputation be secured and how can he be served, and thereby honoured, if his people are not liberated to serve him? The game that YHWH set in motion in Judg. 2:22–23 by leaving nations in the land has thus come back to haunt him. By leaving those nations with their rival gods as a temptation that would test Israel's allegiance, he gave Israel a trump card that they now play with aplomb. Rescue us – for only then will we be free and able to serve you. Or, as Fokkelman puts it: 'as long as we are in the power of these enemies we are also forced to worship their gods . . . if you save us from the enemy we will be able to set these gods aside and serve you' (1993: 512–513). Fokkelman's analysis points out how the grammar of the Israel's speech is put within two 'semantic poles' moving from 'we have sinned' to 'we will serve you' (1993: 512) and how despite the confession and conformity, it is YHWH who is the butt of the game play: 'In 10c *we* leave God, in 10e we have become unable to repair that ourselves and the only solution is that thou (the part duped first, actually) save us we who are now the victims of oppression' (1993: 513). This, intentionally in my view, takes us back to the confession of Judg. 10.15 that was accompanied by putting away the rival gods, but which drove YHWH to exasperation. It explains why I translated עמל as misery/mischief. There is indeed game playing going on here. The reader may, at this point, remind me of my defence of Israel's 'reparative gesture' in Chapter 1. There, I noted how their crying out and repentance had often been interpreted negatively as a mechanistic, self-oriented and convenient strategy and I questioned this commentarial reinforcement of Israel's waywardness. However, the game play going on here cannot be fully explained until Chapter 4, where I argue that Israel's show of overt repentance here and in 10:15–16 is both genuine *and* cloying, a display that rightly provokes scholarly suspicion and criticism. Commentators are not wrong to query the deviousness of Israel's confession, but by grounding that query in the narrator's castigation of Israel as hopelessly self-serving, they miss the psychological rationale for such behaviour. For now, it has to be sufficient to acknowledge a measure of game play in their tactics and in Chapter 4 I will demonstrate how it forms part of an important masochistic defence mechanism.

Conclusion

In this chapter I have noted how attachment theorists are interested not only in how infant reactions can be categorised into attachment styles, but also in the kind of caregiving likely to produce them. I also noted that these attachment categories are marked by a positive/negative view of the self and a positive/negative view of Others. In the three passages discussed, 'past' Israel is undoubtedly 'bad' and is repeatedly accused of abandoning YHWH, serving other gods, inciting YHWH's hot rage, in contrast to which YHWH, despite engaging in underhand punitive measures, is the one repeatedly depicted as 'good', rescuing and bearing with his badly behaved children. The attachment categories marked by this self/bad and others/good quality are the anxious/preoccupied/ambivalent and the fearful, which is a subdivision of the avoidant category.

Readers will recall Bartholomew's view: the ambivalently attached child is one who, having experienced 'inconsistent and insensitive parenting, especially if accompanied by messages of parental devotion, may conclude that their own unworthiness explains any lack of love on the caregiver's part. The result is ... an insatiable desire to gain others' approval and a deep-seated feeling of unworthiness' (1990: 163). Adults who have an ambivalent style of relating are described as having rollercoaster relationships where love and intimacy may be marked by 'obsession, desire for reciprocation and union, emotional highs and lows, and extreme sexual attraction and jealousy' (Hazan and Shaver, 1987: 515). In contrast, fearfully attached persons are likely to have 'difficulties with both autonomy and intimacy' (Bartholomew, 1990: 165) and may have a caregiver who physically abuses. They may have had parents who 'freely expressed negative affect toward and in front of their children, leading to fearfulness and the avoidance of interpersonal conflict on the part of rejected children' (1990: 166). In my view, it is asking too much to connect the descriptions of a limited ancient story world to the attachment categories in any fixed or certain way. The most that can be achieved is a considered, informed but tentative suggestion that some caregiving behaviours, as displayed by this father deity, are likely to result in certain modes of attachment.

The descriptions of rollercoaster relationships, obsession and jealousy do fit, in a very generalised way, the relationship of YHWH and Israel, implying an insecure relationship. However, displays of negative affect, so typical of fearful attachment, are also visible – the threatening thunder and rain, Samuel's haranguing speech, YHWH's running out of words to describe his exasperation with Israel. That said, the most obvious negative affect – YHWH's hot anger – is not actually directly seen by Israel in terms of a 'display'. The narrator describes this off stage, as it were, noting its eruption and its result (selling or giving Israel into the hands of plunderers) while Israel remains ignorant. The physical abuse they experience comes from proxy agents, not from YHWH himself. Such is the manoeuvring of YHWH (or rather, the interplay of perspectives in the text), that the Israel of the text never meets the YHWH that the reader knows, or only a version of him that the narrator allows them to see. Their experience of YHWH's caregiving may thus not be associated with his indirect physical abuse and incendiary negative affect, but in a lesser way Israel experiences a caregiver who is temperamental and not consistently himself, but who they hope will respond to their cries favourably. (That said, the narrator does not record any astonishment when YHWH tells them to go and cry out to their other gods, which may indicate that their hopes are not always high. Rather, they do what Bowlby would expect them to do, engage in behaviour that reduces the distance between them and puts them in the position of contrite supplicants). Ultimately, a consideration of the kind of attachment prompted by YHWH's behaviour depends on whether one's focus is on the behaviour that Israel sees and directly experiences, or the fuller range of behaviour the narrator tells us about. If Israel knew all, one might expect them to be fearfully attached – but they do not.

Rather than dwelling on Israel's responses it is more rewarding to turn attention to the omniscient scribe, the one who scripts the full gamut of YHWH's feelings and behaviour, including the burning nostrils, the appointment of oppressive enemies and the unreliable advice. One might ask whether this scribe is the one who is fearfully attached to his deity, but such a question is unanswerable. Moreover, the scribe himself does not appear to have a negative view of self. It is his past ancestors that he harangues as irredeemably bad as he distances himself from them. This is achieved by a very useful psychological device that enables him to 'borrow' from YHWH an authority, a readiness to chastise and discipline, and a self-presentation as 'good'. A full discussion of this is reserved for Chapter 4. For now, it demonstrates the complexities involved in discerning how the YHWH–Israel relationship resonates with specific attachment categories. I conclude that trying to map them to the biblical text in a detailed way is not possible; the most that can be concluded is that the texts under discussion definitely do not promote a secure form of attachment in psychological terms. The import of this for contemporary theologians and faithful end-users of these biblical texts is beyond the remit of this study, but in my view, needs to be taken seriously.

I concluded Chapter 2 by noting that trauma theory could not satisfactorily explain the Judges cycle. The scribe repeatedly throws his constructed Israel into hostile situations in which they suffer (but describes their distress with a distinct level of aloof sarcasm) and brings into this scenario the threat that YHWH will abandon them. His repeated template enables him to explore again and again betrayal, punishment, rescue and abandonment, playing it out in narrative after narrative. If this does not derive from a traumatised first- or second-generation survivor of the Babylonian exile, we are left with a scribe whose textual product punishes Israel cruelly, humorously mocks their efforts, hangs the guilty sign around their neck again and again, and exposes them to the wrath of an infuriated father/YHWH. In so doing, the scribe *appears* to be condemning previous generations who lost the land, who had to be severely punished for their cultic disloyalty, but this past Israel is a literary fiction. The Israel of the texts discussed above does not get angry or throw aggressive tantrums. This seemed odd to me, given the emphasis in object relations theory on the balancing of aggression/ love that has to be managed, and initially I was puzzled by the absence of anger. However, to some extent it is there, not overtly in the textual happenings of the story world, but in the tone of the author's account. In the author's denigration of a 'past' Israel there is certainly aggression: a 'hate' not directed to the author of the calamities, YHWH, but at an Israel the scribe has split off from his good and obedient Israelite self.

Ultimately, attachment theory has been useful for unpacking the relationship dynamics described in the three passages. To some extent it demonstrates the obvious – that there are ways in which both YHWH and Israel are pulled towards each other while at other times repelling each other – but it has done more than this. It offers the tools for understanding attachment game playing and the rationales for the behaviour that is on display. Attachment theory illuminates a story world where the relationship style of the primary parental character is likely to produce in his children certain modes of attachment. A secure attachment between YHWH and Israel would have been represented in father/YHWH's continuity of care, shared love, relief of distress in a timely way and being consistently himself. What we are actually presented with in the three passages above is a relationship teetering on the point of boiling over, which it almost does in the tenth chapter; a point from which neither party appears to fully recover.[32] But this analysis still does not go far enough. It describes and explains the dynamics of a relationship dominated by attachment issues, but does not help us understand why a scribe would repeatedly tell the same story, continually putting Israel into the painful situation of brutal oppression, or why the scribe remains so pro-YHWH, or why the scribe seems to relish his presentation of a hopeless 'past' Israel who are undeserving of YHWH's gracious election. The repeated template seems to model a perennial problem, i.e., the fact that the relationship between Israel and YHWH is always on the verge of breaking down, offering its bleak verdict on whether things can ever be different. The next chapter delivers the final jigsaw piece, explaining why we have this repeated cycle.

---

[32] Martin notes how after 10:6–16 'the land never again has rest ... For the most part, in the remainder of the book, God is silent, speaking only in two episodes (Judg 13 and 20). Furthermore, God's relative silence is accompanied by his seeming inactivity' (2008: 215).

4

ISRAEL'S MASOCHISTIC DEFENCE MECHANISM

The previous chapter raised a significant question: where is Israel's anger? While attachment theory indicated that there is always a need to balance aggression/love, the God-talk in Judges is one-sided. It has plenty to say about Israel's crying out to YHWH, repentance (genuine or otherwise) and renewed pledges to serve YHWH alone, while any rage against the impingements and demands of their exacting primary caregiver seems not so much muted as altogether absent. I queried whether this aggression had gone underground, turned not against YHWH, but against a 'bad Israel' condemned by the good and obedient Israelite self who narrates the story – but that forms only half of my argument. This chapter demonstrates how the strangely absent aggression is explained by psychoanalytic theories of masochism.[1]

As my interest is not in sexual masochism, I do not work with literature pertaining to the practices of those involved in bondage, discipline, dominance and submission, and sadomasochism, or with queer readings of biblical texts that employ theories of top–bottom relationship dynamics to understand the YHWH–Israel attachment.[2] Nor do I work with Freudian emphases on drive theory and

---

[1] I note Novick and Novick's (2012: 51–52) call to talk about sadomasochism rather than just masochism so that the dance between two inherently connected behaviours can be seen, but the focus of this chapter relates more strongly to the masochistic aspect of this dance.

[2] See, for example, Boer (2001) and Rowlett (2001). Rowlett's identification of YHWH as a sadist character with whom the Deuteronomist is aligned offers an intriguing interpretation of the cyclical pattern of cultic fidelity and apostasy found in Judges. Israel, placed in the 'bottom' position, behaves badly, regularly forsaking their 'top' – YHWH – for rival deities, while YHWH intermittently but regularly hauls them back to their primary relationship. Rowlett points out how the narrator similarly has to exert his own agenda strongly and repeatedly in order to bring a recalcitrant generation to heel. My focus, however, is on the component elements of *relational* masochism and how this operates as a defence mechanism against aggression and helplessness. Where this overlaps with Rowlett's essay is in her observation that YHWH never makes use of

how masochism may be one of the ways in which Oedipal issues are resolved. His work and that of post-Freudians have much to offer to any study of masochism, but I believe Oedipal issues are only one aspect of the broader picture that is sadomasochism.[3] Given my focus on the relationship between YHWH and Israel in Judges I look mainly to those who have understood sadomasochism within a relational framework. Such theorists often engage with the work of Winnicott and Bowlby and their work thus coheres with the previous chapters and the overarching focus of this study.[4]

However, before going any further it should be noted that the application of psychoanalytic theories of sadomasochism to the assessment of a biblical text is problematic. The psychoanalytic literature is largely client-based, with analysts examining patterns of behaviour that are described during therapy sessions. Each case study is thus inevitably unique, contributing distinctive features to the wider and more general picture that analysts have constructed. Readers of Judges and its God-talk have no access to any 'clients' in the sense of having those responsible for the story world's narration sitting on the couch, and we have only an uncertain notion of the specific context in which the scribe operated. Furthermore, psychological analysis routinely returns to questions of the individual client's experiences in their very early years (if beyond recall, those

his apparently overwhelming powers in order to establish his will, suggesting that maybe YHWH 'derives pleasure from the game, or perhaps the sadistic pleasure belongs to his or her (literary) creator, the DH' (2001: 115). I concur that the Judges cycle of repeated punishment does offer pleasure, not in punishment per se, but in the continuing rollercoaster relationship that, paradoxically, ensues from Israel's continual provocation; a view that is explained further in this chapter.

[3] As Kucich notes, relational theorists view Oedipal crises as one 'development phase ... and not necessarily the pivotal one' while 'sexual practices are among the rarest forms of ... masochistic behavior. By questioning masochism's supposed genesis in the sexual conflicts of the Oedipal stage, relational models have the potential to displace Freudian assumptions that have long undergirded both scholarly work and popular' (2009: 25). Those who work with masochism as a defence mechanism have also pushed back Freud's starting point for the emergence of masochistic behaviour to pre-Oedipal situations (see especially the work of Sugarman, 2012).

[4] I note that relational theorists do not have a monopoly on definitions and explanations; Kucich is right to acknowledge that their work exists amid 'tensions with other explanatory paradigms' and that their 'assumptions about the origins and functions of masochism must necessarily remain provisional' (2009: 25). However, relational theorists have, in my view, the most to offer when it comes to evaluating Judges and its God-talk. My understanding of masochism will emerge during the discussion of these theorists and their key ideas but, for now, suffice it to say that it is an understandable, sometimes *crucial*, defence strategy employed to maintain relationship with a primary caregiver.

early experiences have to be imaginatively reconstructed from the fixations of their adult selves). Whatever the adult manifestations are, masochism often appears to have its originating causes early in life and analysts, accordingly, are attentive to the relationship between infant and primary caregiver. Obviously it is impossible to work with a biblical text in such a way; to put the scribe himself into therapy, to unpack his personal life experiences as one would a modern client, is impossible.

Identifying masochistic features in literature is thus rather a difficult project, but it has been done. Studies in English literature have assessed a range of texts for their sadomasochistic dynamics. A good recent example can be found in Kucich's intriguing study of imperial masochism in the works of Joseph Conrad, Robert Louis Stevenson, Olive Schreiner and Rudyard Kipling. For Kucich, masochistic fantasy is at work where one finds 'the conjunction of voluntarily chosen pain, suffering, or humiliation with omnipotent delusion' (2009: 25) and, in his hands, theories of masochism become useful tools for the analysis of Victorian literature. Given that some knowledge pertaining to the lives and contexts of his authors exists, he is able to locate masochistic features both in the imperialism of the literature discussed and in the lives of its writers. Working with biblical literature, however, does not afford this luxury. Biblical texts are constructed by anonymous authors and subject to redaction by later scribes, making any application of masochism theories a far more challenging prospect. As noted before, I cannot engage in speculation about the scribe's life history – the most that can be known is a very sketchy hypothesis of a likely historical context, and even that is informed conjecture. What we *do* have is the literary remnant of one (or more) scribes and a recognition that this document would have been located within a psychic context just as much as a social, economic, political and religious context. So, while the scribe's individual psychic story inevitably remains entirely opaque and inaccessible I proceed rather with an analysis of the story world he has produced, read in the light of theory pertaining to masochism, observing where and how such theory illuminates the God-talk of Judges.

This chapter's discussion begins with the work of Scottish psychiatrist and analyst William Fairbairn, since his work on attachment provides a helpful bridge between this and the previous chapter. His influential views on how children (and adults) split primary objects into 'good' and 'bad', repress the bad objects and in so doing split their own central ego, provides a necessary precursor to the following sections on masochism that explain why humans engage in self-damaging manoeuvres in order to maintain important relationships. Interwoven into the discussion of Fairbairn's ideas are the opening lines of my argument that at the heart of the God-talk in Judges lies a masochistic defence mechanism. However, as his theories do not offer the kind of detailed analysis of masochism found in other writers, I turn to further studies, looking particularly at theorists who explain masochism in terms of defence mechanisms and object relations theory. Appearing around the same time as Fairbairn's *Psychoanalytic Studies of the Personality* (originally published in 1952; Fairbairn, 1996) a number of theorists, whose work was to be become formative, drew on their clinical practice to flesh out the relational aspect of masochistic behaviour patterns. Edmund Bergler's 1949 monograph details the operations and rationale of psychic masochism. He demonstrates just how vital double-think can be: analysts must be able to get beyond surface presenting scenarios to the unconscious wish/defence that lies beneath. When it comes to reading Judges, Bergler's insights are spot on. Double-think makes the mind spin but it opens up surprising fresh insights on the YHWH–Israel attachment, as we shall see. Two years previously, Bernhard Berliner (1947) was influential in shifting understanding away from Freud's focus on libidinal and death drives and into the framework of object relations theory, arguing that our starting point for understanding masochism lies not in manifestations of self-punishment but in *relationship*. In his later paper, originally published in 1958, he wrote what now seems like an obvious statement: 'the *other person* is a reality from the very beginning and is instrumental in bringing about the whole masochistic process' (Berliner, 1995: 345, emphasis added). In a nutshell, he argues that the person who exhibits masochistic patterns of behaviour is caught up in an unsatisfactory relationship and is engaged in defence management. Largely confirming Berliner's work, a short but significant 1953 essay by Esther Menaker argued that causal factors are forged much earlier in life than Berliner proposed but she reinforced the view that masochism is primarily a defence mechanism established to maintain a bond with the primary caregiver (Menaker, 1953). Alongside the work of Bergler, Berliner and Menaker I engage also with contributions from Theodor Reik (1941, 1958), Margaret Brenman (1952), Arnold Cooper (2008) and Jack and Kerry Kelly Novick (Novick and Novick, 1991, 1995, 1996, 2004). The Novicks in particular have developed our understanding of how and why sadomasochism is such a vital defence mechanism and furthered our insight into how projection, externalisation and omnipotent delusion play their part in masochistic fantasy. Their work, and that of Reik, is crucial to the argument I develop about the lost rage of Israel.

I organise the key insights from this body of literature on relational masochism into three sections, each of which addresses a key component of masochistic defence formation. In each section I develop the opening lines of argument presented in the discussion of Fairbairn, demonstrating how each component of masochistic patterns of behaviour offers an instructive, although disturbing, insight into the story world's relationship between YHWH and Israel. In the conclusion to the chapter, I pull the threads together to identify and explain the lost rage of Israel and how Judges can be read as a major defence mechanism in narrative form.

Exploring the story world of Judges through these perspectives is entirely reasonable. Masochistic defences are not the operations of pathological human beings (although they can be); we all engage in such mechanisms from time to time.[5] What this study illuminates is how and why such defences operate, how they can be detected in literature, even ancient literature, how biblical scholars get caught up in this, whether or not they are aware of it, and why this matters when the literature continues to be received by audiences today as scripture.

'Better to Be a Sinner in a World Ruled by God Than to Live in a World Ruled by the Devil': Fairbairn, Repression, Splitting and Psychic Demons

Fairbairn conjures the above slogan to explain an infant's strategy when faced with a 'bad' primary caregiver. Consider the scenario of a child whose parents are not consistently responsive and loving but, contrarily, are withdrawn, rejecting or temperamental. When the child is confronted by this 'bad' parent she is loath to acknowledge it. After all, the child depends on her primary caregiver for her

---

[5] The potential for a masochistic way of relating is universal. Charmé explains how masochism forms a part of most human experience, helping people deal 'with such universal experiences as powerlessness, helplessness, and guilt' (1983: 221). Meyers observes how 'some degree of masochism is universal as long as there is a superego, and helplessness and frustration in childhood, a need for object relatedness and self-definition, for separation and individuation, or a need for repair of the loss of infantile omnipotence' (2008: 175). Others who note the pervasiveness of masochistic relating within human relationships include Brenner (1959, 1982), Berliner (1947), Cooper (2008) and Gabbard (2012). It is the propensity for it to become the dominant way of relating that renders it pathological, as Bergler (1949) noted.

survival. This child, to cope with this very difficult situation, internalises and represses the 'bad' aspect of their caregiver. In fact, Fairbairn says this is a very common scenario: 'It is impossible for anyone to pass through childhood without having bad objects which are internalized and repressed. Hence internalized bad objects are present in the minds of all of us at the deeper levels' (1996: 64–65). Where does it go, this 'bad' aspect? It cannot dissolve into the ether. No, the process of internalising the bad aspect means that the child locates this badness deep within *her own* psychological landscape. This is the price for keeping the parent 'good' and it is preferable, from the child's unconscious perspective, to take on the badness herself than to have to acknowledge that the caregiver is not good. Indeed, the pay-off that accrues from purging the parent of their badness is that the child feels more secure; but the cost is that the internalised badness is not magically erased. It remains within, unconscious, repressed, but there. Fairbairn has a memorable way of describing the process: 'I find it useful to speak of the bad objects as being, as it were, buried in the cellar of the mind behind a locked door which the patient is afraid to open for fear either of revealing the skeleton in the cupboard, or of seeing the ghosts by which the cellar is haunted' (1996: 65 n. 1). He gives a name to this internalised presence – the internal saboteur. The ego has to deal continually with this fifth columnist and its messages. This child, and the later adult, is thus kept busy with the building of defences 'hastily erected, and later laboriously consolidated' (1996: 65). Lavinia Gomez thus rightly and succinctly comments that internalising the bad object is 'damage limitation, paid for in internal conflict' (1997: 60).

While this internalisation of badness and its repression is costly for the child, Fairbairn notes the apparent logic of the action:

> it is better to be a sinner in a world ruled by God than to live in a world ruled by the Devil. A sinner in a world ruled by God may be bad; but there is always a certain sense of security to be derived from the fact that the world around is good – "God's in His heaven – All's right with the world!"; and in any case there is always a hope of redemption. In a world ruled by the Devil the individual may escape the badness of being a sinner; but he is bad because the world around him is bad. Further, he can have no sense of security and no hope of redemption. The only prospect is one of death and destruction. (1996: 66–67)

It is preferable, then, to be in submissive engagement with a loved object and feel bad about oneself, than to face the alternative: potentially not only rejection and withdrawal but existential loss. In the masochism that ensues, there is, at least, *relationship*. It might not be the healthiest, but it remains a much-needed presence in the life of the child. Fairbairn was convinced that the child, above all, desires *contact*, and will jump through all kinds of mental and emotional hoops in order to maintain intimacy. Greenberg and Mitchell provide a helpful explanation: 'If the parent offers only painful, unfulfilling contacts, the child does not abandon the parent to search for more pleasurable opportunities. The child needs the parent, so he integrates his relations with him on a suffering, masochistic basis' (1983: 173).

I will return to their mention of masochism in the sections below, but first, it is necessary to consider why we are compelled to repress and internalise bad objects when we could, at least as adults, reject them and walk away in a more empowering and resisting gesture. Fairbairn's answer to this is that a person, without therapeutic help, 'cannot get away from them. They force themselves upon him, and he cannot resist them because they have power over him. He is accordingly compelled to internalise them in an effort to control them' (1996: 67). Fairbairn's infant needs to keep his parent good at all costs, because the thought of a rejecting an unloving parent is too great to bear. The existential feelings of helplessness and lostness that would ensue are intolerable. As he says, a child cannot reject what it needs for survival: 'It is above all the need of the child for his parents, however bad they may appear to him, that compels him to internalize bad objects and it is because this need remains attached to them in the unconscious that he cannot bring himself to part with them. It is also his need for them that confers upon them their actual power over him' (1996: 68).

In my view, Fairbairn's comments on the repression of the bad object illuminate why Judges and Judges scholarship, particularly but not exclusively that written for believing audiences, maintains a defence of YHWH's essential goodness. Recall how YHWH, even when acting in ways antithetical to attachment, is preserved as the good father figure in Judges scholarship. YHWH's punishments are just, his hot anger is an appropriate response to Israel's insufferable unfaithfulness. Despite all the uncomfortable portrayals of YHWH's manoeuvrings – proxy agents, dubious advice, threats of abandonment – he retains a largely untainted reputation of a good, loving, endlessly merciful national deity. Even in that scene of exasperation in 10:6–16, replete with YHWH's anger and sarcasm, the divine character gets quickly recuperated with a reminder of how 'God has poured out his heart into the Israelites. In spite of his gracious compassionate and goodness to them, delivering them time and time again . . . they [Israel] have readily turned away' (Younger, 2002: 245). Such comments are typical of this need to 'keep YHWH good' which runs like a relentless theme through the commentaries. Perhaps its sheer relentlessness is testimony to the anxiety that lies beneath – the recognition that YHWH actually is not behaving well, has disturbing character traits and engages in ethically unsound practices. Or, as I will argue more strongly during this chapter, the relentlessness hints at an anxiety that suppresses a deep indignation at the unfulfillable demands this larger-than-life divine parent imposes.

It is not that YHWH's darker side is entirely ignored by biblical scholars; when dealing with other texts it has been long recognised that YHWH is loving and merciful but also punishing, abusing and killing[6]. Judges should not be an exception: both negative and positive aspects of YHWH's way of relating are on display and integrated into the story world yet the scholarly focus strangely remains hooked into repeating the message that YHWH is the *good* disciplinarian. This is despite the fact that there does not appear to be a repression of the 'bad' YHWH in the text itself. In fact, if we were to read Judges as Noll reads 1–2 Samuel, the 'bad' aspects of YHWH's behaviour come even more strongly to the forefront. For Noll, the educated recipients of the original Samuel scroll would have read YHWH as 'a capricious antipatron, a god who is never to be trusted' in a tale that focussed 'on the unpredictable and unexpected fates of the human protagonists' (2013: 139).[7] Readers,

---

[6] Scholars who highlight how YHWH operates for good and for evil in a broader range of texts include Exum (1992), Penchansky (1999), Gunn (1980) and Whybray (2000). I particularly admire the robust honesty in Blumenthal's (1993a) work that faces the consequences of this for believers. I also find Mazor's (1997) work illuminating. Commenting on Ps. 139, he astutely notes the complexities that arise from human relationships with the deity. The psalmist 'fervently utters excited admiration of God's fastidiously monitoring presence . . . [while] he feels hounded, surrounded by a suffocating snare that affords no relief' (1997: 262), alternating between 'appreciation and admiration' on the one hand, 'recoil and resentment' on the other (1997: 271).

[7] In his view, the text of Samuel has been misunderstood because scholars have read it with Deuteronomy in mind and as an integral part of the Deuteronomistic History. YHWH's character was never meant to be equated with the god of Deuteronomy in Noll's view, but once that unfortunate connection was made, 'Samuel gradually petrified into a work of sacred literature, eventually being saddled with the unenviable status of word of God' (2013: 135).

he claims, were 'expected to be repelled by this god' (2013: 139).[8] Why then have scholars not commented more directly on the repellent nature of YHWH's behaviour in this text without the immediate rush to exonerate it? Why are we repeatedly given health warnings at the beginning of commentaries only for them to dissolve into relief that such behaviour is all explainable?[9]

To a large extent this seems to be because the readers are manipulated into a position where YHWH's repellent traits are blamed on a pseudo-historical Israel. It is *their* recalcitrance, *their* waywardness, *their* 'pretend' repentance that provokes YHWH into fits of temper and the cycle of punishment. The enemies that tyrannise Israel are modes of discipline, agents of his jealous love. YHWH's actions are thereby sanctioned, understandable and warranted. However, what Fairbairn's ideas shed light on is how difficult it is to envisage and accept the possibility that a primary caretaker (in this case father/YHWH) acts badly *without due cause*. Keeping YHWH 'good' by heaping hostility and acrimony on 'bad' Israel can be understood as a psychological move, but to see how this functions we have to step outside traditional interpretations of Judges where it often has been a short step to move from the rhetoric of the scribe to confirming that YHWH *is* like this *in reality*. In such shifts, critical distance gets radically foreshortened and claims of YHWH's goodness are seen not as a rhetorical move by the scribe but descriptions of the divine. If we step outside the scribe's rhetoric, stop imagining that he is describing an ultimate reality that has somehow been grasped and put into human words, it creates space to recognise how this

---

[8] The differences between scholars writing for a series that has confessional allegiances and scholars who own no such allegiances are evident. It is possible that readers like Noll pick up on unpalatable psychological undercurrents of the text and, with no need to exonerate YHWH, hone in on the dysfunctional features of the text without reservation. Noll has no compunction to 'keep Yhwh good' in the way that can be seen so clearly in the majority of commentaries. Noll does not like this YHWH and he is free to say so. But I do not believe that the scribe is involved in deliberately besmirching the character of YHWH. There is a clear scribal attempt to keep YHWH good. The punitive disciplinary behaviour of this god, dictated by the terms of the covenant, may involve dubious practices but the scribe's confidence in the overall righteousness of YHWH seems not in doubt.

[9] See, for example, McCann's introduction to his commentary which notes the 'bad reputation' of Judges, how it 'seems to be an embarrassment to most church folk ... perhaps ... best passed over in silence' (2002: 1) before going on to commend the 'painful lessons' since they 'can serve to instruct us' (2002: 3). In an impressive exonerating move he continues: Israel experiences 'the destructive results of its own disloyalty and disobedience, but it also experienced a God who is faithful to a faithless people. In a word, Israel experienced a God who is gracious' (2002: 3).

apparent 'glimpse of an eternal truth' is part of an attempt to *keep YHWH good.* The reason why a scribe would do this becomes clear from Fairbairn's further comments on why he works with adult clients to release bad objects that have been introjected. However, to discuss this further it is necessary to return to Fairbairn's discussion.

As noted, Fairbairn argued that repression of the frightening and intolerable aspects of loved objects sets up the internal saboteur, which in turn provokes the continual work of the ego in erecting defences. The adult continues to repress, because the alternative is simply terrifying. Commenting on Fairbairn's work, Greenberg and Mitchell note how a child's continued attachment preserves hope 'for a fuller, more satisfying contact with the parent. The emptier the real exchange, the greater his devotion to the promising yet depriving features of his parents which he has internalized and seeks within. In addition, he preserves his childhood terror that if he disengages himself from these internal objects, he will find himself totally alone' (1983: 173). In Fairbairn's memorable way of putting it, it would mean being compelled to live in a world ruled by the Devil; i.e., recognising utter helplessness in the face of overwhelming and dangerous forces. In his view, it is immensely difficult to do the adult work of dealing with this but vital that it is done, for only by allowing the return of the repressed, identifying and acknowledging it, seeing it for what it is, can one call a pause to the constant defensive, exhausting work of keeping it all at bay and do the work that will cause the bad objects to 'lose their terror' (1996: 76). The psychotherapist, he writes, is thus 'the true successor to the exorcist 'whose work is 'the casting out of devils' (1996: 70). What then, is the terrifying spectre that might return to consciousness if reader (ancient and modern) is enabled to confront the 'bad' YHWH? What demons have to be faced? What have the narrator, and his audience of Judges scholars, colluded in repressing?

In my view, the surface spectre that has to be faced is that the divine hand intervening in history in ways that explain national experiences of humiliation and colonisation, or personal triumphs and disasters, is at best untameable and at worst indifferent and capricious. The deeper spectre is that the 'real' and efficacious deity, geared to the protection of his chosen few, is not there at all. Noll's work on Samuel implies that a critical evaluation of an indifferent deity could actually be the focus of an ancient scribe who writes a piece of philosophical storytelling for his fellow intellectuals. I'm not entirely convinced. The scribe's world is permeated by suprahuman activity and the references to the gods should, in my view, be taken far more seriously than Noll suggests. It must be daunting to entertain the likelihood that there is no accessible route to guaranteed justice, or, in an ancient world context, to envisage the possibility that natural phenomena such as earthquakes, tsunamis and volcanic eruptions are entirely indifferent events that have no divine purpose, or that brutal invasion by neighbouring armies has no rhyme nor reason. If a history of disaster, even a pseudo-self-constructed one, were to be seen as the uncaring result of capricious fate, acted out upon an undeserving Israel, then the story world of Judges would be very different, marked by a lack of justice and Israel's complete lack of control. This seems unthinkable for the scribe who is unable to entertain the prospect that YHWH (and the forces he supposedly commands) is indifferent to Israel, entirely oblivious to their presence – such a prospect would be terrifying. In the helpless position of the child who cannot face the existential crisis, he plunges the recognition of the 'bad' aspects of his caregiver into the deep unconscious. And so, YHWH's loving concern for Israel is emphasised again and again, his loyalty and devotion reinforced, in a will to *make it so*. And if the cost of maintaining hope that YHWH is, after all, loving and on their side, means surrendering autonomy, 'forgetting' the rage that inevitably bubbles up and, instead, acknowledging one's own pseudo-badness, then it simply has to be paid. Of course, the difficult prospect the scribe recognises, along with all other wisdom writers, is that such submission and self-abrogation does not necessarily result in the favour of the gods. As Eli will say in 1 Sam. 3:18: 'he is YHWH. He will do whatever seems best to him'.[10]

Fairbairn's theories thus help elucidate how the drive to keep YHWH good by claiming an ultimate care and concern is a by-product of repressing the unpalatable notion that YHWH and what he represents may simply be, well – bad! Instead, YHWH is salvaged and exonerated from the dubious and harmful actions that nonetheless remain clearly present in the text. Judges commentators, widely adopting the scribe's tactic of keeping YHWH good at the expense of a constructed 'past Israel', continue to reinforce the repression. To bury the intolerable thought YHWH becomes bad-but-only-because-he-loves. Note, for example, how this results in commentarial assertive

---

[10] While commentators often take this as a pious remark from Eli who humbly acquiesces to the divine will, Eslinger recognises a more profound statement of cynicism hidden 'beneath the guise of piety and submission to the Almighty' (1985: 155). I am with Eslinger on this.

language claiming that the deity's behaviour comes from love, grace and passion. Thus 2:16–18 is described as a passage that affirms 'God's grace like the arms of a mother or father surrounding wayward Israel even when they continue in sin' (Hamlin, 1990: 60). Martin simply rules out any question that divine abandonment is even possible: YHWH goes 'out on a limb' in a way that bespeaks his 'passion for his people, his jealousy for their affection ... "Forever" means he is not a fickle God nor a flippant God, nor a capricious God' (2008: 160).

Such commentarial reaction is understandable. If YHWH was just a character in a Greek story world, the psychological games played out between this deity and his chosen children would probably be of no more concern to us than the stories of Odysseus and the gods. However, faithful readers do not have the luxury of reading Judges as they would Homer. Judges is a text read as scripture by the faithful, believed to contain an insight into divine–human relations. But what Fairbairn's insights highlight is the cost involved in reading Judges and swallowing the rhetoric. The strategy it uses to keep YHWH good incur potentially damaging consequences: seeing the self as to blame for perceived evidences of divine displeasure and continual repression of the possibility that gods are anything but just and loving. Of course this also prevents the worse spectre: that fate is all there is and that humans need to abandon dependence upon the notion that the gods exist. Freud perceived how hard it is for humans to let go of God projections. He includes the 'dark power of Destiny' in the list of authority figures 'which only the fewest of us are able to look upon as impersonal' (1924: 281) and suspects that 'all who transfer the guidance of the world to Providence, to God, or to God and Nature ... still look upon these ultimate and remotest powers as a parental couple, in a mythological sense, and believe themselves linked to them by libidinal ties' (1924: 281).[11] Further exploration of Freud's views on this subject, however, is beyond the remit of this study.

To understand the function of masochism in Fairbairn's work, a more detailed excursus into his understanding of repression and how it affects the central ego is necessary. As noted above, repression

---

[11] It is not appropriate to engage in speculative thought about how the Judges scribe's God image might have been informed by his experience of father figures. We can, however, analyse the images produced and analyse them for health, pathology and as important influences upon subsequent generations who inherit them as powerful collective archetypal sources for thoughts about God.

involves sending the 'bad object' (the negative aspects of the primary caregiver) down to the cellar of the unconscious. This repressed bad object has two facets: 'on the one hand, it frustrates; and, on the other, it tempts and allures' (1996: 111). So, the infant has now internalised 'an object which not only continues to frustrate his need, but also continues to whet it' (1996: 111).[12] This affects a person's central ego for parts of the ego remain attached to both exciting and rejecting facets of the bad object and go down to the cellar with it. The *libidinal ego* is the name given to the splintered part that remains attached to the exciting aspect of the bad object, while the *antilibidinal* ego remains attached to the rejecting aspect. Gomez's examples are helpful here. She imagines the libidinal ego/exciting object configuration in terms of the 'painful yearning' one might experience when 'waiting endlessly by the phone for the lover who had promised to ring, but who we know from experience will not' (1997: 62). The antilibidinal ego is the part that ingenuously asserts lack of any interest in whether or not the telephone rings at all. We find it in the 'I never wanted her anyway' claim, 'berating our pathetic neediness of the tantalising exciting object whom we attempt to render worthless' (1997: 64). It is '"the anti-wanting I", the aspect of the self that is contemptuous of neediness', 'the cynical, angry self which is too dangerously hostile for us to acknowledge' (1997: 63).

In Fairbairn's scheme we have thus a threefold ego structure: a central ego and two subsidiary parts that are attached to the repressed bad object.[13] He describes the central ego and its splintered parts as follows. The central ego is the 'primary and dynamic structure, from which ... the other mental structures are subsequently derived' (1996: 106). The libidinal ego has a 'more infantile character ... a lesser degree of organization and a smaller measure of adaption to reality and ... a greater devotion to internalized objects' (1996: 106). The antilibidinal ego, through 'despising rather than acknowledging our neediness ... ensure[s] that we neither seek nor get what we want' (Gomez, 1997: 63). This antilibidinal ego is part

---

[12] Indeed, as Fairbairn notes: 'its essential "badness" consists precisely in the fact that it combines allurement with frustration' (1996: 111).

[13] Later, he posited an ego with a threefold subsidiary structure, for once 'the exciting and rejecting objects are split off, there remains a nucleus of the original object shorn of its over-exciting and over-frustrating elements' (Fairbairn, 1996: 178). As this third aspect is acceptable there is no need for repression and he suggests this 'is the object which I now regard as providing the nucleus round which the super-ego ... is built up' (1996: 179).

of that internal saboteur which is unrelentingly hostile to the desiring libidinal ego. A state of inner, largely unconscious, turmoil is thus established.[14]

An illustration helps to explain this conflict between antilibidinal and libidinal ego. Consider again the child whose love and trust in the primary caregiver has been met with experiences of rejection or withdrawal. Despite longing for intimacy, the child experiences a feeling of not being loved. If the child objects, he risks intensifying the rejection and thus increasing the 'badness' of the primary caregiver. An objection, since it overtly makes a criticism, also compromises the child's desire for the caregiver's 'goodness' for the caregiver might consequently 'love him less' (Fairbairn, 1996: 113) and act in overtly negative ways. But if the child expresses his need/ love for the caregiver, this might be 'equivalent to discharging his libido into an emotional vacuum' which would be 'devastating' (1996: 113). An older child may experience this as 'intense humiliation over the depreciation of his love' while at the deeper level 'the experience is one of shame over the display of needs which are disregarded or belittled' by which 'he feels reduced to a state of worthlessness, destitution or beggardom. His sense of his own value is threatened; and he feels bad in the sense of "inferior"' (1996: 113). The child is thus in an impossible situation: 'If, one the one hand, he expresses aggression, he is threatened with loss of his good object, and, if, on the other hand, he expresses libidinal need, he is threatened with loss of his libido (which for him constitutes his own goodness) and ultimately with loss of the ego structure which constitutes himself' (1996: 113).

So how might the child deal with the dangers of expressing feeling in the face of rejection when he cannot afford to reduce the primary caregiver to insignificance? Fairbairn's belief is that the ambivalence is dealt with by the internal saboteur's attack upon the libidinal ego in order to dampen the desire and love for the mother. But, simultaneously, the libidinal ego sees the object threatened by this attack and this increases his commitment to it. And so, the battle rages at the unconscious level between one part of the split ego and the other, a state of affairs that gives rise to the melancholic or the schizoid position. If the aggression towards the caregiver is in focus, it leads to the depressive or melancholic state 'for whom the disposal of aggression presents greater difficulties than the disposal of libido'

---

[14] He posits that the central ego uses the energy of this inner turmoil to keep the two splintered parts of the ego deep within the unconscious.

(1996: 114). The schizoid position, on the other hand, derives from the need to express desire (but have it rejected) which manifests in a sense of futility. In Fairbairn's view, we are all schizoid to some extent for 'it would take a bold man to claim that his ego was so perfectly integrated as to be incapable of revealing any evidence of splitting at the deepest levels,' (1996: 8). We are mostly unconscious of this but it can be recognised in those moments when we feel artificial, or in experiences he describes as 'the plate-glass feeling' or 'feelings of familiarity with the unfamiliar' (1996: 5). What we are dealing with in such moments are feelings of pointlessness, hopelessness, and failing to see the point. Gomez concurs: where need and anger have been cut off the central ego will feel empty, experienced as 'a sense of emptiness, deadness and futility' ... 'feeling unreal and cut off, as though separated from the world and their own feelings by a glass screen' (1997: 66).

These psychological processes leave us subject to a sadomasochistic dance. The libidinal ego is so obstinately tied to the exciting object that it puts itself in continual danger of being defeated (the obstinacy relates to the impossibility of giving up on the caregiver. The child cannot afford to do this). Moreover, the emptier the relationship the more his devotion to this cycle will endure. The battle going on within the psyche means that 'defeat is orchestrated again and again to perpetuate the longing and need of the libidinal ego for the fulfilment of the promise of the exciting object' (Greenberg and Mitchell, 1983: 173–174). Greenberg and Mitchell also highlight very clearly the costs of this dance for adult life given that these orchestrations continue long beyond childhood:

> Destructive patterns of integrating relations with others and experiencing life are perpetuated—because beneath the pain and the self-defeating relations and organizations of experience lie ancient internal attachments and allegiances to early significant others. The re-creation of the sorrow, suffering, and defeat are forms of renewal of and devotion to these ties. Reluctance to betray these attachments through new relations and allegiances impedes constructive change in living and results in a central and often the most intransigent resistance in psychoanalysis. (1983: 174)

Masochism, then, for Fairbairn, indicates something askew in the relationship with external objects. In his view, it 'should be regarded as in no small measure attempts to salvage natural emotional relationships which have broken down' (1996: 40). In order to unpack this in greater detail I turn now to three key aspects of masochism as defined by theorists who work within a relational framework. At the end of each section, I apply the theory discussed to the relationship between YHWH and Israel.

Key Aspects of Relational Masochism and Application to the God-Talk in Judges

Narcissistic Injury

Clinical accounts of masochism regularly refer to a narcissistic wound that has been inflicted on the analyst's client. Narcissism, in everyday contemporary language, usually carries negative connotations of egocentrism, arrogance and preoccupation with the self. In psychoanalytic terminology, however, narcissism can refer to the 'libidinal investment in the self' and be 'a healthy and normal part of development. To be able to find oneself lovable, means the future ability to have successful relations with others' (Smith et al., 2012: 189).[15]

When analysts refer to a narcissistic wound or injury, they have in mind damage done to the person's sense of self. When a child develops she has to shift from a state of omnipotent fantasy to a recognition that, actually, she hasn't magically conjured the mother to attend to her every need; the mother is a separate entity with her own life and interests. This is a devastating blow to the child's narcissistic self: 'It seems intolerable to the narcissism of adults and children alike that the limits a mother sets . . . might actually proceed from the mother's assertion of her own separate selfhood' (Benjamin, 1990: 82), but the growing child has to learn to see the caregiver as an independent other. A healthy individual moves through this stage as their delusion of omnipotence slowly fades and they begin the process of separation from the mother–child dyad.[16] In his helpful paper illustrating the development and traits of the narcissistic-masochistic character, Cooper notes how pain is an

---

[15] It tips into narcissistic personality disorder in 'an individual who overestimates their attractiveness or desirability in some way regardless of the lack of outside affirmation and consequently needs a great deal of admiration from others' (Smith et al., 2012: 190).

[16] The talk of necessary separation can be over-stated. Benjamin rightly recasts the emphasis on the need for separation and individuation as the need to develop mutual recognition. It is 'not how we become free of the other, but how we actively engage and make ourselves known in relation to the other' (1990: 18).

inevitable aspect of human development and is shared by all of us. In order to come to terms with the external world and negotiate our deal with it, frustrations and painful experiences inevitably occur. These are our narcissistic injuries: there is damage to our self-esteem and 'the sense of magical omnipotent control' – this is, in his view, the 'prototype of narcissistic humiliation.' (2008: 127). The response is to try and fend off the threat to self-esteem and deal with the terribly uncomfortable feeling of helplessness in the face of being restricted. This is a familiar route for all humans but it gets distorted when or if the 'early narcissistic humiliation is excessive'. Here, 'the object is perceived as excessively cruel and refusing' (2008: 128) and the person concerned would find it very difficult to assert him or herself. In such cases 'being disappointed, or refused, becomes the *preferred* mode of narcissistic assertion to the extent that narcissistic and masochistic distortions dominate the character' (2008: 128).

In summary, narcissistic injury is a blow to one's sense of self. Masochistic patterns of behaviour are an attempt to heal that wound; an attempt to deal with the extremely distressing emotional situation of finding oneself subject to the controlling or limiting actions of others, or of finding oneself emanating deep love for a primary caregiver only to have it devalued. Without a strategy to heal the situation the affected person would feel helpless and hopeless. A child who looks to their parent to mirror love, joy and engagement, but finds instead criticism, rejection and withdrawnness is not only disappointed but experiences a profound sense of anxiety – facing the terrifying prospect of being unprotected and unloved.

Berliner locates this basic conflict as the cause of masochistic behaviour. He posits a relationship between two parties: one with libidinal needs and one who is unable, for whatever reason, to respond appropriately to these needs. He is known for the phrase 'the bid for affection' where the one with libidinal needs stakes their claim upon the other. We have already noted in Fairbairn's work how a child takes on the badness herself in order to keep the caregiver good. Berliner adds a note of externalisation to this: the child allows himself to *become* unlovable in order to become the child the caregiver externalises.[17] He self-sabotages in the hope

---

[17] Externalisation occurs when a person takes an uncomfortable aspect of the self, such as being disorganised or lazy, and disowns it by locating precisely those traits in their partner, child or boss, etc. When a primary caregiver does this he prompts the

that, in the down-playing of the self, the person might emerge who his caregiver *could* love. Berliner puts it in these terms: 'he is stigmatized with unwantedness and displays his stigma as his bid for affection' (1947: 468). This bid is thus part of a defensive strategy adopted in order to manage a profoundly difficult situation. The child has a fundamental need for love, security and attachment and to gain that security and keep the relationship alive the child will adapt, regardless of how dysfunctional that adaptation might be.

The later work of Kerry and Jack Novick support Berliner's proposals. They describe how 'all the masochistic cases' they have worked with 'were intermittently loved and cared for, but in a way which undermined confidence' (1996: 53). The mirroring that helps a child to thrive has gone wrong: 'mothers smiled only when they emerged from their depressed or anxious state and felt like smiling, not in response to the child's smile' (1996: 53). In their explanation of the essence of masochism, they recount the story of Nicole. At four months of age, she had tried to engage with the mother while being spoon-fed. However, a non-responsive mother 'literally scraped the smile off Nicole's face with the spoon, until the sixth bite was followed by a frown ... In our observations we could see the next step, in which the mother externalized her feelings of failure onto the baby: the mother then made clear that she found Nicole an unpleasant girl' (1995: 241). They go on to discuss how Nicole's later pain-seeking behaviours were her way of adapting to the malattunement between herself and her mother, and represented 'an attempt to substitute for the withdrawal of cathexis by the mother' (1995: 242). Nicole's story calls to mind Winnicott's understanding, discussed in Chapter 1, that finding recognition, love and joy reflected back in the parent's gaze is vital for healthy development. He also argued that a good relationship involves keeping parental demands

---

child to devalue themselves, taking on the externalised qualities. As Novick and Novick make clear, this maintains family equilibrium (for with externalisation, all the actors in the family are likely to be affected), and prevents the alternative, failing to accept the caregiver's externalisation which 'would leave him prey to the primitive terror of abandonment' (1996: 121). But the child is between a rock and a hard place, because accepting the externalised qualities leads to a devaluation of the self and resultant inner pain and conflict, difficulty maintaining a modicum of self-esteem and a compromised central ego. The Novicks use a strong phrase to describe such strategies: a parent's overbearing externalisation onto a child 'violates the child's selfhood' (1996: 152). They concur with Shengold's (1989) description of it as 'soul murder'.

in balance with the child's need for omnipotence. When external impingements and parental intrusion or demands arrive too soon and too relentlessly, the child over-develops the False Self. The Novicks concur, speculating that such children 'may have become aware too soon of their dependence on their mothers and felt deeply their inability to exert any control over the social realm. They turn to pathological solutions as an adaptation to this dilemma' (1995: 242). What their client stories reveal is a sad state of affairs where a profound mismatch has occurred between a child's needs and the caregiver's inability to meet them. Narcissistic injury results.

When the book of Judges is read with these insights in mind, a new way of looking at the narratorial voice emerges; the underlying bid for YHWH's affection and attention comes out of hiding. Previous Judges scholarship made some progress in recognising this when it drew a strong distinction between the tone of a rather sanctimonious 'editor' and the lighter tone of the stories themselves. However, for well over a century this distinction was mostly accounted for by theories of redaction. Wellhausen (1885: 229–236) describes the pedantic, sombre, pious tone and 'clerical instincts' of the Deuteronomist compared with the lively, earthy, comic and entertaining qualities of the judge stories within the cyclical framework (which he attributed to pre-existing material). Other scholars identified a voice of authoritative dogmatism (Polzin), or more recently, a master narrative undercut by the voice of trauma (Janzen), both discussed in Chapter 2. However, what has not been adequately recognised is the less visible *psychological* function of this narratorial voice. It presents the speaker as the new model Israel, the star pupil, YHWH's ideal child – loyal, obedient, submissive and encouraging his readers to engage with his identity formation project and willingly sacrifice autonomy and authority in order to retain a continued and effective relationship with YHWH. While the tone appears to be assertive and commanding, it is actually the voice of the compliant child, who, in acquiescence to parental demands, overdevelops the False Self. The 'good boy' rescues himself from potential parental rejection and withdrawal by accommodating himself to the parent's attitudes, expectations and view of the world even if it runs counter to his personal experience and even though this comes at a high personal cost. This is the 'good boy' who also recognises that overdevelopment of the False Self is somehow necessary to maintain the parent's narcissistic

equilibrium and goodwill. Repression, externalisation and masochism are at work here.[18]

The resulting aggrandisement of YHWH is typical of externalisation and of masochism being used as a defence reaction. Menaker
(1953) saw how masochism goes hand-in-hand with self-devaluation.
She offers the clinical example of a 25-year-old woman who 'had
been the possession, the extension, the tool of her mother from the
beginning of life' (1953: 211). It was a case where the woman's
accomplishments 'served the narcissistic gratification of the mother,
not the ego development and satisfaction of the daughter' (1953:
215). The consequences were profound. The daughter's fragile and
weak ego had no independent life, because she was defined in her
mother's terms. In order to keep the bond, the daughter had
repressed the mother's 'basically unloving attitude' for, had she not
done so, then aggressive feelings might break through, which would
prompt the mother's retaliation and possible abandonment. 'To
avoid separation, therefore, the mother image had to be maintained
as good and loving, and all frustration experienced in the mother
relationship was attributed to the worthlessness of the self' (1953:
215). Commentators on Judges (myself included) have often identified the glorification of YHWH as a major theme; exhibited when
the narrator praises the deity's supernatural involvement in battles,
his manipulation of situations and so forth. The trouble is that this
ignores or continues to repress how emphases in a text have deeper
psychological functions. While biblical scholars talk of glorification,
psychologists talk of *idealisation* where an individual may get 'ele-
vated to the point of perfection, aggrandized, and exalted' with
'accompanying feelings' of 'admiration, awe, veneration, worship,
adoration, and enthrallment' (Moore and Fine, 1990: 91).

The obsequious tone I hear in the narratorial voice can manifest
itself simultaneously as assertive and commanding – but this is the
result of *identification* with the primary caregiver. Berliner notes how
'analysis regularly reveals that the person feels … he will gain the
love and approval of the [loved] object when he expresses aggressive
trends which copy those of the object' (1947: 468). The narratorial

---

[18] It is difficult to apply notions of externalisation directly to YHWH because he is
a constructed character with a script provided by the scribe, not a caregiver on an
analyst's couch. Accordingly, we need a rather convoluted way of thinking about it;
the story world represented by the scribe externalises qualities he despises by describing it as antithetical to his character YHWH and by constructing a past Israel who
embodies those behaviours.

voice in Judges that constructs and condemns a past 'bad' Israel while sycophantically aligning itself with the expectations of YHWH, conforms to what Berliner would expect: the masochist becoming the person the caregiver projects. The voice commentators identify as Deuteronomic or Deuteronomistic is identified with the caregiver's agenda and disciplinary practices, and accepts punishment for past misdemeanours. In fact, it is not just that the narrator and YHWH's voices are aligned. It is more accurate to acknowledge that YHWH's voice is constructed by the scribe. It does not descend from the heavens, translated into period Hebrew – it is speech written for a character who is being constructed as divine. So the situation is more accurately described in terms of YHWH and his messengers voicing the privileged narratorial viewpoint that the reader is supposed to 'hear' as divine. The identification of the 'model' Israel with YHWH's agenda is thus hardly surprising. What is happening is that the reader is being asked to align with 'YHWH's' perspective and identify with him and feel a concomitant repulsion for this 'past' Israel and its 'sinfulness', regarding Israel's punishment as fully deserved.

Citing his 1947 paper, Berliner writes: 'The need for punishment ... is the acceptance, in form and content, of the drive to punish which operates in the love object, resulting in punishing oneself and in punishing others, thus developing one's own drive to punish and passing it on to the next generation. The identification with the parental drive to punish seems to be the strongest foundation of our moral standards ... It accounts for the universality of moral masochism in our culture' (1995: 353). Punishment is, of course, what Judges provides over and over again. With each narrative Israel is accosted by some new enemy and in divine visitations Israel is warned of greater punishment to come; i.e., complete loss of land and defeat. Throughout, Israel is enjoined to become the model child that the narratorial voice/YHWH demands, to become the new Israel that 'YHWH' desires. The multiplicity of examples thus serves to drive the point home.

The scribe's identification with YHWH is subsequently seen in the encouragement to treat others in ways thought to be commensurate with the caregiver's ways of treating external objects. YHWH hates Canaanites, the scribe hates Canaanites, the reader should hate Canaanites. There is a certain satisfaction for the scribe in this; a benefit that accrues from submitting to the parental authority from whom 'the masochist borrows his authority for the drive to punish'

(Berliner, 1947: 468). First, it feels good to be in the role of aggressor rather than victim; now the scribe can vent some of that pent-up aggression (the lost rage) in the satire and ethnic humour deployed against despised enemies (as seen so clearly in the demise of Eglon and Sisera), while also venting it against his 'past' Israel and their 'sins'. Second, he is indemnified by having his aggression sanctioned. After all, he is only carrying out the disciplinary role he is 'meant' to undertake. Third, it gives him a feeling self-esteem, potency and agency. This is probably best seen in the satirical content of Judges. In psychological terms, a joke is never 'just a joke'; it is a vehicle for aggression. The satirical jibes directed at foreigners and the scribe's 'past' ancestors mock both because doing so places the scribe in overall control of the situation. As Garrick (2006) observes, dehumanising humour can be a way of taking the fright and danger out of a situation and change the balance of power so that the person doing the ridiculing has some measure of control. This explains why the stories in Judges contain comedy and also why it is often of such a crude variety.

The Omnipotent Delusion

Chapter 1 noted Winnicott's argument that healthy development is dependent on a primary caregiver's ability to know when and how to tail off their interventionist care so that the child's illusion of omnipotence does not suddenly fall off a cliff. In discussions of masochism, the issue of omnipotence returns to centre stage but in a different way. The delusion of omnipotence that characterises early childhood is that of a 'happy, contented infant, safe in mother's arms and surrounded by adoring adults' and content in the 'delusion that he is the center of the universe with the power to make everyone meet all his needs' (Novick and Novick, 1996: 50–51). This is in stark contrast to the delusion of omnipotence found in masochistic clients. In place of the infant's blissful state is the inner, often unconscious, 'raging, hostile tyrant whose behavior is fuelled by envy' in order to compensate 'for feelings of helplessness and shame' (Novick and Novick, 1996: 51). Those feelings of helplessness derive from the kind of malattunement already described above and from experiences of caregiver intrusiveness, resulting in a child's lack of the crucial self-esteem that comes from a consistently encouraging caregiver. The Novicks discuss how and why resulting feelings have to be managed and explain why omnipotent thought becomes a solution that can offer a defence from feelings of 'intense helpless rage' (1996: 54).

A fantasy of omnipotence offers the delusion of being in control. The 'raging hostile tyrant' is the client who provokes needed others to inflict pain. (It is important to recall that pain in this situation is not sought for itself, but as evidence that a relationship exists). As Berliner notes: 'The child does not love suffering or ill-treatment – nobody does – but because it loves the person who gives it, the ill-treatment is libidinized' (1947: 461). It is from provoking the caretaker to react, however punitively, that the masochist gains a sense of being noticed, being in control and, vitally, being *in relationship*.

A brief digression into the work of other theorists is necessary at this point. Anna Ornstein helps to explain why provocative situations are engineered in this repeated fashion within masochistic relationships. First, she returns us to the importance of good mirroring experiences: the 'phase-appropriate recognition and validation (mirroring) of a child's growing capacities' (2012: 123). Lack of these experiences, together with any additional negative and traumatic experiences, gives rise to an unvoiceable narcissistic rage. As it is not safe to express this rage, infants and young children employ '"pathological accommodations" that function as protection "against intolerable pain and existential anxiety"' (2012: 124, citing Brandchaft, 2007: 667). The repetitive cycle comes into play as the child, and later the adult, manipulates situations so that they can play the victim and become 'injustices collectors'. The rage that should be directed against the primary caregiver is thus indirectly focussed on frustrating others.

The phrase 'injustice collectors' comes from Bergler's (1949) monograph which details the process in more detail. For Bergler, what we see in the provocations of masochistic behaviour is a *pseudo*-aggression. A person deliberately, but unconsciously, provokes a painful experience such as a relationship break-up, being abandoned, being refused, in order to play the victim. 'Injustice collectors' are those who use a '*provocative technique* applied unconsciously to achieve the anticipated kick in the jaw' where 'the outer world has to be provoked to administer the defeat' (1949: 13, emphasis original). He describes the clinical pictures as follows:

(1)   'I shall repeat the masochistic wish of being deprived by my mother, by creating or misusing situations in which some substitute of my mother-image shall refuse my wishes.'

(2)   'I shall not be conscious of my wish to be refused and denied, nor of my initial provocation of refusal. I shall see only that I am justified in righteous indignation to fight in self-defense the meanness of my self-created adversary.'

(3)   'Afterwards I shall pity myself because such injustice can happen only to poor little me, and enjoy once more psychic masochistic pleasure' (1949: 67–68).

However, this pattern of behaviour is not primarily about pain, contrarily and paradoxically it concerns the diminution of deeper more distressing feelings of loss, abandonment. Psychic masochism may induce punishment but pain is not *consciously* sought. It is actually about trying to offset feelings of loss, invisibility and existential nothingness. For Bergler it is vital not to treat the presenting symptom but to identify the unconscious wish/defence that lies beneath.

Cooper came to a similar conclusion in his discussion of the narcissistic-masochistic character. The provocation, in his view, is not primarily directed towards a 'reunion with a loving and caring mother' but is oriented towards 'fantasised control' (2008: 128). One of his clinical vignettes illustrates how a mother, narcissistically obsessed with maintaining her own beauty, ignored her daughter's need for love and affection. The daughter's response was to surrender her desire for affection and, instead, libidinise rejection. In later life this set up a pattern of failing relationships that repeated the experience of painful abandonment, because this gave her 'the hidden gratification of narcissistic control and masochistic satisfaction' (2008: 132).

In short, provocation gives the person a sense of control over the situation. This restores self-esteem and pleasure even though it comes at the cost of punishment; i.e., let the primary caregiver hate me and let me find a way of handling this so that I don't feel overwhelmed but, rather, in control. The narcissistic element of this is the feeling of being able to cope and be strong; the masochistic element lies in acceptance of bitter–sweet suffering. Cooper concludes that masochism and narcissism are utterly interwoven. 'Neither can exist without the other. Interpreting masochistic behavior produces narcissistic mortification, and interpreting narcissistic defenses produces feelings of masochistic victimization, self-pity, and humiliation' (2008: 137).

Returning now to the Novicks, it is evident that their clinical experience is broadly similar. One of several examples that they provide is of a daughter who has a most intrusive controlling mother. If the daughter is able to provoke the mother's anger then the daughter feels a measure of control. She is the one who has instigated the negative response and thereby becomes the powerful 'I' and, by continuing to experience pain (of the mother's reaction), the daughter feels both in control and *attached*. Moreover, by experiencing pain the daughter can conveniently and simultaneously position herself as victim and sufferer, one who is misunderstood, targeted (the injustice collector noted above). This 'poor me' posturing can sanction the daughter's experience of feeling of anger and resentment, and also of fear. Questioning what this daughter is really afraid of, the Novicks answer: 'The terrifying narcissistic humiliation she feared when she noted seeing herself or others as they really were' (1996: 65). Or, from their conclusion of a different case study, the real fear is the 'helpless terror and panic ... at the idea of meaning nothing' (1996: 67). The omnipotent delusion of masochism offers a restored kind of self-esteem, but it is rooted only in a delusional fantasy of control. For analysts, this is apparently a very difficult thing to treat, because patients feel that if this sense of control is taken away they have to face an intolerable existential crisis – a feeling that the Novicks' patients describe as 'being dead' (1996: 69). It is not surprising, therefore, that Menaker had earlier commented that the masochistic defence may well be a necessary means of survival – the ego might have 'no alternative reaction' (1953: 216). In one of their clinical accounts, the Novicks explain how Mary's attempts to commit suicide were, in fact, attempts 'to murder the mother inside her' (1996: 166). The aggression, the rage, so difficult to deal with effectively, is defended against and expressed by attacks on one's own body. Here is clear trauma; not the kind of trauma that is being promoted in biblical studies, the trauma of warfare and exile, but a psychic trauma where the ego is overwhelmed.

Thinking through this in relation to Judges, the repeated cycle of provocation comes into focus not as an example of Israel's perpetual hopeless waywardness which kind, loyal and super-enduring YHWH has to deal with, but as a mechanism of human control. Israel's behaviour that can send him into fits of rage and propel him into repeated acts of punishment just as their cries can induce him to rescue them. Israel can make YHWH react. He reacts badly – as Lasine says, they 'push his buttons' (2002: 47, n. 27) – but that is precisely the point, it means that Israel is *noticed.* But Lasine focuses so strongly on YHWH that he overlooks the scribe, the character-master, the way in which pressing YHWH's buttons might be a defence mechanism used with a hugely over-intrusive caregiver in order to maintain, not push away, relationship, and to feel in control. In their repeated serving of rival caregivers (the Baals, Asherah), Israel make YHWH react and the game is kept in play. The scribe plays with the prospect of divine abandonment and with Israel's desertion, but crisis after crisis is averted in order to maintain connection between the two parties. *The thing that is constant is the game itself.* The repetitive feature of such reaction-provoking scenarios chimes with the later clinical experience of Novick and Novick who note self-destructive patterns of behaviour that 'cycle repeatedly with no real change or growth' (2012: 52).

Before leaving this discussion of omnipotent delusion, it is worth thinking more concretely about this scribe who has the audacity to describe the words, actions, thoughts and passions of YHWH. It is quite a tour de force to conjure a script for a deity, but, in so doing, the scribe maintains his own delusion of omnipotence. Israel's importance as the focus of a deity's attention is maintained and the terrible unfaceable threat – that Israel means nothing in the larger world – is averted. In reality, Israel may be small fry on the larger imperial stage in which other nations dominate, but in the story world of Judges, Israel and YHWH are the centre of the universe. When all is well between this god and his people then those other nations are as naught. Hard-pressed though they are, in dire straits, Israel is repeatedly rescued. A clever trick with jars, trumpets and a slogan, or with double-entendre and tricky doors, or a woman handy with tent pegs and a heavily outnumbered Israel can bring down a larger, far better-equipped, brutal enemy. This is the stuff of fantasy. And it is the stuff of masochistic fantasy.

The scribe's scenario implies that any experimentation with auton-omy or independence (say, to choose rival gods) threatens YHWH, but this is typical of the 'provocation' that masochists unconsciously deploy. By provoking YHWH, he is kept in the relational dance. Then the scribe supplies YHWH with a helpless (self)-victim – the wayward Israel of 'past history' on whom all the divine frustrations can land. This Judges material, however, tells us nothing about any 'real' YHWH, but a whole lot about *the scribe's* grandiose delusion that he can 'help' YHWH maintain power. The projection of omnipotence onto YHWH enables the scribe to produce a morally simplified and thereby controllable world in which judgements about others are always absolute (and serve the scribe's narcissistic needs). YHWH becomes the lovingly authoritarian parental figure who can safely be idealised. The narrator's construction of the 'bad' Israel and the way in which he victimises the self in this overt, repeated and stern criticism of them, means that he can keep YHWH on side, placate YHWH because here is the scribe being the obedient, submissive child offering YHWH a scapegoat, a past Israel upon whom the disciplinary action can be taken. But in so doing the scribe is being in control; he is the one with the story world; the one who has the power or the shrewdness to pacify YHWH. In this story world, the relationship between YHWH and Israel is the real drama – not the apparent vicissitudes of history which are, after all, used by 'YHWH' to keep Israel in relationship with him. This is a huge, fantastic, psychological drama in which the cosmic attachment between YHWH and Israel plays out within a supposed national history. The vast scale is quite incredible.

Repressed Rage

There is an inevitable rage at the core of masochistic relating. A child's primary caregiver dictates the terms of coexistence, sets out the demands and, in effect, controls and owns the child. Faced with thwarted drives, the child both provokes and kowtows for the sake of a continued relationship and security, but beneath that is rage. Analysts have long commented on how unaware masochists are of their own aggression. Freud comments, for example, on the excessively stern super-ego possessed by masochistic clients and, yet, while submitting to the harsh scripts of the super-ego which hamstrings them with an overly strong moral conscience 'they are not conscious of this ultramorality' (1924: 282). More recently, the Novicks (1995: 254) have commented on the many years of analysis needed before a client can begin the work of acknowledging their inner rage. This is not surprising, however, when one considers how subject it is to severe repression.

Berliner indicates how repression of inner rage is vital when one fears that any expression of it would lead to the loss of the primary caregiver. However, while it has to be deeply submerged to the extent that masochists themselves remain oblivious to its presence, it manifests itself in a number of ways. It finds expression in the ongoing manufacturing of provocative scenarios to which the other party is compelled to react. As we have seen, this enables the masochist to self-present as both 'victim' and 'troublemaker'; 'he is sinned against and sinning' (Berliner, 1995: 355).

Theodor Reik, an American psychoanalyst, trained by Freud, regularly engaged with biblical texts as he worked through his theories of masochism.[19] In an engaging study that makes up for what it lacks in biblical scholarship with sharp psychological insight, Reik picks up the deep, profound rage that these provocations mask. He argues that the real 'sin' that lurks beneath the prophetic condemnation of surface 'sins' is actually that of revolt: 'Behind the sin of idolatry and of worship of pagan cults the sin of aggression and attack against Jahveh is concealed. Not desertion, not apostasy was the real crime of which the prophets accused the Jews, but revolt against their God and the moral commandments He had given' (1958: 181).

In Reik's view, the intrusive demands of YHWH were insufferable and entirely unrealistic. By prohibiting a range of behaviours, and outlawing a range of desires, a reaction is inevitably produced – a resentment so strong and fierce that it would inevitably provoke feelings of national guilt. However, this gets repressed when the prophets offer Israel a means of propitiating the guilt felt concerning their resentment by implying that other things – cultic infringements, worship of other gods – are the problem. Thus, when YHWH's spokespeople suggest that national disaster is divine punishment, then the national sense of guilt gets assuaged, but only in a pseudo or secondary manner. It is not lancing the real boil, only the guilt that arises from not following laws and from committing the apostasy that arouses divine wrath. But the canker that lies beneath is a guilt that has a far deeper cause: guilt for the unconscious, repressed rage at YHWH for his interference in their lives, revolt against his exacting and unrealistic discipline. In a memorable section he thus argues that punishment, in the guise of national catastrophes and so forth, might provide some measure of relief, but it will never remove guilt altogether because lurking beneath is the unconscious 'aggressiveness and the hate against God-Father ... the repressed aggression has to be anxiously kept in its cage, has to be guarded day and night, because the ferocious beast would be dangerous if it broke out. The love and awe of the Lord is a reactive emotion and its tremendous intensity is determined by the power of the repressed rebellious and hateful tendencies' (Reik, 1958: 302). Biblical texts that characterise a jealous deity demanding total loyalty are, in his view, trying

---

[19] While I do not subscribe to Freud's (1939) hypothesis of the murdered Moses on which Reik leans, his observations of suppressed rage remain convincing.

at all costs to ensure that an 'explosion of fury' did not break through' (1958: 302).

When it comes to Judges, the need to double-think is vital. We are not supposed to detect in the text the manipulations and complex manoeuvres that feature in psychic masochism. What we have is the surface manifestation of lesser 'crimes', pseudo-aggression and victim status. However, with the help of psychological insight one can deduce that there are ulterior ploys at work that are not overtly appearing in the story world. What we *do* see is the repeated provoking of YHWH's anger that brings punishment – which brings to mind the 'injustice collecting'noted by Bergler and others. As we have seen, such repeated provocation is deliberate, allowing the writer to present himself as both sinning and sinned against, although, as this is precisely what the psychic masochist does not recognise about themselves it would be a manifestation of an unconscious rationale for the story world's cyclic pattern. The text conjures recurring situations of refusal and defeat because this represents some kind of libidinal pleasure. The libidinal pleasure is that the provocation and subsequent punishment means that a relationship exists. YHWH and Israel are bound together, however torridly, in an ongoing dance that won't let go. This determined refusal to let go is something we have already seen reflected in Judges commentaries. The reader might recall Webb's observation that Judges' theology concerns a relationship that is 'dynamic rather than static, and raw rather than refined. It is a theology of conflict in which both parties suffer, and in which Israel survives only because Yahweh does not give up on her and simply walk away' (2012: 54). I posit a different explanation of such divine determination. It is the scribe who does not let go and the scribe who has conjured and scripted the YHWH character as one who can be manipulated into ongoing relationship, paradoxically via provocation.

Judges commentators respond appropriately to the text's rhetoric when they criticise Israel but are just following the dictates of the text when they do so for reasons of Israel's apostasy, waywardness and ingratitude. If this constructed Israel is deliberately provoking wrath it belongs to the scribe's masochistic fantasy that such behaviours *should* be criticised; in this way, YHWH as a character and we as readers are being managed. His plot enables us to heap blame on Israel – aren't they absolutely awful, how hopeless they are, how rude, how ungrateful – because this can also facilitate the desired victim status – poor me, so hard done by, YHWH is so big and strong and I was only doing what comes naturally, then he sent all these enemies to destroy me (note the hyperbole and injustice collecting). This is why, in Chapter 1, I could identify so readily with the indignities and unfairness that Israel suffers at the hands of YHWH. If I had not been so well informed by the psychological literature, it would have been easy to fall for a trap – to be sympathetic to their plight and see their victim status, but without recognising the underlying rage that it masks.

Commentators who express their irritation with Israel's irksome behaviour, particularly when Israel 'repents', are probably subconsciously picking up on the masochistic elements of the text. There are many references in the psychoanalytic literature to analysts acknowledging how easy it is to get caught up in countertransference. The client might well be presenting their most compliant 'poor me' front but the analyst is annoyed by it. Noting Reik's (1941) views that masochism involves aggressive impulses camouflaged by presenting a victimised persona, Brenman (1952) points out that the camouflage is often unsuccessful because what is concealed becomes evident to those who are on the receiving end of the masochistic behaviour. The effort to ingratiate oneself (Israel cries out or repents overtly) masks the underlying hostility quite effectively, but that ingratiation can be so off-putting that the person to whom it is directed actually feels the underlying hostility and suspects that the apparently self-sacrificial behaviour is also an unspoken criticism. An amusing and helpful example from Brenman is included in her case study of Allerton W. whose parents expected her to curtsy before distinguished house guests. In fact, she was not allowed to be part of the proceedings until she had learned the art of the perfect curtsey. However, in her debut performance Allerton 'bowed so low that she fell flat on her face arousing much consternation in her parents and merriment in the assembled guests. It seemed quite clear ... that while her conscious wish had been to produce the most perfect curtsy ever seen, she was at the same time teasing (or better here, mocking) her parents by producing a live caricature of the behaviour they were demanding and directing attention to herself as an awkward but lovable buffoon' (1952: 268).

I noted in Chapter 3 that Israel is repeatedly criticised by commentators who either can't make up their mind whether their repentance is genuine, or are sure that it is not. I am not surprised. If the matter is viewed in the light of Brenman's paper, Israel's show of overt repentance in 10:15–16 is both genuine *and* the result of defence mechanisms. It is genuine insofar as its cloying 'please like me' deference to YHWH tells us what Israel most desires – the response of a primary caregiver who will be reliably and consistently himself with his love and protection. Yet, it simultaneously camouflages an unspoken hostility that demonstrates the wearisome nature of YHWH's demands and expectations. Commentators are thus right to see through the device, but are not seeing in sufficient depth the psychological rationale for such behaviour. Allerton performs a comic mishap that provokes the affection of family friends while simultaneously discharging hostility against her parents by exposing their ridiculous requirements. In her collapsed curtsy perhaps we can see Israel's cocked eyebrow at YHWH's expectations and reactions, but unlike the house guests, biblical scholars are not sure whether they can be complicit in the criticism.

Brenman, like Reik, insists that we must look beyond the 'front', beyond the injustice collecting. The reader of Judges likewise has to look beyond the face value of Israel's repeated plight. The biblical reader needs the clinical distance of the theoretically informed analyst and also the analyst's ability to double-think what is going on. If all we note is the repeated cries of pain then the underlying matter is left unaddressed, for beneath all this is vengeful feeling and aggression. Rather than responding, as some commentators do, with irritation at Israel's behaviour, we should model the response of the astute analyst who detects the circuitous aggressiveness and sees the reality that is being presented: fear of 'being dead'. So I think we would be partially right to apply to the book of Judges Noll's (2013) view that the scribe of Samuel is critical of a YHWH who we are meant to find repulsive. As with Allerton, we are meant to question the motives and intrusion of parents who demand ridiculous curtseys. But what Noll lacks is a detailed and nuanced understanding of the psychological factors that contribute to this.

Conclusion

In the previous discussion I have made a case for interpreting the repeated cycle in Judges as a masochistic defence mechanism. In order to bring together the argument of the previous discussion, I now summarise concisely how the mechanism operates.

First, the cyclical abandonment of YHWH and serving of other gods is a provocation – an 'acting-up' scenario meant to provoke YHWH's disappointment and angry reaction. His reaction meets a scribal desire to be reprimanded. This game is largely operating at the unconscious level because the masochist typically represses recognition that he plays a part in arriving at a victim status; i.e., Israel's apostasy is a deliberate ploy to ensure that it attracts YHWH's attention, displeasure and punishment. Unconsciously, it is a strategy that keeps the pair in relationship and also invites sympathy for Israel's treatment (their cries for help).

Second, while their apostasy seems to be defiant behaviour, it is actually only pseudo-aggression deliberately intended to bring on punishment and provide the masochistic pleasure that comes with the expected retaliation. Their victory is the preservation of the sadomasochistic game. As Berliner (1995) points out, masochism is not so much about the desire for suffering but, in fact, desire to avoid it. The punishment facilitates the opportunity to cry out (the 'poor me' response), yet without having to acknowledge that they have prompted it.

Third, unconsciously there is pleasure in the rebuff that has been staged, even though the outward emotional display is one of self-pity (even indulgent self-pity), which is why commentators are so harsh on Israel. They are picking up, very clearly, on how Israel has indeed played a part in getting to this point.

Fourth, the real aggression is not in these provocations. It is deep underground, because this is the rage that cannot be vented. The masochistic fear, in part conjured by the delusion of omnipotence, is that this rage would be so volcanic that it would destroy the relationship. It has to remain suppressed, deep within the unconscious, leaving on the surface a much more compliant Israel. Yes, they have their little kicks against the system by going off to experiment with the Baals, with kingship, but these actions knowingly produce a punishment that fends off, only to some small and temporary extent, the guilt actually felt about their unconscious and much more frightening rage.

Fifth, the unconscious aggression is taken inwards. Repressed and unconscious, it is found in the relentless condemnation heaped on 'bad' Israel, the satirical Othering of enemies, the pervasive feeling of guilt that needs resolution and finds it in the punishment doled out for lesser provocations. Fundamentally it is found in the masochistic basis on which the entire YHWH–Israel relationship has been constructed in Judges. We, as readers, only begin to grasp this when we do what Bergler enjoins us to do, which is to look for 'a queer excitement' in what's going on (1949: 81). I read this as the instruction to look for some strange heightening of the senses, or perhaps a

transgressive tantalising weirdness about the encounter being analysed. In the narrative cycle of Judges there is indeed an odd, larger-
than-life kind of excitement for the reader as Israel experiments
again with different and rival primary caregivers, while YHWH
explodes with over-the-top fury at the incitement as the plot works
towards his laconic absenteeism. There is certainly game play here.
Once the immediate danger is dealt with there is a pause, and then
the provocation occurs again in the cyclical game of cat and mouse
and we, the readers, are caught up in its suspense, comedy, pathos
and 'queer excitement', despite all the tedium of a relentlessly
pompous scribe.

5

CONCLUSION: PSYCHOLOGICAL THEORY
AND BIBLICAL HERMENEUTICS

Jung noted how it is often the texts that appear to have no overt psychology within their pages that are the most interesting. Despite appearing 'quite devoid of psychological exposition' texts are 'built upon a groundwork of implicit psychological assumptions, and, in the measure that the author is unconscious of them, they reveal themselves, pure and unalloyed, to the critical discernment' (1933: 178). What I've learned from writing this book is that Judges is such a text. At surface level, it tells its repetitive story without inner musings or any apparent interest in self-reflection. Rather, it presses home a number of central themes that scholars are broadly agreed upon. Judges is 'about' a south–north steady deterioration that bespeaks negative bias against northern tribes, different modes of leadership, cultic loyalty, women and ethnic boundaries. This deeply grooved scholarly consensus mirrors or explains in scholarly fashion what the narrator is already saying. Bal (1988) rightly perceives the limits of this. As noted in Chapter 1, she reads in a more disobedient way. She locates the interests or themes that are just as significant for driving the plot, but which are suppressed or repressed by both narrator and the history of reception. Bal's approach differs significantly from mine in that hers is primarily a narrative reading of the text attentive to psychological and gendered issues while mine is grounded more obviously in a psychological assessment. Yet, we both recognise that what a text is 'about' has deeper dimensions that the surface plot describes. So while I concur that the Judges scribe uses ingenious modifications to the repeated cycle in order to demonstrate progressive flaws in judgeship, or the steady disintegration of tribal life, I find this kind of analysis helpful but circumscribed by the overt contours of the text's account. My approach is to listen to the presenting story carefully but then use it as a launch pad for an analysis of its inevitable psychological imprint and a consideration of the function it serves. This enables me to revise what is meant by 'themes' or 'interests' in the Book of Judges. Paradoxically, a method that is 'alien' to the text pushes the interpreter even deeper into it, in order to analyse its inner world of attachment issues, masochistic drives, splitting and repression. The thing that acts as the safeguard, that prevents the reader from being sucked into the presenting story's rhetoric, is the critical theory itself, which is both external to the text and the means of entering deeply into the relational dynamic of the text's story world. Writing this book has demonstrated for me how psychological theory is not only a viable adjunct to biblical hermeneutics but also a vital addition for the analysis of submerged issues operative within the story world.

In terms of hermeneutics, I found that a psychological reading of biblical texts coheres really well with narrative approaches. I certainly found this to be the case when examining the biblical passages in Chapter 3. Here the most fruitful interlocutors were narrative critics. Their attentiveness to narrators and their strategies is what proved to be helpful, which was a surprise. I had initially thought that character studies, which are such a staple of narrative approaches, would have been the obvious area of overlap. The problem is that YHWH seldom makes an appearance in them or, if he does, authors of such studies say that he is beyond analysis. Alter, for example, argues that 'intellectual humility' is called for, together with the recognition that we are not dealing with 'an antiquarian book' but with texts where humans are 'confronted, challenged, and confounded by a reality beyond human ken' (1992: 23). I agree with this. Biblical texts do confront us with the numinous, they can be visionary, they can speak to the human soul in a profound way and the exercise of 'intellectual humility' is no bad thing. Alter also acknowledges that this deity is the construct of the narrator, who 'presumed to know, quite literally, what God knows, as on occasion he may remind us by reporting God's assessments and intentions, or even what He says to Himself' (1981: 157). Again, I concur. However, when Alter advises that, despite this, we cannot do character studies with YHWH because he is beyond the human frame of reference, I disagree. Alter requires readers to be tacit in a game that recognises how the narrator constructs the character of YHWH, and how he proceeds to put this character beyond our scrutiny, but Alter then requires his reader to accept that YHWH 'really is' inscrutable. Rather than seeing inscrutability as a main *character trait*, inscrutability becomes a divine attribute, something that puts YHWH beyond mere human reasoning. He is given a capital 'H' to remind readers that He is not an ordinary character in the text, nor is he a character at the whim and service of a scribe. He is both in the text yet beyond the text, a transcendent horizon that meets with human in a revelatory way. I have demonstrated how this privileging of YHWH, however, hamstrings our ability to investigate how the psychological dance between YHWH and Israel functions. Since unwillingness to scrutinise YHWH as a character among others means that YHWH's point of view is allowed to reign sovereign, I cannot be complicit in Alter's game; rather, I align myself with critics such as Gunn and Fewell (1993: 81–89) Clines (1998), and Bal. The latter insists that we *have* to evaluate YHWH as a character among other characters, for it is 'precisely this methodological rigour that allows a narratorial analysis to become truly critical' (1988: 34). When characterisation, narratorial strategy and rhetoric are analysed alongside theory that can unpack the psychological landscape of the text, then we have a method that does the work of close reading, understanding the text on its own terms, combined with a way of stepping out of its rhetoric and analysing the kind of relationship dynamics that are presented. Terms like proximity maintenance, protest behaviour, holding environments, impingement, splitting, injustice collecting, are not usually to be found in biblical commentaries, but use of these interrogative concepts enable the scholar to ask important questions.

A psychological reading thus complements narrative approaches but calls for more robustness in the analysis of YHWH than is currently the case. There are studies that have paved the way such as those by Barton (2010), Blumenthal (1993a), Brueggemann (1995, 2000), Penchansky (1999) and Whybray (2000), but psychology does not feature as a major interrogative tool in these accounts. In masculinity studies, where one might expect to find critical scrutiny of the deity, there is currently very little. Even Clines (forthcoming, *Play the Man: The Masculine Imperative in the Bible*), who can usually be relied upon for transgressing taboos, acknowledges that in the past he has deferred the challenge. Again, it is the issue of YHWH's inscrutability that has put such work beyond scholars. It becomes a device that discourages uncomfortable analyses of the narrator's main character. The findings of this book explain why this happens. The repression of the 'bad' aspects of YHWH's character and the strategies undertaken to keep him 'good' involve the scribe in a masochistic defence mechanism. The main task of that mechanism is to bury the anger and resentment felt towards a powerful primary caregiver whose impingements are overly intrusive and whose demands are impossible to meet. The scribe, nonetheless, tells a story where YHWH's underhand activities are laid bare. Taking the part of an omniscient narrator, the reader is given privileged insight into YHWH's bouts of incandescent rage (the burning of the nostrils) and appointment of enemies to hem Israel in on all sides until they are compelled to cry out. This acknowledgement of the shady side of YHWH's character is a daring move on the part of the scribe and one likely to evoke some trepidation (just as the child fears the consequences of any overt criticism of the caregiver). If the scribe can cloak YHWH's dubious manoeuvers and terrifying features of his character in an appeal to his supernatural wisdom and purposes of which mere humans know nothing, potential repercussions from exposing YHWH's dubious behaviour are avoided. The onus is on biblical scholars to recognise this strategy and to resist complicity or at least notice what is being endorsed.

In terms of compatible approaches, I also found 'faithful' commentaries insightful and illustrative, even though I appear irretrievably at odds with them. I have noted throughout that I appreciate how their writers wrestle profoundly with a very discomforting text. My criticism has been that faith commitments may have hindered their recognition of the significant costs involved in privileging the inscrutable YHWH, and in reinforcing and deepening that furrow that doggedly 'keeps him good'. Faithful readers are thereby encouraged to adopt an internalised working model of divine parenthood that is troubling. The questions I raise about the depiction of divine–human relations and the findings of this study are not the result of indifferent ivory tower playfulness; I am serious about the consequences of this study for people of faith. So, while I have often drawn on confessional commentaries in order to demonstrate my disagreement with their main positional stance that keeps YHWH 'good', I hope that my deep appreciation of their scholarship, insights and willingness to confront directly the difficult depictions of genocide, violence, ethical behaviour and YHWH's temper, has also been evident. I am not in favour of drawing impenetrable lines between the kind of biblical interpretation written from and for faithful people and the biblical studies of the academy. I understand why Davies (1995b) calls for a dividing line and I have sympathy for his view that confessional views of God and scripture complicate (or, in his view, compromise) academic enquiry, but I would never ask students to leave their confessional hat at the door of my classroom.

It is more helpful to negotiate a balance where a range of voices can interrogate each other.[1] What concerns me is the way a commentary series is given a remit that hinders the kind of work I call for. The guidelines of series such as the New International Commentary on the Old Testament (NICOT), for example, seriously hamper the ability of scholars to challenge the portrayal of YHWH. Hubbard's preface to Webb's commentary notes how it contributes to NICOT's aim to balance '"criticism" ... with humble respect, admiration, and even affection for the biblical text' how it 'aims to serve women and men of faith who desire to hear God's voice afresh' (2012: xv). The boundaries drawn around this series make it a 'safe' resource for evangelical readers; here is a commentary informed by academic scholarship but overseen by the series' faithful credentials. Nothing to rock the faith of readers will be found here. This and several other commentary series perpetuate the dogma that YHWH is a *sui generis* character beyond the normal scope of character studies, whose behaviour is beyond criticism because it has divine purposes ultimately beyond human understanding. The effect of this is inevitably a taboo on critical studies of YHWH. We are not expected to question how he forms his relationship with Israel, his use of disciplinary punishment to maintain that relationship, or the divine determination that compels Israel into a False Self, unless it ends with a rather pious, justifying gloss. The end-users of commentaries are not given the resources to think more deeply about how Judges presents that relationship. Given that biblical texts form the basis of weekly sermons, and commentaries are regularly used by preachers for sermon-production, I do not think we can afford to continually reinforce a flawed relationship model. I would like to see commentaries radically open their boundaries so that scholars can engage in these questions. Let readers of faith come to a more profound and enlarged vision of their deity that is not boxed in by an ancient scribe's rather troubled notions.

When Winnicott (1990b) wrote about the process of writing his papers he said he did so while imagining his audience for that

---

[1] I concur with Davidson that keeping the two approaches separate would be 'an impossible act of intellectual and spiritual schizophrenia' (2002: 166) even while he acknowledge a tension: 'There have been occasions when I have sat in church on Sunday and cringed at the way in which the Bible was being expounded to the congregation in total ignorance or in total disregard of some of the fundamental insights of academic scholarship. Such cringing is not conducive to meaningful worship!' (2002: 166).

address. I note, with a smile, his acknowledgement that the actual audience who turned up related only partly to the audience he imagined. I have envisaged a readership of biblical scholars, some of whom might find it impossible to accept my starting point for this book. But in the area which Winnicott calls transitional, I have engaged with readers of all faiths and none, imagining that they have stayed with me, seeing the argument through to its final chapter. Winnicott also talks about how the transitional space exists likewise for readers, or in his analogy, theatregoers. There is a liminal space between theatregoers' expectation of how a play will be performed and the rising of the stage curtain. Their anticipation of what they are about to see may cohere to certain extents or it may depart significantly. I cannot anticipate how far there has been a happy continuity between readers' expectations and their actual experience, but I think what matters is that encounter has happened.

BIBLIOGRAPHY

Abram, Jan. 1996.*The Language of Winnicott: A Dictionary and Guide to Understanding His Work*. Northvale and London: Jason Aronson Inc.

Ahlström, Gösta W. 1991. The Origin of Israel in Palestine. *Scandinavian Journal of the Old Testament* 5 (2): 19–34.

Ainsworth, Mary D. S. 1963. The Development of Infant–Mother Interaction among the Ganda. Pages 67–103 in *Determinants of Infant Behaviour II*. Edited by B. M. Foss. London: Methuen.

1964. Patterns of Attachment Behavior Shown by the Infant in Interaction with His Mother. *Merrill-Palmer Quarterly* 10: 51–58.

1967. *Infancy in Uganda: Infant Care and the Growth of Love*. Baltimore: John Hopkins University Press.

Ainsworth, Mary D. S. and B. A. Wittig. 1969. Attachment and Exploratory Behavior of One-Year Olds in a Strange Situation. Pages 111–136 in *Determinants of Infant Behaviour IV*. Edited by B. M. Foss. London: Methuen.

Ainsworth, Mary D. S., S. M. Bell and D. J. Stayton. 1971. Individual Differences in Strange-Situation Behavior of One-Year-Olds. Pages 17–58 in *The Origins of Human Social Relations*. Edited by H. R. Schaffer. London: Academic Press.

Ainsworth, Mary D. S., Mary C. Blehar, Everett Waters and Sally N. Wall. 1978. *Patterns of Attachment: A Psychological Study of the Strange Situation*. Hillsdale: Erlbaum.

Alter, Robert. 1981. *The Art of Biblical Narrative*. New York: Basic Books.

1992. *The World of Biblical Literature*. London: SPCK.

2013. *Ancient Israel, the Former Prophets: Joshua, Judges, Samuel and Kings: A Translation with Commentary*. New York: W. W. Norton & Co.

Amit, Yairah. 1999. *The Book of Judges: The Art of Editing*. Biblical Interpretation Series 38.Translated by Jonathan Chipman. Leiden: Brill.

2009. The Book of Judges: Dating and Meaning. Pages 297–322 in *Homeland and Exile: Biblical and Ancient near Eastern Studies in Honour of Bustenay Oded*. Vetus Testamentum Supplements 130. Edited by Gershon Galil, Mark Geller and Alan Millard. Leiden: Brill.

2014. Who Was Interested in the Book of Judges in the Persian–Hellenistic Periods? Pages 103–114 in *Deuteronomy – Kings As*

Emerging Authoritative Books: A Conversation. Edited by D. V. Edel-
man. Atlanta: Society for Biblical Literature.
Bailey, Randall C. 1995. They're Nothing but Incestuous Bastards: The
Polemical Use of Sex and Sexuality in Hebrew Canon Narratives. Pages
121–138 in *Reading from This Place Volume 1 Social Location and
Biblical Interpretation in the United States.* Edited by F. Segovia and
M. A. Tolbert. Minneapolis: Fortress.
Bal, Mieke. 1988. *Death and Dissymmetry: The Politics of Coherence in the
Book of Judges.* Chicago Studies in the History of Judaism. Chicago:
University of Chicago Press.
Bar-Efrat, Shimon. 1989. *Narrative Art in the Bible.* Journal for the Study of
the Old Testament Supplementary Series 70. Bible and Literature Series
17. Sheffield: Almond Press.
Bartholomew, Kim. 1990. Avoidance of Intimacy: An Attachment Perspec-
tive. *Journal of Social and Personal Relationships* 7: 147–178.
Bartholomew, Kim and Leonard M. Horowitz. 1991. Attachment Styles
among Young Adults: A Test of a Four-Category Model. *Journal of
Personality and Social Psychology* 61 (2): 226–244.
Bartholomew, Kim, A. J. Z. Henderson and D. G. Dutton. 2001. Insecure
Attachment and Abusive Intimate Relationships. Pages 43–61 in *Adult
Attachment and Couple Psychotherapy: Applying the "Secure Base"
Practice and Research.* Edited by C. Clulow. London: Brunner
Routledge.
Barton, John. 2010. The Dark Side of God in the Old Testament.
Pages 122–134 in *Ethical and Unethical in the Old Testament:
God and Humans in Dialogue.* The Library of Hebrew Bible/Old
Testament Studies 528. Edited by Katherine J. Dell. London: T &
T Clark.
Becker, Uwe. 1990. *Richterzeit und Königtum: Redaktionsgeschichtliche Stu-
dien Zum Richterbuch. Beihefte Zur Zeitschrift Fur Die Alttestamen-
tliche Wissenschaft 192.* Berlin: de Gruyter.
Becking, Bob. 2009. Exile and Forced Labour in Bêt Har'oš: Remarks on a
Recently Discovered Moabite Inscription. Pages 3–12 in *Homeland and
Exile: Biblical and Ancient near Eastern Studies in Honour of Bustenay
Oded.* Vetus Testamentum Supplements 130. Edited by Gershon Galil,
Mark Geller and Alan Millard. Leiden: Brill.
Ben Zvi, E. 1997. The Urban Center of Jerusalem and the Development of
the Literature of the Hebrew Bible. Pages 194–209 in *Urbanism in
Antiquity: From Mesopotamia to Crete.* Edited by W. G. Aufrecht,
Steven W. Gauley and Neil A. Mirau. Journal for the Study of the
Old Testament Supplementary Series 244. Sheffield: Sheffield Academic
Press.
Benjamin, Jessica. 1990. *The Bonds of Love: Psychoanalysis, Feminism, and
the Problem of Domination.* London: Virago.
Bergler, Edmund. 1949. *The Basic Neurosis: Oral Regression and Psychic
Masochism.* New York: Grune and Stratton.
Bergmann, Martin S. and Milton E. Jucovy. 1982. Prelude. Pages 3–29 in
Generations of the Holocaust. Edited by Martin S. Bergmann and
Milton E. Jucovy. New York: Basic Books.

Berliner, Bernhard. 1947. On Some Psychodynamics of Masochism. *Psychoanalytical Quarterly* 16: 459–471.

1995. The Role of Object Relations in Moral Masochism. Pages 344–359 in *Essential Papers on Masochism*. Edited by Margaret Ann Fitzpatrick Hanly. New York: New York University Press. First published 1958. *Psychoanalytic Quarterly* 27 (1): 38–56.

Blenkinsopp, Joseph. 2002a. The Babylonian Gap Revisited. *Biblical Archaeology Review* 28 (3): 36–39, 59.

2002b. The Bible, Archaeology and Politics; Or The Empty Land Revisited. *Journal for the Study of the Old Testament* 27 (2): 169–187.

Block, Daniel I. 1999. *Judges, Ruth*. New American Commentary 6. Nashville: Broadman and Holman.

Blumenthal, David R. 1993a. *Facing the Abusing God: A Theology of Protest*. Louisville: Westminster John Knox Press.

1993b. Who Is Battering Whom? *Conservative Judaism* 45: 72–89.

Boer, Roland. 2001. Yahweh as Top: A Lost Targum. Pages 75–105 in *Queer Commentary and the Hebrew Bible*. Journal for the Study of the Old Testament Supplementary Series 334. Edited by Ken Stone. London: Sheffield Academic Press.

Bolin, Thomas M. 1996. When the End Is the Beginning: The Persian Period and the Origins of the Biblical Tradition. *Scandinavian Journal of the Old Testament* 10 (1): 3–15.

Boling, Robert G. 1975. *Judges: A New Translation with Introduction and Commentary*. Anchor Bible 6A. New York: Doubleday.

Bowlby, John. 1978. *Attachment and Loss Vol II: Separation: Anxiety and Anger*. Harmondsworth: Penguin. First published 1973 London: Hogarth Press.

1979. *The Making and Breaking of Affectional Bonds*. London: Tavistock Publications Ltd.

1980a. *A Secure Base*. New York: Basic Books.

1980b. *Attachment and Loss Vol III: Loss, Sadness and Depression*. London: Hogarth Press.

1997. *Attachment and Loss Vol 1* London: Pimlico. First published 1969 London: Hogarth Press.

Bowman, Richard G. 2007. Narrative Criticism: Human Purpose in Conflict with Divine Presence. Pages 19–45 in *Judges and Method: New Approaches in Biblical Studies*. 2nd edition. Edited by Gale A. Yee. Minneapolis: Fortress Press.

Brandchaft, B. 2007. Systems of Pathological Accommodations and Change in Analysis. *Psychoanalytic Psychology* 24: 667–687.

Brenman, Margaret. 1952. On Teasing and Being Teased: And the Problem of 'Moral Masochism'. *The Psychoanalytic Study of the Child* 7 (1): 264–285.

Brenner, Athalya. 1994. Who's Afraid of Feminist Criticism? Who's Afraid of Biblical Humour? The Case of the Obtuse Foreign Ruler in the Hebrew Bible. *Journal for the Study of the Old Testament* 63: 38–55.

Brenner, C. 1959. The Masochistic Character: Genesis and Treatment. *Journal of American Psychoanalytic Association* 7: 197–226

1982. *The Mind in Conflict*. New York: International Universities Press.

Brettler, Marc Zvi. 1995. *The Creation of History in Ancient Israel*. London: Routledge.

2002. *The Book of Judges*. Old Testament Readings. London: Routledge.

Bright, John. 1980. *A History of Israel*. 3rd edition. London: SCM Press.

Brueggemann Walter. 1988. *Israel's Praise: Doxology against Idolatry and Ideology*. Philadelphia: Fortress Press.

1990. *First and Second Samuel. Interpretation: A Bible Commentary for Teaching and Preaching*. Louisville: John Knox Press.

1995. *The Psalms and the Life of Faith*. Minneapolis: Augsburg Fortress.

1997. *Theology of the Old Testament: Testimony, Dispute, Advocacy*. Minneapolis: Augsburg Fortress.

2000. Texts That Linger, Not Yet Overcome. Pages 21–41 in '*Shall Not the Judge of All the Earth Do What Is Right?' Studies on the Nature of God in Tribute to James L. Crenshaw*. Edited by David Penchansky and Paul L. Redditt. Winona Lake: Eisenbrauns.

2008. *Old Testament Theology: An Introduction*. Nashville: Abingdon Press.

Buber, Martin. 1967. *Kingship of God*. London: George Allen and Unwin Ltd.

Burns-Smith, Charlene. 1999. Theology and Winnicott's Object-Relations Theory: A Conversation. *Journal of Psychology and Theology* 27 (1): 3–19.

Butler, Trent C. 2009. *Judges*. Word Biblical Commentary 8. Grand Rapids: Zondervan.

Carlander Jakob. 2001. The Saul–David Story from a Kleinian Perspective: God, Prophets, Women and the Lack of Tragedy. Pages 73–95 in *God, Biblical Stories and Psychoanalytic Understanding*. Edited by Rainer Kessler and Patrick Vandermeersch. Frankfurt: Peter Lang.

Carroll, Robert P. 1991. Textual Strategies and Ideology in the Second Temple Period. Pages 108–124 in *Second Temple Studies 1: Persian Period*. Journal for the Study of the Old Testament Supplementary Series 117. Edited by Philip R. Davies. Sheffield: Sheffield Academic. Press.

Carter, Charles E. 1999. *The Emergence of Yehud in the Persian Period: A Social and Demographic Study*. Journal for the Study of the Old Testament Supplementary Series 294. Sheffield: Sheffield Academic Press.

Caruth, Cathy. 1995. Introduction. Pages 3–12 in *Trauma: Explorations in Memory*. Edited by Cathy Caruth. Baltimore: John Hopkins Press.

1996. *Unclaimed Experience: Trauma, Narrative and History*. Baltimore: John Hopkins University Press.

Charmé, Stuart L. 1983. Religion and the Theory of Masochism. *Journal of Religion and Health* 27 (3): 221–233.

Clericus. J. 1708. *Veteris Testamenti Libri Historici*. Amsterdam: Henricum Schelte.

Clines, David J. A. 1995. *Interested Parties: The Ideology of Writers and Readers of the Hebrew Bible*. Journal for the Study of the Old Testament Supplementary Series 205. Gender, Culture, Theory 1. Sheffield: Sheffield Academic Press.

1998. Yahweh and the God of Christian Theology. Pages 498–507 in *On the Way to the Postmodern: Old Testament Essays 1967–1998 Vol 2*. Edited by David J. A. Clines. Sheffield: Sheffield Academic Press.

Collicutt, Joanna. 2012. Bringing the Academic Discipline of Psychology to Bear in the Study of the Bible. *The Journal of Theological Studies* 62 (1): 1–48.

Coogan, M. D. 1974. Life in the Diaspora: Jews at Nippur in the Fifth Century B.C. *Biblical Archaeologist* 37: 6–12.

Cooper, Arnold M. 2008. The Narcissistic–Masochistic Character. Pages 117–138 in *Masochism: Current Psychoanalytic Perspectives*. Edited by Robert A. Glick and Donald I. Meyers. New York and London: Psychology Press.

Coote, Robert B. and Keith W. Whitelam. 1987. *The Emergence of Early Israel in Historical Perspective*. The Social World of Biblical Antiquity 5. Sheffield: Almond Press.

Critchley, Simon. 2002. *On Humour*. London: Routledge.

Cross, Frank Moore. 1973. *Canaanite Myth and Hebrew Epic: Essays in the History of the Religion of Israel*. Cambridge: Harvard University Press.

Danell, G. A. 1946. *Studies in the Name Israel in the Old Testament*. Uppsala: Appelbergs Boktryckeri.

Davidson, E. T. A. 2008. *Intricacy, Design, and Cunning in the Book of Judges*. Philadelphia: Xlibris.

Davidson, Robert. 2002. The Bible in Church and Academy. Pages 161–173 in *Sense and Sensitivity: Essays on Reading the Bible in Memory of Robert Carroll*. The Library of Hebrew Bible/Old Testament Studies 348. Edited by Alastair G. Hunter and Philip R. Davies. London: Sheffield Academic Press.

Davies, G. I. 2004. Review of *The Origin of the History of Israel: Herodotus Histories as Blueprint for the First Books of the Bible*. *Journal of Theological Studies* 55 (2): 805–806.

Davies, Philip R. 1992. *In Search of 'Ancient Israel'*. Journal for the Study of the Old Testament Supplementary Series 148. Sheffield: Sheffield Academic Press.

1995a. Method and Madness: Some Remarks on Doing History with the Bible. *Journal of Biblical Literature* 114: 699–705.

1995b. *Whose Bible Is It Anyway?* Journal for the Study of the Old Testament Supplementary Series 204. Sheffield: Sheffield Academic Press.

1998. *Scribes and Schools: The Canonization of the Hebrew Scriptures*. London: SPCK.

Davis, Keith E., April Ace and Michelle Andra. 2000. Stalking Perpetrators and Psychological Maltreatment of Partners: Anger-Jealousy, Attachment Insecurity, Need for Control, and Break-Up Context. *Violence and Victims* 15 (4): 407–425.

Day, John. 1993. Bedan, Abdon or Barak in 1 Samuel XII 11? *Vetus Testamentum* 43 (2): 261–264.

Des Pres, Terrence. 1976. *The Survivor: An Anatomy of Life in the Death Camps*. Oxford: Oxford University Press.

Dever, William G. 1999. Historians and Nonhistories of Ancient Israel. *Bulletin of the American Schools of Oriental Research* 316: 89–106.

2001. *What Did the Biblical Writers Know and When Did They Know It?
What Archaeology Can Tell Us About the Reality of Ancient Israel.*
Grand Rapids: Eerdmans.

Driver, Samuel Rolles. 1890. *Notes on the Hebrew Text of the Books
of Samuel with an Introduction on Hebrew Palaeography and the
Ancient Versions and Facsimiles of Inscriptions.* Oxford: Clarendon
Press.

Dutton, D. G., K. Saunders, A. Starzomski and K. Bartholomew. 1994.
Intimacy Anger and Insecure Attachment as Precursors of Abuse in
Intimate Relationships. *Journal of Applied Social Psychology* 24:
1367–1386.

Ephal, I. 1978. The Western Minorities in Babylonia in the 6th–5th centuries
B.C.: Maintenance and Cohesion. *Orientalia* 47: 74–89.

Eslinger, Lyle. 1985. *Kingship of God in Crisis: A Close Reading of 1 Sam
1–12.* Bible and literature series 10. Sheffield: Almond.

Exum, J. Cheryl. 1990. The Centre Cannot Hold: Thematic and Textual
Instabilities in Judges. *Catholic Biblical Quarterly* 52 (3): 410–431.

    1992. *Tragedy in Biblical Narrative: Arrows of the Almighty.* Cambridge:
Cambridge University Press.

Ewald, H. 1865. *Geschichte des Volkes Israel 2.* 3rd edition. Göttingen:
Dieterichschen Buchhandlung.

Fairbairn, William Ronald Dodds. 1996. *Psychoanalytic Studies of the
Personality.* London: Routledge. First published 1952. London: Tavistock Pubs Ltd.

Feldman, Louis H. 2004. Review of the *Origin of the History of Israel:
Herodotus's Histories as Blueprint for the First Books of the Bible.
Journal of Hebrew Scriptures* 4. www.jhsonline.org/cocoon/JHS/
r081.html

Fenichel, Otto. 1953. A Contribution to the Psychology of Jealousy.
Pages 349–362 in *The Collected Papers of Otto Fenichel: 1st Series.*
Edited by Hanna Fenichel and David Rapaport. New York:
W. W. Norton & Co.

Finkelstein, Israel and Neil Asher Silberman. 2001. *The Bible Unearthed.
Archaeology's New Vision of Ancient Israel and the Origins of Its Sacred
Texts.* New York: The Free Press.

Finkelstein, Israel, Ahimai Mazar and Brian B. Schmidt. 2007. *The Quest
for the Historical Israel: Debating Archaeology and the History of Early
Israel.* Atlanta: SBL.

Fokkelman, J. P. 1993. *Narrative Art and Poetry in the books of Samuel:
A Full Interpretation Based on Stylistic and Structural Analyses. Vol IV:
Vow and Desire. 1 Sam 1 – 12.* Assen: Van Gorcum.

Freud, Anna. 1942. *The Ego and the Mechanisms of Defence.* New York:
International Universities Press.

Freud, Sigmund. 1924. *The Economic Problem of Masochism.* Collected
Papers, 2. London: Hogarth Press: 255–268.

    1939. *Moses and Monotheism.* London: Hogarth Press.

    1963. *Three Case Histories.* New York: Simon and Schuster/Touchstone.

Freyd, Jennifer J. 1996. *Betrayal Trauma: The Logic of Forgetting Childhood
Abuse.* Cambridge, MA: Harvard University Press.

Fry, W. F. 2000. Humor and Synergy. *Humor and Health Journal* 9 (3): 1–3.

Fuchs, Esther. 2000. *Sexual Politics in the Biblical Narrative: Reading the Hebrew Bible as a Woman*. Journal for the Study of the Old Testament Supplementary Series 310. Sheffield: Sheffield Academic Press.

Gabbard, Glen O. 2012. Masochism as a Multiply-Determined Phenomenon. Pages 103–111 in *The Clinical Problem of Masochism*. Edited by Deanna Holtzman and Nancy Kulish. Lanham: Rowman and Littlefield.

Garber, David G. Jr. 2015. Trauma Theory and Biblical Studies. *Currents in Biblical Research* 14 (1): 24–44.

Garbini, Giovanni. 1988. *History and Ideology in Ancient Israel*. Translated by John Bowden. London: SCM Press.

1994. Hebrew Literature in the Persian Period. Pages 180–188 in *Second Temple Studies: 2: Temple and Community in the Persian Period*. Journal for the Study of the Old Testament Supplementary Series 175. Edited by Tamara C. Eskenazi and Kent H. Richards. Sheffield: Sheffield Academic Press.

Garrick, Jacqueline. 2006. The Humor of Trauma Survivors. *Journal of Aggression, Maltreatment and Trauma* 12 (1–2): 169–182.

Gerstenberger, Erhard S. 2011. *Israel in the Persian Period: The Fifth and Fourth Centuries BCE*. Translated by Siegfried S. Schatzmann. Biblical Encyclopedia 8. Atlanta: SBL.

Gillmayr-Bucher, Susanne. 2009. Framework and Discourse in the Book of Judges. *Journal of Biblical Literature* 128 (4): 687–702.

Glatt-Gilad, David A. 2002. Yahweh's Honor at Stake: A Divine Conundrum. *Journal for the Study of the Old Testament* 98: 63–74.

Gnuse, Robert. 2007. Abducted Wives: A Hellenistic Narrative in Judges 21? *Scandinavian Journal of the Old Testament* 21 (2): 228–240.

Gomez, Lavinia. 1997. *An Introduction to Object Relations*. London: Free Association Book.

Gooding, D. W. 1982. The Composition of the Book of Judges. *Eretz Israel* 16: 70–79.

Gottwald, Norman K. 1954. *Studies in the Book of Lamentations*. Studies in Biblical Theology 14. London: SCM Press.

1979. *The Tribes of Yahweh: A Sociology of Liberated Israel 1250–1050 BCE*. London: SCM Press.

Grabbe, Lester L. 1997. *Can a 'History of Israel' Be Written?* Sheffield: Sheffield Academic Press.

Gray, John. 1986. *The New Century Bible Commentary: Joshua, Judges and Ruth*. Basingstoke: Marshall, Morgan and Scott.

Green, Barbara. 2003. *How Are the Mighty Fallen? A Dialogic Study of King Saul in 1 Samuel*. The Library of Hebrew Bible/Old Testament Studies, 365. Sheffield: Sheffield Academic Press.

Greenberg, Jay R. and Stephen A. Mitchell. 1983. *Object Relations in Psychoanalytic Theory*. Cambridge: Harvard University Press.

Gros Louis, Kenneth R. R. 1974. The Book of Judges. Pages 141–162 in *Literary Interpretations of Biblical Narratives*. Edited by Kenneth R. R. Gros Louis, James Stokes Ackerman and Thayer S. Warshaw. Nashville: Abingdon Press.

Guest, Deryn. 1998. Can Judges Survive without Sources? Challenging the Consensus. *Journal for the Study of the Old Testament* 78: 43–61.

2006. Judges. Pages 167–189 in *The Queer Bible Commentary*. Edited by Deryn Guest, Bob Goss, Mona West and Tom Bohache. London: SCM Press.

Guillaume, Philippe. 2004. *Waiting for Josiah: The Judges.* Journal for the Study of the Old Testament Supplementary Series 385. London: T & T Clark International.

Gunn, David M. 1980. *The Fate of King Saul: An Interpretation of a Biblical Story.* Journal for the Study of the Old Testament Supplementary Series 14. Sheffield: Sheffield Academic Press.

1989. Joshua and Judges. Pages 102–121 in *The Literary Guide to the Bible*. Edited by Robert Alter and Frank Kermode. London: Fontana Press.

Gunn, David M. and Danna Nolan Fewell. 1993. *Narrative in the Hebrew Bible.* Oxford Bible Series. Oxford: Oxford University Press.

Halpern, Baruch S. 1999. Erasing History: The Minimalist Assault on Ancient Israel. Pages 415–426 in *Israel's Past in Present Research: Essays on ancient Israelite Historiography.* Edited by V. Philips Long. Winona Lake: Eisenbrauns.

Halpern, Baruch S. and David S. Vanderhooft. 1991. The Editions of Kings in the 7th–6th Centuries BCE. *Hebrew Union College Annual* 62: 179–244.

Hamlin, E. John. 1990. *At Risk in the Promised Land: A Commentary on the Book of Judges.* Grand Rapids: Eerdmans.

Handy, Lowell K. 1992. Uneasy Laughter: Ehud and Eglon as Ethnic Humour. *Scandinavian Journal of the Old Testament* 6 (2): 223–246.

Hazan, Cindy and Phillip R. Shaver. 1987. Romantic Love Conceptualized as an Attachment Process *Journal of Personality and Social Psychology* 52 (3): 511–512.

1994. Attachment as an Organizational Framework for Research on Close Relationships. *Psychological Inquiry* 5 (1): 1–22.

Hepner, Gershon. 2004. Scatology in the Bible. *Scandinavian Journal of the Old Testament* 18 (2): 278–295.

Herman, Judith Lewis. 1997. *Trauma and Recovery.* New York: Basic Books.

Hertzberg, H. W. 1964. *I and II Samuel: A Commentary.* Old Testament Library. Translated by John Bowden. London: SCM Press.

Holmes, Jeremy. 1997. Attachment, Autonomy, Intimacy: Some Clinical Implications of Attachment Theory. *British Journal of Medical Psychology* 70: 231–248.

2001. *The Search for the Secure Base: Attachment Theory and Psychotherapy.* Hove: Brunner-Routledge.

Hopkins, David C. 1985. *The Highlands of Canaan.* Social World of Biblical Antiquity 3. Sheffield: Almond Press.

Hudson, Don Michael. 1994. Living in a Land of Epithets: Anonymity in Judges 19–21. *Journal for the Study of the Old Testament* 62: 49–66.

Jackson, Melissa A. 2012. *Comedy and Feminist Interpretation of the Hebrew Bible: A Subversive Collaboration.* Oxford: Oxford University Press.

Jacobson, Howard. 1992. The Judge Bedan (1 Samuel xii 11)' *Vetus Testamentum* 42 (1): 123–124.

Jamieson-Drake, D. W. 1991. *Scribes and Schools in Monarchic Judah: A Socio-Archaeological Approach*. Journal for the Study of the Old Testament Supplementary Series 109. The Social World of Biblical Antiquity Series 9. Sheffield: Sheffield Academic Press.

Janzen, David. 2012. *The Violent Gift: Trauma's Subversion of the Deuteronomistic History's Narrative*. Library of Hebrew Bible/Old Testament studies 561. New York: T & T Clark International.

Japhet, Sara. 1998. In Search of Ancient Israel: Revisionism at all Costs. Pages 212–234 in *The Jewish Past Revisited: Reflections on Modern Jewish Historians*. Edited by David N. Myers and David B. Ruderman. New Haven: Yale University Press.

Jobling, David. 1986. *The Sense of Biblical Narrative: Structural Analyses in the Hebrew Bible II*. Journal for the Study of the Old Testament Supplementary Series 39. Sheffield: Sheffield Academic Press.

1998. *Berit Olam: 1 Samuel: Studies in Hebrew Narrative and Poetry*. Collegeville: The Liturgical Press.

2003. The Salvation of Israel in 'The Book of the Divided Kingdoms' or, Was There Any 'Fall of the Northern Kingdom'?' Pages 50–61 in *Redirected Travel: Alternative Journeys and Places in Biblical* Studies. Journal for the Study of the Old Testament Supplementary Series 383. Edited by Roland Boer and Edgar Conrad. London: T & T Clark International.

Joyce, Paul M. 1993. Lamentations and the Grief Process: A Psychological Reading. *Biblical Interpretation* 1 (3): 304–320.

Jung, Carl J. 1933. *Modern Man in Search of a Soul*. London: Kegan Paul.

Kamionkowski, S. Tamar. 2003. *Gender Reversal and Cosmic Chaos: A Study in the Book of Ezekiel*. Journal for the Study of the Old Testament Supplementary Series 368. London: Sheffield Academic Press.

Kernberg Otto F. 1985. *Borderline: Conditions and Pathological Narcissism*. Northvale: Aronson.

Kille, D. Andrew. 2001. *Psychological Biblical Criticism*. Guides to Biblical Scholarship. Minneapolis: Augsburg Fortress.

Klein, Lillian. 1989. *The Triumph of Irony in the Book of Judges*. Journal for the Study of the Old Testament Supplementary Series 68, Bible and Literature Series 14. Sheffield: Almond Press.

Klein, Ralph W. 2000. *1 Samuel*. 2nd edition. WBC 10. Nashville: Thomas Nelson

Kucich, J. 2009. *Imperial Masochism*. Princeton: Princeton University Press.

Larsson, Gerhard. 2004. Possible Hellenistic Influences in the Historical Parts of the Old Testament. *Scandinavian Journal of the Old Testament* 18 (2): 296–311.

Lasine, Stuart. 2001. *Knowing Kings: Knowledge, Power, and Narcissism in the Hebrew Bible*. SBL Semeia Studies 40. Atlanta: Society of Biblical Literature.

2002. Divine Narcissism and Yahweh's Parenting Style. *Biblical Interpretation* 10 (1): 36–56.

2013. *Weighing Hearts: Character, Judgment, and the Ethics of Reading the Bible*. The Library of Hebrew/Old Testament Studies 568. New York: T & T Clark.

Laub, Dori. 1992. Bearing Witness: Or the Vicissitudes of Listening. Pages 57–74 in *Testimony: Cries of Witnessing in Literature, Psychoanalysis and History*. Edited by Shoshana Felman and Dori Laub. New York: Routledge.

1995. Truth and Testimony: The Process and the Struggle. Pages 61–75 in *Trauma. Explorations in Memory*. Edited by Cathy Caruth. Baltimore: John Hopkins Press.

Lemaire, A. 2006. Hebrew and Aramaic in the First Millennium BCE in the Light of the Epigraphic Evidence (Social and Historical Aspects). Pages 177–196 in *Biblical Hebrew in its Northwest Semitic Setting*. Edited by S. E. Fassberg and A. Hurvitz. Winona Lake: Eisenbrauns.

Lemche, Niels Peter. 1985. *Early Israel: Anthropological and Historical Studies on the Israelite Society Before the Monarchy*. Vetus Testamentum Supplements 37. Leiden: Brill.

1988. *Ancient Israel: A New History of Israelite Society*. The Biblical Seminar 5. Sheffield: Sheffield Academic Press.

1992. Israel, History of (Premonarchic Period). Pages 526–543 in *The Anchor Bible Dictionary III*. Edited by David Noel Freedman. New York: Doubleday.

1993. The Old Testament – A Hellenistic Book. *Scandinavian Journal of the Old Testament* 7 (2): 163–193.

1994. Is it Still Possible to Write a History of Israel? *Scandinavian Journal of the Old Testament* 8 (2): 165–190.

1998. *The Israelites in History and Tradition*. London: SPCK.

2000. Good and Bad in History: The Greek Connection. Pages 127–140 in *Rethinking the Foundations; Historiography in the Ancient World and in the Bible; Essays in Honour of John Van Seters*. Edited by Steven L. McKenzie, Thomas Römer and Hans Heinrich Schmid. Berlin: Walter de Gruyter.

2003. 'Because They Have Cast Away the Law of the Lord of Hosts' – Or: 'We and the Rest of the World'. The Authors who 'wrote' the Old Testament. *Scandinavian Journal of the Old Testament* 17 (2): 268–290.

Levenson, Jon D. 1994. *Creation and the Persistence of Evil: The Jewish Drama of Divine Omnipotence*. Princeton: Princeton University Press.

Lilley, J. P. U. 1967. A Literary Appreciation of the Book of Judges. *Tyndale Bulletin* 18: 94–102.

Linville, James R. 1998. *Israel in the Book of Kings: The Past as a Project of Social Identity*. Journal for the Study of the Old Testament Supplementary Series 272. Sheffield: Sheffield Academic Press.

Lipman, S. 1991. *Laughter in Hell: The Use of Humor during the Holocaust*. Northvale: Jason Aranson.

Long, V. Phillips, David W. Baker and Gordon J. Wenham, eds. 2002. *Windows into Old Testament History, Evidence, Argument and the Crisis of Biblical Israel*. Grand Rapids: Eerdmans.

Lowen, Alexander. 1997. *Narcissism: Denial of the True Self*. New York: Touchstone.

Mandell, Sara and David Noel Freedman. 1993. *The Relationship between Herodotus' History and Primary History*. Atlanta: Scholars Press.

Margalith, Othniel. 1966. Parallels of Samson's Stories with Stories of the Aegean Sea People. *Beth Mikra* 27: 122–130.

1986a. Samson's Foxes. *Vetus Testamentum* 36: 225–234.

1986b. More Samson Legends. *Vetus Testamentum* 36: 397–405.

1987. The Legends of Samson/Heracles. *Vetus Testamentum* 37: 63–70.

Martin, Lee Roy. 2008. *The Unheard Voice of God: A Pentecostal Hearing of the Book of Judges*. Journal of Pentecostal Theology Supplementary Series 32. Dorset: Deo Publishing.

Mayes, A. D. H. 1983. *The Story of Israel between Settlement and Exile: A Redactional Study of the Deuteronomistic History*. London: SCM Press.

Mazor, Yair. 1997. When Aesthetics Is Harnessed to Psychological Characterization: 'Ars Poetica' in Psalm 139. *Zeitschrift für die Alttestamentliche Wissenschaft* 109: 260–271.

McCann, J. Clinton. 2002. *Judges*. Interpretation: A Bible Commentary for Teaching and Preaching. Louisville: John Knox Press.

McCarter, P. Kyle. Jr. 1980. *I Samuel: A New Translation with Introduction and Commentary*. Anchor Bible 8. New York: Doubleday.

McCarthy, D. J. 1978. *Treaty and Covenant: A Study in Form in the Ancient Oriental Documents and in the Old Testament*. Analecta Biblica 21. Rome: Pontifical Biblical Institute.

Menaker, Esther. 1953. Masochism as a Defence Reaction of the Ego. *The Psychoanalytic Quarterly* 22: 205–220.

Meyers, Helen. 2008. A Consideration of Treatment Techniques in Relation to Functions of Masochism. Pages 175–188 in *Masochism: Current Psychoanalytic Perspectives*. Edited by Robert A. Glick and Donald I. Meyers. New York: Psychology Press.

Miller, Alice. 1987. *For Your Own Good: The Roots of Violence in Child-Rearing*. Translated by Hildegarde and Hunter Hannum. London: Virago.

Miner, Maureen H. 2007. Back to the Basics in Attachment to God: Revisiting Theory in the Light of Theology. *Journal of Psychology and Theology* 35 (2): 112–122.

Miscall, Peter. 1986. *1 Samuel: A Literary Reading*. Bloomington: Indiana University Press.

Mobley, Gregory. 2005. *The Empty Men: The Heroic Tradition of Ancient Israel*. New York: Doubleday.

Moore, Burness E. and Bernard D. Fine. 1990. *Psychoanalytic Terms and Concepts*. New Haven: The American Psychoanalytic Association and Yale University Press.

Moore, George Foot. 1898. *A Critical and Exegetical Commentary on Judges*. Edinburgh: T & T Clark.

Morrow, William S. 2004. Comfort for Jerusalem: The Second Isaiah as Counselor to Refugees. *Biblical Theology Bulletin* 34 (2): 80–86.

Niditch, Susan. 2008. *Judges: A Commentary*. Old Testament Library. Louisville: Westminster John Knox Press.

Noll, K. L. 1999. Is There a Text in This Tradition? Readers' Response and the Taming of Samuel's God. *Journal for the Study of the Old Testament* 83: 31–51.

——— 2001. The Kaleidoscopic Nature of Divine Personality in the Hebrew Bible. *Biblical Interpretation* 9 (1): 1–24.

——— 2007a. Deuteronomistic History or Deuteronomic Debate? (A Thought Experiment). *Journal for the Study of the Old Testament* 31: 311–345.

——— 2007b. Is the Book of Kings Deuteronomistic? And Is It a History? *Scandinavian Journal of the Old Testament* 21 (1): 49–72.

——— 2013. *Canaan and Israel in Antiquity: A Textbook on History and Religion.* 2nd edition. London: Bloomsbury.

Noth, Martin. 1943. *Überlieferungsgeschichtliche Studien.* Halle: Niemeyer.

Novick, Jack and Kerry Kelly Novick. 1991. Some Comments on Masochism and the Delusion of Omnipotence from a Developmental Perspective. *Journal of the American Psychoanalytic Association* 39: 307–328.

——— 1996. *Fearful Symmetry: The Development and Treatment of Sadomasochism.* Northvale: Jason Aronson Inc.

——— 2004. The Superego and the Two-System Model. *Psychoanalytical Inquiry* 24: 232–256.

Novick, Kerry Kelly and Jack Novick. 1995. The Essence of Masochism. Pages 237–264 in *Essential Papers on Masochism.* Edited by Margaret Ann Fitzpatrick Hanly. New York: New York University Press.

——— 2012. Some Suggestions for Engaging with the Clinical Problem of Masochism. Pages 51–75 in *The Clinical Problem of Masochism.* Edited by Deanna Holtzman and Nancy Kulish. Lanham: Rowman and Littlefield.

O'Brien, Mark A. 1989. *The Deuteronomistic History Hypothesis: A Reassessment.* Göttingen: Vandenhoeck & Ruprecht.

O'Connell, Robert H. 1996. *The Rhetoric of the Book of Judges.* Vetus Testamentum Supplement 63. Leiden: Brill.

O'Connor, Kathleen M. 2014. How Trauma Studies can Contribute to Old Testament Studies. Pages 210–223 in *Trauma and Traumatization in Individual and Collective Dimensions: Insights from Biblical Studies and Beyond.* Studia Aarhusiana Neotestamentica 2. Edited by Eve-Marie Becker, Jan Dochhorn, and Else K. Holt. Göttingen: Vandenhoeck & Ruprecht.

Oded, Bustenay. 1979. *Mass Deportations and Deportees in the Neo-Assyrian Empire.* Wiesbaden: Reichert.

Ogden, Thomas H. 2007. On Holding and Containing, Being and Dreaming. Pages 76–96 in *Winnicott and the Psychoanalytical Tradition: Interpretation and Other Psychoanalytic Issues.* Edited by Lesley Caldwell. London: Karnac Books.

——— 2013. The Mother, the Infant and the Matrix. Interpretations of Aspects of the Work of Donald Winnicott. Pages 46–72 in *Donald Winnicott Today.* New Library of Psychoanalysis. Edited by Jan Abram. London: Routledge.

Ornstein, Anna. 2012. Self-Abuse and Suicidality: Clinical Manifestations of Chronic Narcissistic Rage. Pages 113–125 in *The Clinical Problem of*

Masochism. Edited by Deanna Holtzman and Nancy Kulish. Lanham: Rowman and Littlefield.

Oswalt, John. 1998. *The Book of Isaiah, Chapters 40–66*. Grand Rapids: Eerdmans.

Paul, Lynn K. 1999. Jesus as Object: Christian Conversion as Interpreted through the Perspective of Fairbairn's Object Relations Theory. *Journal of Psychology and Theology* 27 (4): 300–308.

Penchansky, David. 1999. *What Rough Beast? Images of God in the Hebrew Bible*. Louisville: Westminster John Knox Press.

Person, Raymond F. Jr. 2002. *The Deuteronomic School: History, Social Setting, and Literature*. Studies in Biblical Literature 2. Atlanta: SBL.

Polden, Jane. 2002. *Regeneration: Journey through the Mid-Life Crisis*. London: Continuum.

Polzin, Robert M. 1980. *Moses and the Deuteronomist: A Literary Study of the Deuteronomic History, Part One*. New York: Seabury Press.

    1989. *Samuel and the Deuteronomist: A Literary Study of the Deuteronomic History, Part Two*. Bloomington: Indiana University Press.

Pressler, Carolyn. 2002. *Joshua, Judges, and Ruth*. Westminster Bible Companion. Louisville: Westminster John Knox Press.

Pritchard, James K. 1969. *Ancient Near Eastern Texts Relating to the Old Testament*. 3rd edition. Princeton: Princeton University Press.

Provan, Iain W. 1988. *Hezekiah and the Books of Kings: A Contribution to the Debate about the Composition of the Deuteronomistic History*. Berlin: W. de Gruyter.

    1995. In the Stable with the Dwarves: Testimony, Interpretation, Faith and the History of Israel. *Journal of Biblical Literature* 114 (4): 585–606.

Radday, Yehuda T. and Athalya Brenner. 1990. *On Humour and Comic in the Hebrew Bible*. Sheffield: Almond.

Raguse, H. 2001. The Oedipus Complex in the Book of Esther. Pages 55–71 in *God, Biblical Stories and Psychoanalytic Understanding*. Edited by Rainer Kessler and Patrick Vandermeersch. Frankfurt: Peter Lang.

Rashkow, Ilona N. 1993. *The Phallacy of Genesis: A Feminist-Psychoanalytic Approach*. Literary Currents in Biblical Interpretation. Louisville: Westminster John Knox Press.

Reik, Theodor. 1941. *Masochism in Modern Man*. New York: Farrar and Strauss.

    1958. *Myth and Guilt: The Crime and Punishment of Mankind*. London: Hutchinson and Co.

Richter, Wolfgang. 1964. *Die Bearbeitungen des 'Retterbuches' in der Deuteronomischen Epoche*. Bonner Biblische Beiträge 21. Bonn: Peter Hanstein.

Robinson, Gnana. 1993. *Let Us Be Like the Nations: A Commentary on the Books of 1 and 2 Samuel*. International Theological Commentary. Grand Rapids: Eerdmans.

Rollins, Wayne G. 2002. The Bible in Psycho-Spiritual Perspective: News from the World of Biblical Scholarship. *Pastoral Psychology* 51 (2): 101–118.

Rollins, Wayne G. and Andrew Kille, eds. 2007. *Psychological Insight into the Bible: Texts and Readings*. Grand Rapids: Eerdmans.

190   Bibliography

Römer, Thomas. 2007. *The So-Called Deuteronomistic History: A Sociological, Historical and Literary Introduction*. London: T & T Clark.

Rowlett, Lori. 2001. Violent Femmes and S/M: Queering Samson and Delilah. Pages 106–115 in *Queer Commentary and the Hebrew Bible*. Journal for the Study of the Old Testament Supplementary Series 334. Edited by Ken Stone. London: Sheffield Academic Press.

Ruether, Rosemary Radford. 1983. *Sexism and God-Talk: Towards a Feminist Theology*. Boston: Beacon Press.

St Clair, Michael. 1986. *Object Relations and Self Psychology: An Introduction*. Belmont: Wadsworth.

Sasson, Jack. 2014. *Judges 1–12: A New Translation with Introduction and Commentary*. The Anchor Yale Bible 6D. New Haven: Yale University Press.

Schneider, Tammi. 2000. *Berit Olam. Judges: Studies in Hebrew Narrative and Poetry*. Collegeville: The Liturgical Press.

Schniedewind, William M. 2004. *How the Bible Became a Book: The Textualization of Ancient Israel*. Cambridge: Cambridge University Press.

Shengold, Leonard. 1989. *Soul Murder: The Effects of Childhood Abuse and Deprivation* New Haven: Yale University Press.

Smith, Morton. 1971. *Palestinian Parties and Politics that Shaped the Old Testament*. London: SCM Press.

Smith, Henry Preserved. 1899. *A Critical and Exegetical Commentary on the Books of Samuel*. International Critical Commentary. Edinburgh: T & T Clark.

Smith, Vicki, Patrizia Collard, Paula Nicolson and Rowan Bayne, eds. 2012. *Key Concepts in Counselling and Psychotherapy: A Critical A-Z Guide to Theory*. New York: Open University Press.

Smith-Christopher, Daniel L. 1991. The Politics of Ezra: Sociological Indicators of Postexilic Judaean Society. Pages 73–97 in *Second Temple Studies 1: Persian Period*. Journal for the Study of the Old Testament Supplementary Series 117. Edited by Philip R. Davies. Sheffield: Sheffield Academic. Press.

2014. Trauma and the Old Testament: Some Problems and Prospects. Pages 223–243 in *Trauma and Traumatization in Individual and Collective Dimensions: Insights from Biblical Studies and Beyond*. Studia Aarhusiana Neotestamentica 2. Edited by Eve-Marie Becker, Jan Dochhorn and Else K. Holt. Göttingen: Vandenhoeck and Ruprecht.

Soggin, J. Alberto. 1981. *Judges*. Old Testament Library. Translated by John Bowden. London: SCM Press.

Somers, M. R. and G. G. Gibson. 1994. Reclaiming the Epistemological 'Other': Narrative and the Social Construction of Identity. Pages 37–99 in *Social Theory and the Politics of Identity*. Edited by C. Calhoun. Oxford: Basil Blackwell.

Stager, Lawrence. 1996. The Fury of Babylon. *Biblical Archaeology Review* 22 (1): 56–69.

Stern, Ephraim. 2000. The Babylonian Gap. *Biblical Archaeology Review* 26 (6): 45–51.

Sternberg, Meir. 1985. *The Poetics of Biblical Narrative: Ideological Literature and the Drama of Reading*. Indiana Studies in Biblical Literature. Bloomington: Indiana University Press.

Stiebing, W. H. 1989. *Out of the Desert? Archaeology and the Exodus/ Conquest Narratives*. New York: Prometheus.

Straker, Gillian. 2015. 'The Racialization of the Mind in Intimate Spaces: The "Nanny" and the Failure of Recognition'. Pages 4–16 in *The Bonds of Love, Revisited*. Edited by Eyal Rozmarin. London: Routledge.

Sugarman, Alan. 2012. Masochism in Childhood and Adolescence as a Self-regulatory Disorder. Pages 29–50 in *The Clinical Problem of Masochism*. Edited by Deanna Holtzman and Nancy Kulish. Lanham: Rowman and Littlefield.

Sypher, Wylie. 1956. The Meanings of Comedy. Pages 193–260 in *Comedy*. Edited by Wylie Sypher. Garden City: Doubleday.

Tadmor, H. 1966. Philistia under Assyrian Rule. *The Biblical Archaeologist* 29: 86–102.

Thompson, Thomas L. 1992. *Early History of the Israelite People from the Written and Archaeological Sources*. Leiden: Brill.

1999a. *The Bible in History: How Writers Create a Past*. London: Jonathan Cape.

1999b. *The Mythic Past: Biblical Archaeology and the Myth of Israel*. London: Jonathan Cape.

Tsumura, David Toshio. 2007. *The First Book of Samuel*. The New International Commentary on the Old Testament. Grand Rapids: Eerdmans.

Van Seters, John. 1983. *In Search of History: Historiography in the Ancient World and the Origins of Biblical History*. New Haven: Yale University Press.

Vanderhooft, David Stephen. 1999. *The Neo-Babylonian Empire and Babylon in the Latter Prophets*. Atlanta: Scholars Press.

Vandermeersch, Patrick. 2001. Psychoanalytic Interpretations of Religious Texts: Some Bases. Pages 9–27 in *God, Biblical Stories and Psychoanalytic Understanding*. Edited by Rainer Kessler and Patrick Vandermeersch. Frankfurt: Peter Lang.

Volkan, Vamik D. 2001. Transgenerational Transmissions and Chosen Traumas: An Aspect of Large-Group Identity. *Group Analysis* 34: 79–97.

Webb, Barry G. 1987. *The Book of the Judges: An Integrated Reading*. Journal for the Study of the Old Testament Supplementary Series 66. Sheffield: JSOT Press.

2012. *The Book of the Judges*. The New International Commentary on the Old Testament. Grand Rapids: Eerdmans.

Weippert, Helga. 1972. Die 'Deuteronomistischen' Beurteilungen der Könige von Israel und Juda und das Problem der Redaktion der Königsbücher. *Biblica* 53: 301–339.

Wellhausen, Julius. 1885. *Prolegomena to the History of Israel*. Edinburgh: A & C Black.

Wesselius, Jan-Wim. 2002. *The Origin of the History of Israel. Herodotus' Histories as Blueprint for the First Books of the Bible*. Journal for the

Study of the Old Testament Supplementary Series 345. Sheffield: Sheffield Academic Press.

Westermann, Claus. 1994. *Lamentations: Issues and Interpretation*. Translated by Charles Muenchow. Edinburgh: T & T Clark.

Whitelam, Keith W. 1994. The Identity of Early Israel: The Realignment and Transformation of Late Bronze-Iron Age Palestine. *Journal for the Study of the Old Testament* 63: 57–87.

Whybray, R. N. 2000. 'Shall Not the Judge of All the Earth Do What Is Just?' God's Oppression of the Innocent in the Old Testament. Pages 1–19 in *'Shall Not the Judge of All the Earth Do What Is Right?' Studies on the Nature of God in Tribute to James L. Crenshaw*. Edited by David Penchansky and Paul L. Redditt. Winona Lake: Eisenbrauns.

Winnicott, Donald Woods. 1954. Mind and Its Relation to the Psyche-Soma. *British Journal of Medical Psychology* 27 (4): 201–209.

——— 1984. *Deprivation and Delinquency*. London: Tavistock Publications Ltd.

——— 1990a. *The Maturational Processes and the Facilitating Environment: Studies in the Theory of Emotional Development*. London: Karnac Books.

——— 1990b. *Home Is Where We Start From: Essays by a Psychologist*. Compiled and edited by Clare Winnicott, Ray Shepherd and Madeleine Davis. London: Penguin.

Wolff, Hans W. 1975. The Kerygma of the Deuteronomic Historical Work. Pages 83–100 in *The Vitality of Old Testament Traditions*. Edited by Hans W. Wolff and Walter Brueggemann. Atlanta: John Knox Press.

Wong, Gregory T. K. 2006. *Compositional Strategy of the Book of Judges: An Inductive, Rhetorical Study*. Vetus Testamentum Supplement 111. Leiden: Brill.

Younger, K. Lawson Jr. 2002. *The NIV Application Commentary: From Biblical Text to Contemporary Life: Judges/Ruth*. Grand Rapids: Zondervan.

Zadok, R. 1978. Phoenicians, Philistines and Moabites in Mesopotamia. *Bulletin of the American School of Oriental Research* 230: 58–65.

Zakovitch, Y. 1972. *yptḥ = bdn. Vetus Testamentum* 22 (1): 123–125.

INDEX

Kille, D. Andrew, 24, 46
Klein, Lillian, 28, 59
Klein, Melanie, 10

Lasine, Stuart, 25–6, 35, 37, 41, 129, 163
Lemche, Niels Peter, 69, 75, 87
Levenson, Jon D., 110–11
love/hate in relationships, 31, 33, 35, 37–8, 136

malattunement, 96, 154–5, 159
Martin, Lee Roy, 3, 116–17, 149
masculinity studies, 128, 173
masochism, 2, 139, 142, 144, 149, 153, 155, 157, 159, 162, 165–7, 169
masochistic defence mechanism, 34, 37, 134, 141–2, 163, 168, 173
Menaker, Esther, 141, 157, 162
Mitchell, Stephen A., 18, 114, 144, 147, 152
mother
  environment, 17, 22, 31, 33, 35, 39
  good-enough, 20–1, 43, 94
  object, 21, 33
  mysterium, 5, 7–8

narcissism, 128, 153, 161
narrative approaches, 6, 8, 45, 59, 123–4, 129–30, 171, 174
Niditch, Susan, 27, 40, 65, 117, 120
Noll, K., 1, 68, 72, 78, 85–8, 146–8, 168
Novick, Jack and Kerry Kelly, 141, 156, 160, 162–4

O'Connell, Robert H., 32, 34, 40, 42, 59, 117
Ogden, Thomas, 17, 21, 114
Old Testament theology, 1, 3, 5–7, 11–12, 41, 90, 127
omnipotence, fantasies/delusion of, 38, 112, 153, 156, 160, 163, 169

polyphony, 46, 55, 63, 84, 87
Polzin, Robert M., 29, 42, 61–2, 118, 124, 133, 156
Pressler, Carolyn, 28, 40, 108, 118
Primary Maternal Preoccupation, 29, 38–9
projection, 4, 8, 13, 31, 109, 142, 149, 158, 163
protest behaviour, 95, 105, 107, 109–11, 119, 173

provocation, masochistic, 160–3, 165–6, 170
proximity maintenance, 94–7, 104–7, 109, 173
pseudo-aggression, 160, 166, 169
psychology, as external yardstick, 6–7, 11, 23, 25–6, 129, 172

Rashkow, Ilona, 24–6
Reik, Theodor, 141–2, 166–8
repression, 2, 15, 22–3, 53, 129, 140, 151, 157, 166, 169, 171, 173
restitutive gesture, 22, 32–4, 36, 39, 133
Rollins, Wayne G., 24, 46

Sasson, Jack, 26–7, 90, 106, 110, 116–17
Smith-Christopher, Daniel L., 53–4, 74
split objects, 2, 8, 14–15, 31, 79, 128, 137, 140, 152, 172–3
strange situation, 93, 95, 97, 109, 119
survivor literature, 47, 52–3, 56, 59–60

Thompson, Thomas L., 63, 71, 75, 77–8, 81, 84, 87
trauma theory, 63, 72, 88, 136
True and False self, 20, 22, 31, 36–9, 99, 114, 116, 156–7, 175

Vandermeersch, Patrick, 10

Webb, Barry, 3, 6, 36, 38, 40–1, 49, 59, 118, 166, 175
Wellhausen, Julius, 10–11, 156
Winnicott, Donald Woods, 13, 16–17, 23, 26, 29, 31, 33, 35–9, 43, 94, 96, 106, 116, 132, 139, 155, 159, 176

YHWH
  anger, 38, 74, 90, 100, 103, 109, 111, 115, 118–19, 127, 134–5, 145, 162, 166, 170, 174
  constructed character, 5, 9, 42, 88, 100, 158, 166
  inscrutable, 6, 8, 43, 173–4
  intrusive, 22, 40, 100, 138, 163, 165, 168, 174
  jealousy, 36, 108, 120, 126–8, 146, 149, 165
  reputation protection, 51, 60, 126, 129, 133
  vulnerable, 100, 110, 128